W9-CZM-281

Faster and Easier Way to AutoCAD Design

by

Yoofi Garbrah-Aidoo

authorHOUSE

1663 LIBERTY DRIVE, SUITE 200
BLOOMINGTON, INDIANA 47403
(800) 839-8640
www.authorhouse.com

First published by AuthorHouse 12/06/05

ISBN: 1-4208-9677-6 (sc)

Printed in the United States of America
Bloomington, Indiana

This book is printed on acid-free paper.

Faster and Easier Way to AutoCAD Design

YOOFI GARBRAH-AIDOO

About the Author

Yoofi Garbrah-Aidoo graduated from the University of Houston College of Technology with a bachelor's degree in Mechanical Engineering.

Yoofi has been working for different Oil & Gas companies since 1999, before joining the school system

He taught Engineering design at North Harris Community College, in Houston and currently employed as an Engineering design Instructor at Cy-Fair College, Cy-Fair Texas.

Foreword

The goal of writing this book is to enable the user to be more productive and get things done accurately and on time

To introduce the user to tips of the trade, short cuts and innovation to make working with AutoCAD easier and fun

Chapters in this book walk the user through the Model stage from 2D sketches. Each chapter is loaded with practical examples, which reflect exact location of tools for specific design.

Using this Book will enable the user and designer to be able to produce Models like it is second nature in no time at all.

Acknowledgments

The author would like to thank AutoDesk for creating this state of the art software.

The author would also like to thank his family for their patience and support.

The author and publisher would like to thank all the professionals who reviewed the manuscript.

A special acknowledgement is due the following instructors and professionals.

Dr. Hicks, my Analytic Chemistry instructor at LaGrange College, Georgia, who suggested Medical school.

Ibrahim ElSamahy, University of Houston: Houston, Texas for his style of teaching.

David Mott, North Harris Community College, Houston, Texas the one who gave me a chance when no one would.

In the memory of Dr. Ahmed Nassef, my Dynamics professor, University of Houston, who broke it down to simple terms when it became complicated.

Ghassan Khalil, University of Houston, who gave me refresher course on calculus.

Dr. David Sam, President of North Harris Community College, for his professional guidance.

To all my students for, bringing the best out of me through, their diverse questioning.

Dedication

In loving memory of my Mother Eva Victoria Garbrah-Aidoo for seeing to it that I obtained the basic foundation of formal education.

To my wife and children, for their understanding and to Mia, for her unconditional love.

To my son, Omahn, for helping bring the best out of me as a parent and a father.

Limits of Liability and Disclaimer

The publishers and author of this book have made every effort to make sure that there are no errors in the text or design, whiles using AutoCAD. However should in case such occurrences happen, it will be appreciated much if we are contacted to enable us make corrections in future issues.

The publishers and author make no warranty of any kind, implied or expressed, as regards to the designs in this book. The publisher and author shall not be liable in any event for incidental or consequential damages in connection with the use of this book.

TABLE OF CONTENTS

Preface

Designers and students alike will find these valuable step-by-step examples of AutoCAD easy to follow and understand. The book will guide the user through the technical aspect of designing and 3D modeling and students and designers familiar with any of Microsoft packages will hit the floor running.

AutoCAD is loaded with all the tools you will need for designing a part and has an enhanced intelligent capability known as Xref, a self correcting tool which will help you make immediate changes to wrong designs and not loose a drawing or time. By so doing, changes made to the part will automatically reflect in other areas of the drawing and update accordingly when you use Reload.

There are different uses of the AutoCAD package allowing the user to design complex shapes with **Extrude** as well as **Revolve**, otherwise would be impossible or difficult to achieve.

This book is written for the novice as well as the advanced designer who would like to explore further into AutoCAD by combining **Inquiry and Mass Properties** for calculations and analysis.

Introduction to AutoCAD

AutoCAD is 2D application software with an Introduction to 3D design, used in designing different types of parts and assemblies, from electrical, civil, architecture and piping to mechanical. Certain design software, required the designer to draw all over again when minor changes had to be made. AutoCAD has built-in Xref capabilities, meaning changing a dimension changes the part and upgrading of the model. Sequencing used in the model is also captured. With all these capabilities added on, the designer gets his work done more quickly and accurately, thus improving production and service. There is also the Internet commerce connection to share drawings across with clients. Drawings could be started in other CAD software and saved as a DWG or jpeg file and opened up in AutoCAD for editing.

With the help of this book users would be able to:

- Start basic 2D drawing add all necessary dimensions and convert it to 3D model
- Discover hidden codes in the program
- Build on existing parts and make changes
- Use the built in capabilities to calculate the inertia of a beam, find the Mass Property of a part and determine its weight.
- Use external referenced files in drawings
- Create Blocks to enable the user speed up production.
- Learn the uses of Mold cavity

User Interaction

A complete keyboard entries and mouse-driven control capabilities reduce design steps and minimize the need for dialogue boxes. It is assumed that you are familiar with Windows and worked with the menu and its tools, start programs, move windows, select various commands from menus as well as edit features, copy and paste save and print.

New Windows users can pick up a 'how to book' on Windows® for a crash course to bring them up to speed.

It is also assumed that you have access to a mouse and know how to use it, for most of the sketches are performed with the aid of a mouse. The keyboard is mostly used to enter when prompted by the Command line.

Feature-Based

Certain geometric features such as Extrude, cuts, holes, revolve; fillets, chamfers and angular dimensions are invoked and utilized in the application to the parts you create, when you use AutoCAD software.

Welcome to AutoCAD Design:

Welcome to AutoCAD design. After reading and practicing the first few chapters of this book, you will become very knowledgeable in the CAD environment world and design like a professional.

Note on Exercises:

The exercises given after each lesson, is to provide the student or designer, an opportunity to try out similar examples just covered and to offer hands on experience for each topic. It is advised that all necessary effort be put forth into the completion of such exercises. This will give you hands-on experience as well as build your confidence.

Make sure you cover all the given exercises at the end of each chapter.

Who is This Book For?

*   This book is supported under the Microsoft Windows® graphical interface and users who have used Windows before or similar operating system and eager to know more about designing faster and easier.

*   If you are a newcomer to designing parts and gadgets, and do not want to mess around sitting in long lectured classrooms and itching to plunge straight in at the deep end.

*   You would like to learn the basics and start using your knowledge for better and challenging design, and then you have certainly got hold of the right book.

- Alternatively if you have been working in any CAD environment and would like to know what AutoCAD could do differently, strap on your seatbelt, for you are about to set aside the one you are with, AutoCAD can do what you do even better and easier.

- What you already know is going to be reinforced, letting you get to the real thing straight away. **You will also be tutored in actual Design skills with all the FAT sliced off.**

- The objective of this book is to bypass endless lectures and dive straight into reality designing.

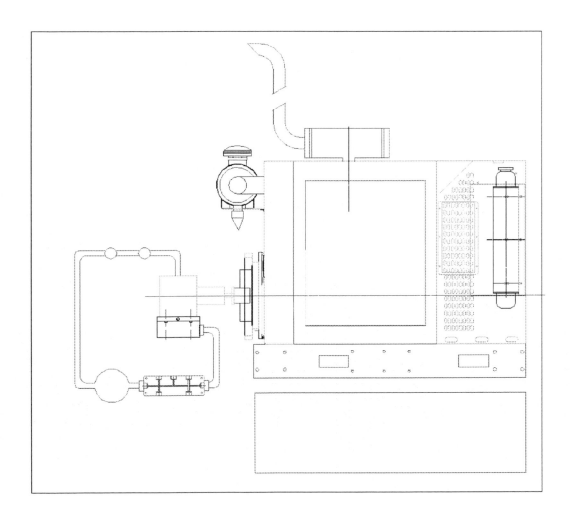

CHAPTER 1

After completing this Chapter, you will be able to:

- Open the Start up Dialogue Boxes
- Learn about Dialogue Boxes
- Use a Wizard Dialogue boxes
- Learn to Setup Template
- Create New Folder
- Open a New Drawing
- Use the Save As option
- Create a Custom Template
- Use Limits
- Learn about Upper and Lower Limits
- Use Grips
- Draw Circle, Rectangle and using other Sketch Tools
- Learn of International and American Standards.

We will begin the Chapter with an introduction to basic setup and commands necessary to do your drawings with.

Design Skills

It is very essential to review previously covered material, as you continue to learn new topics.

By so doing, you will be able to obtain a general concept of the material ahead, since each chapter is built on the ones already covered. This Design Skills is priceless, once you get used to it.

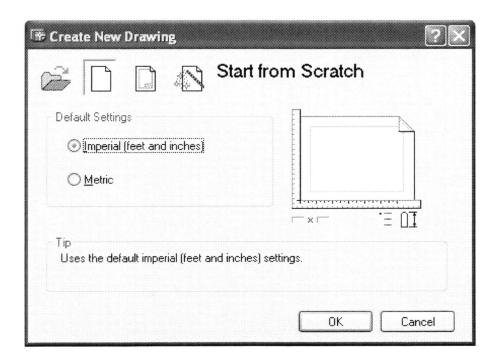

Figure 1.00

Why AutoCAD?

AutoCAD is one of the widely used software in the Drafting and Engineering fields and it is user friendly. It contains all the capabilities of any CAD software in the market, which incorporates everything from 2D drawings to basic 3Ddesign, to links on the Internet as well as conversions to and from other CAD software like SolidWorks and Inventor. Those familiar with other CAD programs will find familiar features like the Command Line to make keyboard entries as well as drawing features. The Title Block offers the capabilities of Layers as found in other CAD programs.

Starting AutoCAD:

You can start the AutoCAD programs in one of two ways, click on Start button, Programs, and choose **AutoCAD** from the programs menu. A dialogue box pops up and you click on file new and OK to start.

Alternatively, double-click on the AutoCAD icon from the Graphics area to bring up Create New Drawing dialogue box.

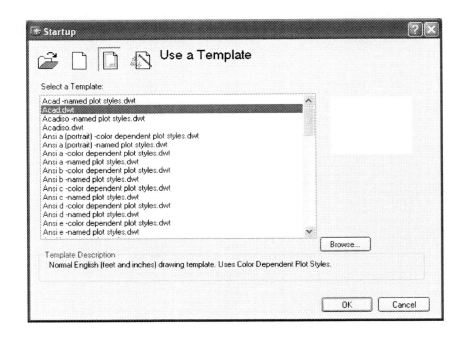

Figure 1.01

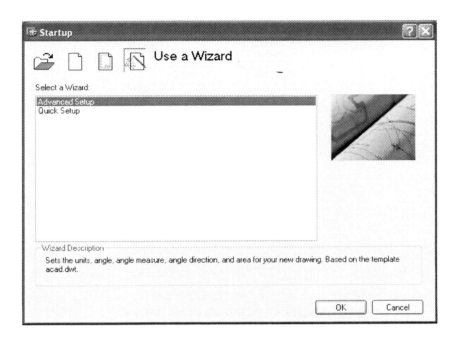

Figure 1.02

Template Setup:

When you first start AutoCAD, the **Create New Drawing** dialogue box pops up.
Refer to Figure 1.00. There will be two **Radio** buttons for **Imperial (feet and inches)** and **Metric**

Here you click to select the units you are planning to sketch your drawings in.
If your drawing will be dimensioned in **inches,** click to select the radio button
besides **Imperial (feet and inches)** on the other hand if your drawing is going to be
presented in **millimeters** then you click to select the radio button besides **Metric**
and click on OK to start.

For our purposes, let us select **Imperial (feet and inches)** and click on OK.
On the very top of the Menu bar should read, **Drawing 1.dwg**. The software is
informing you that, you have started your first drawing and has appended a **'DWG'**
as an extension for the software to differentiate this drawing from others.

There are other extensions like **'DXF'**, which will be covered, in subsequent chapters.

1. Click on File from the Main Menu and select **Save As,** the Save Drawing As dialogue box pops up.

2. Click on the arrow at the end of Save in: and click on **C:** drive or whichever drive you would like to save your drawings in.

3. Move to the end of list of icons on top of the dialogue box and click on Create new folder, refer to Figure 1.04

4. Scroll through the list of names and locate the new folder just created.

5. Slowly click on top of the words **New Folder** under **Name**; two times and the letters will start blinking inside the box.

6. Type **Mechanical - ACAD** or any preferred name to replace New Folder and

7. Click Save. Close the dialogue box to cone back to AutoCAD Drawing 1

8. Click on Save AS again, click to open the C: drive and search for **Mechanical - ACAD**

9. Double-click on **Mechanical - ACAD** folder to open it

10. Type Template1 inside the empty box by File name and click on Save. Figure 1.06

11. Click to close AutoCAD and let us test the new Folder you have created.

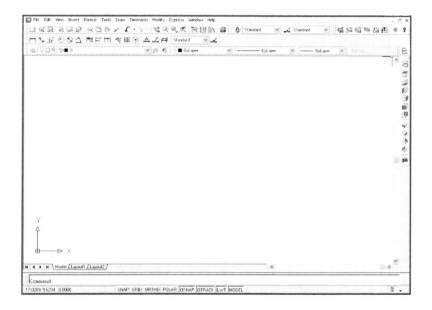

Figure 1.03

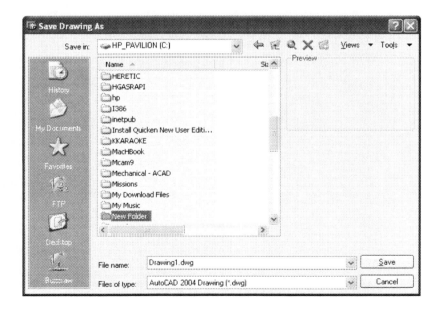

Figure 1.04

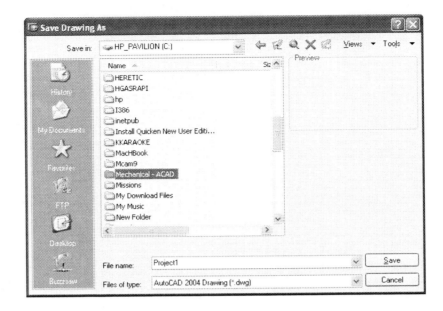

Figure 1.05

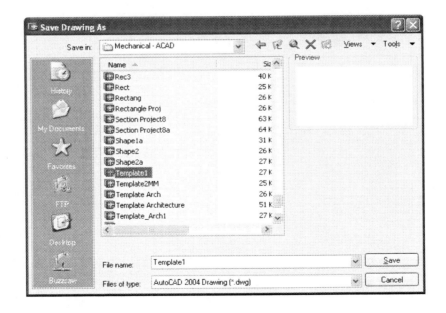

Figure 1.06

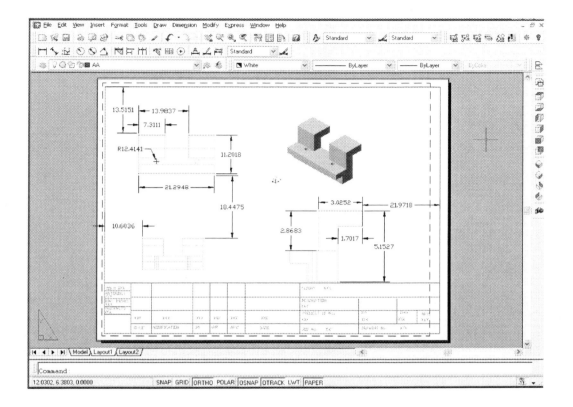

Figure 1.08

That on the X-Axis will be X-Limit: **1 +1.3578 + 3.8237 + .6862 + 3.4023 + 1 = 11.27**

Y-Axis will be the Y limit: **1 + 0.4055 + 1.2476 +0.6238 + 1 = 4.2769**

Making room for additional text, you can now set your Limits to **0.0000, 0.0000** for the lower Limits and **12.0000, 9.0000** for the Upper Limits

Plot Size and Scale:

Drawings that are created in Civil Engineering as well as Architecture tend to be several feet in measurement. To be able to make such drawings, the Sheet Layout is setup with a scale of ¼" to 1 foot or 1/8" to the foot.

The scale has to be converted to suit the Sheet Layout size before any sketches could be made to avoid mistakes.

Follow these steps to set up a scale of 1/8" to 1foot for a Sheet layout of 22" by 34" which is also a size **'D'** in the American National Standard..

11. Given a Drawing to be plotted for Sheet Size 22" x 34"

12. Scale 1/8"(in) = 1'(Ft) or 1" = 96"

Calculate Limits.

Since the Sheet Size is 22" x 34"

The Xlimit is 22" and

The Ylimit is 34"

Therefore Xlimit = 22 x 8' = 176' and Ylmit = 34 x 8 = 272'

To incorporate this value with your setup, you first have to change the Units to correspond to the one to be used. Type Units at the Command Prompt and press the Enter key.

13. Command: Units (The Drawing Units dialogue box opens up when you press the Enter key). Refer to Figure 1.09

14. Expand the arrow under Type and select Architectural for the Length

15. Expand the arrow under Angle and select Deg/Min/sec for the type and click on Ok to exit.

At the Command prompt type Limits and press the Enter key.

16. Command: Limits (Press the Enter key and a Message pops up requesting you to):

17. **Specify lower left corner or [ON/OFF] (0'-0", 0'-0">:**

18. Press the Enter key to accept the Default setting. A Message pops up

requesting you to:

19. **Specify upper right corner <1'-0", 0'-9">:**

20. Enter **176', 272'** and press the Enter key. The Sheet Layout is now set.

Figure 1.09

21. When the Text height is also given, multiply it by 96 since 1/8" = 1' then 1"
    = 96"

Therefore ¼" x 96" = 24" or 2'. Your Text height should be set for 2'.

Finally type Ltscale at the Command Prompt and press the Enter key to enter the
new scale factor.

22. Command: **Ltscale** (Press the Enter key) A Message pops up requesting you to:

23. Enter new Linetype scale factor:

24. Type **96** and press the Enter key.

25. Save this setup as Template Scale 1in to 8ft.

SHEET LAYOUTS:

Sheet comes in two different standards that of the **American National Standard** which is also the Imperial English (feet and inches) and the **International Standard** or **Metric**. Letter sizes range from the letter **A** to **E** for the American National Standard and A4 to A0 for the International Standard or Metric. Before plotting a drawing one should select a work area based on the sheet size to use to plot the drawing. The sheet size you choose determines the work area and other parameters as related to the drawing. The tables below are the standard sheet sizes with corresponding letter size to choose from:

Table 1.00 **American National Standards**

Letter Size	Sheet Size
A	12 x 9
B	18 x 12
C	24 x 18
D	36 x 24
E	48 x 36

Table 1.01 **International Standards**
–

Letter Size	Sheet Size
A4	210 x 297
B3	297 x 420
C	420 x 594
D1	595 x 841
E0	841 x 1189

Layers:

Building a house involves different stages of development from drawing sketch to the end product.

There is the foundation, where a concrete slab is set in place, the plumbing, where pipe lines are laid to cover certain portions of the slab, the framing of the house, the electrical layout, the roofing and other important factors that go into making the house complete.

On the drawing sheet where all these stages are to be represented, everything will be so cluttered that it will not be possible to get a smooth operation of the carpenter or plumber, therefore **Layers** that represent individual objects are set up to enable each and everyone perform their parts accordingly.

Imagine several sheets of paper stack on top of the other, which represents unique objects.

AutoCAD offers the capability of stacking such sheets, assign different colors and Line Types to them and invoke them as and when needed.

As such the Plumber could do his job at the same time the Electrician is wiring the house through **Layers**

38

<u>Creating Layers:</u>

Now that you have finished setting up the Limits for your drawing, it is time to cover Layer Setup. To do these do the following to create a **Layer:**

26. Start AutoCAD and load the **Template1** from your folder **Mechanical – ACAD.**

27. In Front of the **Command:** which is located on the lower bar in the Graphics area, refer to Figure 1.08, type **Layer** and press the **Enter Key, Layer Properties Manager** opens up as indicated in Figure 1.10

28. Press the Enter Key again to Load **Layer1** Figure 1.10

29. Type **Obj** in the place of Layer1 and press the Enter Key two times.

Refer to Figure 1.11 and fill in the rest of the Text, the next step after filling in all the text is to assign Colors to your Linetype. To do this you will follow these simple steps:

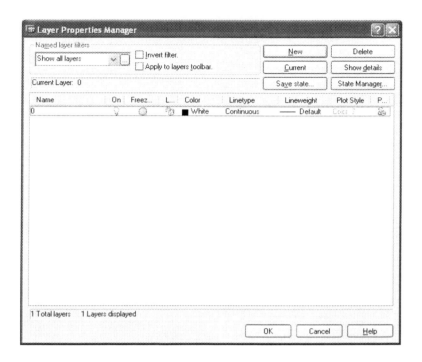

Figure 1.10

30. After filling in all the text as in Figure 1.12, click in the black square box to the side of **White** under **Color** to invoke the **Select Color** dialogue box Figure 1.13

31. Change the last Layer to Magenta by clicking to select it and click OK.

32. This will bring you back to the **Layer Properties Manager** with a change in color.

33. Click on the next black square box to the side of Txt and select Green and click OK

Repeat the above operation and change the rest to correspond to that of Figure 1.15

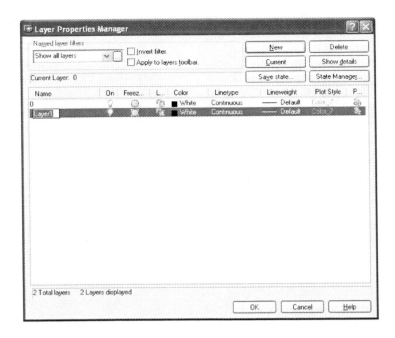

Figure 1.11

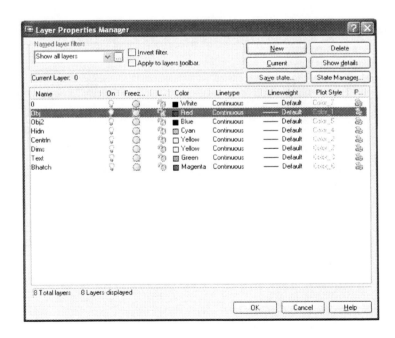

Figure 1.12

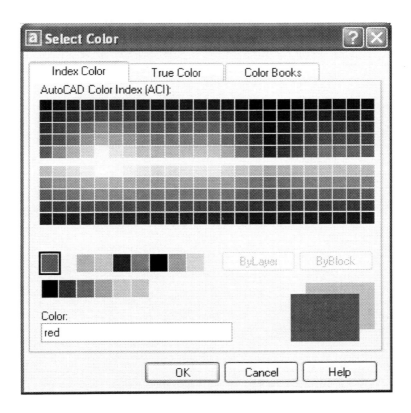

Figure 1.13

Linetype:

Certain Linetype have a unique feature that distinguishes it from the rest of the Linetypes. For an example, Center and Hidden Lines have broken lines with different styles. To invoke one of these Linetype you will do the following:

34. Move your pointer on top of Continuous to the side of **'Hidn'** and click on it.

35. This will open the **Select Linetype** dialogue box. See Figure 1.14

36. Click on Load to access the Load or Load Linetype dialogue box. Search for **Hidden** and click to select it.

37. Back in **Select Line Types** click on **Hidden** again to load it into your Template.

38. Repeat this action for **'Centrln'** and load **Center** into your Template

42

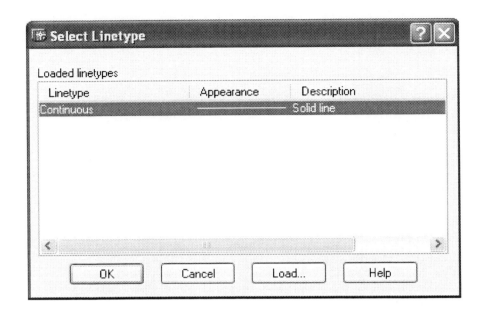

Figure 1.14

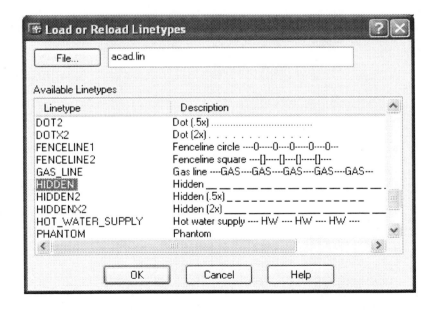

Figure 1.15

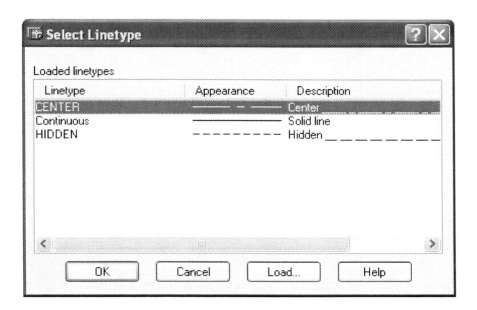

Figure 1.16

39. Click on Ok to close the Layer Properties Manager and Save the Template again.

40. Now anytime that you open your Template it will have all the Linetype already set for design.

BASIC AutoCAD:

We are going to start with **Basic AutoCAD**, cover **Intermediate** and graduate with **Advanced AutoCAD**.

Now that we have set up a Template and learned about fundamental commands, we will start with simple drawings and familiarize ourselves with the tools needed to do your drawing. You will learn how to **start** a new drawing, **Save, Save As, Close, and Exit AutoCAD**.

Learn about **Drawing Files** and learn how to draw **Line, Rectangle, Circle, Arc, and Ellipse** and use the **Erase** and **Delete** options.

41. Start AutoCAD if it is not already running on your Computer, by clicking on *start* from the Desktop, click on **All Programs** and locate **AutoCAD** icon and double-click to open it.

42. From the Startup Dialogue box, refer to Figure 1.02, click the open icon and search and load your Template, by double-clicking on it.

43. Type **Layer** at the Command Prompt and click on the **Obj** to make it the current layer.

44. Alternatively, select the **Obj** layer from the **Layer Properties Manager** to make it the current layer. Refer to Figure 1.12

45. In the **Draw** on the **Main Menu** are different tools needed to do your drawings with.

46. In the **Modify** on the Main Menu are different edit tools to use throughout these lessons.

47. In essence you will use tools from **Draw** to do all your sketching and editing commands from **Modify** to change your sketch.

This chapter will cover in **DETAIL**, commands listed under **Draw** and its uses. Line can be drawn **Horizontally** on the X-Axis or **Vertically** on the Y-Axis. The Z-Axis is only used in 3D Modeling; this will be covered in the Advanced Chapter under 3D Modeling. You can use lines to draw different objects from Rectangle to many complex objects. You will start with the **Line** tool and go through the list of items in descending order. Start a new file in AutoCAD.

Line:

You can draw a line in several different ways including using the line icon, going to pick the Line Tool, from a list of tools in the Draw option or type LINE at the command prompt.

Either of these will give you the same results.

This goes for the rest of the drawing tools. Alternatively, you can use Aliases to generate most frequently used AutoCAD commands or any particular tool to be used for your sketch.

Aliases are short cuts normally comprising of the first two letters of the name of tool to be used. That will also invoke the tool to be used.

For an example typing **'L'** at the Command Prompt and pressing the Enter key, will be the same as clicking on the Line tool. Follow these steps to draw a Line. For more on Command Aliases a copy of the list is found on the section under **'How Do I?'**

Creating your first drawing

Tool Tip

Remember to leave the mouse pointer on top of an icon to reveal what that particular tool does when in doubt

In this exercise, you will use simple tools to make basic sketches, like lines, circles, and save your work.

48. Let us go on and click on **File, Open** from the toolbar and then click on your

49. Template. This will be the first step you take every time you start a new drawing, therefore be conversant with it.

50. You will notice that, this action activates the **Origin** icon also known as the **UCS** (User Coordinate System, with the **'Y'-axis** pointing vertically in the positive direction and **'X' pointing horizontally** the positive direction.

51. The **'Z'-axis will be covered in 3D Modeling**.

52. Next click on Line from the Draw on the Main Menu Bar and press the **F8** key

53. The **F8** key forces lines to be drawn **Vertically** or **Horizontally**.

54. Click on any place on the graphics area with the left mouse button, release your finger and move the mouse and drag the pointer **vertically up and click again.**

55. Next move the mouse pointer **horizontally** to the right and watch the increase in **Length** at the bottom of the screen, as you move the pointer.

56. Hit the **'Esc'** key to complete drawing a line.

57. Repeat this action several times until you are very comfortable with drawing a line.

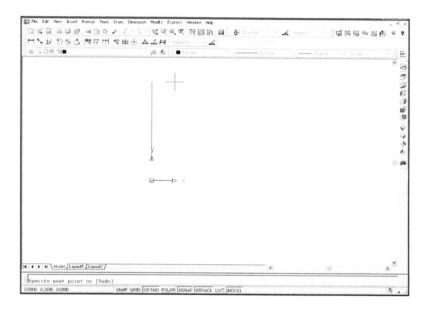

Figure 1.17

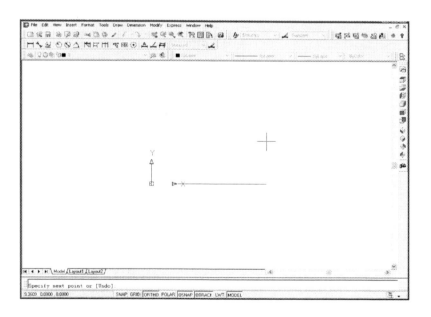

Figure 1.18

58. Type **Line** at the Command prompt: A message pops up requesting you to:

59. **Specify first point:**

60. Type **0, 0** and press the Enter key. A message pops up requesting you to:

61. **Specify next point or [Close / Undo]:**

62. Type **10, 0** press the Enter key A message pops up requesting you to:

63. **Specify next point or [Close / Undo]:**

64. Type **10, 5** and press the Enter key A message pops up requesting you to:

65. **Specify next point or [Close / Undo]**

66. Type **0, 5** and press the Enter key A message pops up requesting you to:

67. **Specify next point or [Close / Undo]:**

Figure 1.19

Figure 1.20

68. Type the letter '**C**' and press the Enter key to exit the line command.

Construction Line:

Ray:

Construction Line comprises of the **Ray** and **Xline**. These two lines have similar characteristics and uses but also different in certain aspects. You will learn to create one of each and learn about its uses.

The next tool to cover is the **RAY** tool. This is a very useful tool when it comes to drawing construction lines as a reference to use in offset or any other sketch.

Ray is an Infinite Construction Line drawn in one direction.

A Ray line will have a definite starting point that you define and project a straight line from the set point to Infinity.

You are now going to use the **RAY** tool to create sketches.

Start AutoCAD if it is not already running on your Computer and create a new file.

69.   Type **Ray** at the Command prompt and press the Enter key, or click on **Draw**
        from the Main Menu and select **Ray**. A message pops up requesting you to:

70.   **Specify start point:**

71.   Type **0, 0** to place the first point at the origin, and press the Enter key. A
        message pops up requesting you to:

72.   **Specify through point:**

73.   Click on **SW** from the origin to place the first Ray Line. . A message pops
        up requesting you to:

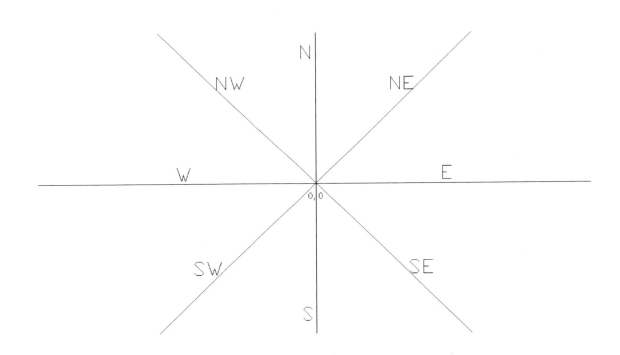

Figure 1.21

74. **Specify through point:**

Move the pointer away from the **SW** and click on the Cardinal points clockwise or counterclockwise on the graphics area to place the rest of the Ray lines. Refer to Figure 1.21

75. Repeat this action until you are satisfied with the pattern being created or just a line being drawn

76. Press the Enter key to exit the **Ray** command.

Xline:

XLINE like the Ray will create an infinite line, which are normally used as construction lines. Xline gives you the option of drawing lines with horizontal, vertical, Angular, Bisect as well as Offset. You are now going to use the Xline tool to create sketches. Start AutoCAD if it is not already running on your Computer and create a new file.

77. Type **Xline** at the Command prompt and press the Enter key.

78. **Specify a point or [Hor / Ver / Ang / Bisect / Offset]:**

79. Type the letter '**H**' short for horizontal and press the Enter key. A message pops up requesting you to:

80. **Specify through point:**

81. Type **0, 0** and press the Enter key A message pops up requesting you to:

82. **Specify through point:**

83. **Press the Enter key again** to place a **Horizontal Line** from the origin to **Infinity**

You will notice that, when you press the Enter key once more, it will reactivate the **Xline** command. Since, no new tool has been selected yet. Go ahead and press the Enter key again you are now going to use the **Angle** option to draw an Xline

84. After pressing the Enter key, a message pops up requesting you to

85. **Specify a point or [Hor / Ver / Ang / Bisect / Offset]:**

86. Type the letter '**V**' short for **Vertical** and press the Enter key. A message pops up requesting you to

87. **Specify through point:**

88. Type **0, 0** and press the Enter key **2Xs**, to place a **Vertical** line from the origin to infinity

89. Press the Enter key to activate the Xline A message pops up requesting you to:

90. **Specify a point or [Hor / Ver / Ang / Bisect / Offset]:**

91. Type the letter '**A**' short for Angle and press the Enter key A message pops up requesting you to

92. **Enter angle of Xline (0) or [Reference]:**

93. Type **15** and press the Enter key A message pops up requesting you to:

94. **Specify through point**

95. Type **0, 0 and press the Enter key 2xs,** to place a line at an angle of **15°** through the origin.

You are now going to use the **Bisect** option to draw an Xline

96. Press the Enter key to activate the Xline command or type **Xline** and press the Enter key. A message pops up requesting you to:

97. **Specify a point or [Hor / Ver / Ang / Bisect / Offset]:**

98.   Type the letter 'B' short for **Vertical** and press the Enter key. A message pops up requesting you to:

99.   **Specify angle vertex point:**

100.   Type **0, 0** and press the Enter A message pops up requesting you to

101.   **Specify angle start point**

102.   Type **35** and press the Enter key A message pops up requesting you to

103.   **Specify angle end point**

104.   Type **45** and press the Enter key **2X** to place an **Xline** through the origin.

You are now going to use the **Offset** option to create a duplicate copy of the Xline.

105.   Press the Enter key to activate the Xline command or type **Xline** and press the Enter key. A message pops up requesting you to:

106.   **Specify a point or [Hor / Ver / Ang / Bisect / Offset]:**

107.   Type the letter 'O' short for **Vertical** and press the Enter key. A message pops up requesting you to

108.   Specify **Offset** distance or Through [Through]

109.   Type **5** and press the Enter key A message pops up requesting you to:

110.   **Select a line object:**

111.   Click on one of the lines and click away from it to place an offset Xline at a specified distance.

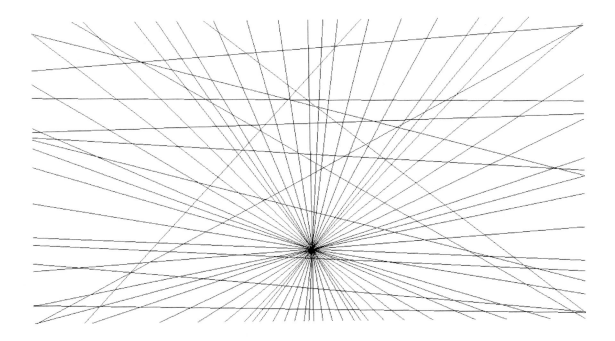

Figure 1.22

Multiline:

The next Topic will cover **Multiline.** This is a very useful tool in Civil Engineering as well as in **Cartography**, map design. You will have to use the **Multiline Style** to setup required options before utilizing it in your drawing. Follow these steps to set up the Multiline options. Open AutoCAD and start a new file.

112.　Click on Format from the Main Menu and select **Multiline Style**

113.　A dialogue box pops up with different options, ranging from Current, **Name and Description Load, Save, Add Rename, Element, Multiline Properties**, You are now going to define Multiline style.

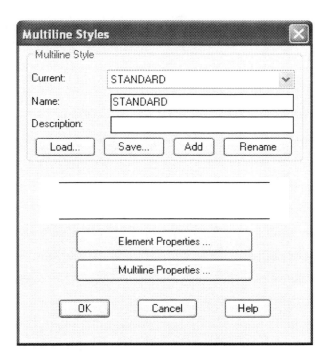

Figure 1.23

You can set capping arrangements, Linetype pattern, colors, as well as spacing between parallel lines. Multiline is made up of two parallel lines, set by default as - 0.5 and 0.5 apart which can be changed. To set the Multiline, let us go through the list of items starting with Current.

Current:

Use the edit box to set the current Multiline style in your drawing.

Predefined Multiline styles can be accessed through the drop-down list through the edit box. Any style e can be chosen to represent the current Multiline style.

Follow these steps to customize the Current edit box to your environment.

114. Click on **Dimension** from the Main Menu and select **Style**, the **Dimension Style Manager** pops up.

115. Click on **New** and enter **Multiline** in the box by the **New Style Name**

116. Click on **Continue** and open the **Lines & Arrows** tab.

117. Change **arrow size** to **0.25** and **Color** to **Red By layer**

118. Click on **Text Style Browser** and change **Font Name** to **Times New Roman** and 0.25 for the height

119. Click on Apply and click to close the dialogue box

120. Click on set current to exit the Dimension Style Manager Dialogue box.

Name:

After defining the Multiline style, you can enter the name of the Multiline you created in the Name box.

Description:

Here is where you enter a text about the make of you Multiline. For an example, enter **0.25** Text height. Red color and **0.25** for the Arrow size

Load:

Customized and predefined MultiLines, can be invoked using the Load option, with an extension of **(.mln)**

You can select from a list of Multiline styles when you use Format Multiline Style and click on Load

Save:

Multiline that you create will be saved under the Save option. This opens up the AutoCAD Support folder and lets you save your Multiline with an (.mln) extension.

Add:

This option allows you to Add loaded Multiline into the Current option and to enable you choose from a list of items.

Rename:

Currently loaded Multiline can always be renamed through this edit box. Be informed that Standard Multiline is a Default Multiline and cannot be renamed.

Line Display Panel:

This dialog box displays color, Linetype and the spacing given to your Multiline.

Element Properties:

Changes can only be made to new Multiline style and not the Standard Multiline; therefore new Multiline should be entered before doing so.

When you click on the Element Properties you have the option of editing the Offset, Change Color as well as the Linetype.

Add:

New Lines can be added to the current Line style. AutoCAD inserts an offset distance of **(0, 0)** when new lines are added. This offset can always be change to reflect the design you are currently working on.

Delete:

As the word depicts, the edit option allows you delete highlighted lines in the list box.

Linetype:

The Standard Linetype dialog box, allows you to assign different Linetypes to selected Multiline, from Centerline to Hidden lines.

Now that you have gone through all the editing tools, let us put them into use to find out the practical aspect of the Multiline Style. Load the Multiline Style from the main menu.

121.   Click on Format and select **Multiline Style**.

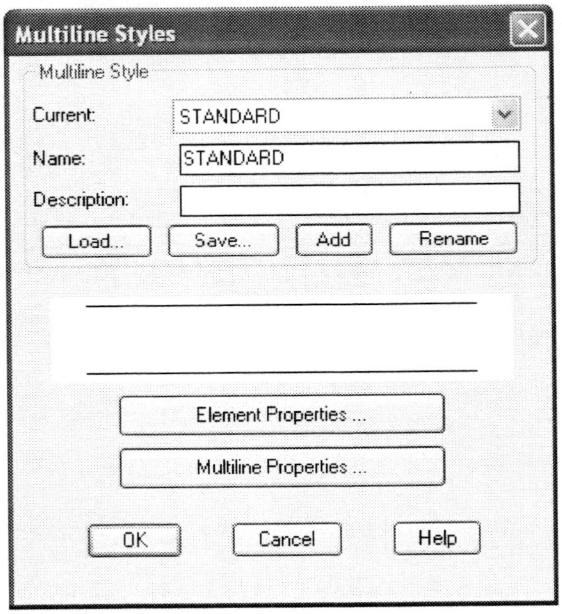

Figure 1.24

122.   Multi Line Style dialogue box opens Refer to Figure 1.24

123.   Click Add and Type MLProject inside the box by the Name

124.   Click Add again to make the new name Current

125.   Type New Multiline inside the Description box

126. Click on Element Properties

127. Click to highlight the default 0.5 and change it to 1.00 by the Offset

128. Click to highlight the default -0.5 and change it to 0.5 by the Offset

129. Click on 1.00 to make it current and click on Color

130. Change the color to Green in the Color pallet

131. Click to highlight 0.50 and click on Color

132. Change the Color to Red from the Color pallet

133. Click on Linetype and change it to Continuous and click on OK 2Xs

134. This will bring you back to the Multiline Style dialogue box.

135. Click on **Multiline Properties**

136. Click to place a check mark under **Fill** and change the color to **Cyan**

137. Change the **90** in the two boxes by Angle to **75** and **75** and OK again to exit the Multiline Styles dialogue box.

138. Click on Save and Enter MLProject in the File Name and click on Save

139. Click OK to exit the Multiline dialogue box

You are now going to use this setup to draw a strip of road to a farmhouse.
Type **Mline** at the Command prompt and press the Enter key. A message pops up requesting you to:

140. **Specify start point or [Justification / Scale /Style]:**

141. Click on the Screen also known as the Graphics area and move the pointer horizontally to your right at about 5inches and click

142. Move the pointer at an angle of 30 Northeast at a distance of about 7 inches and click again and press the Enter key to exit the command.

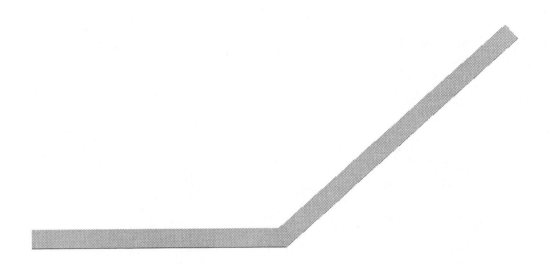

Figure 1.25

Multiline Editing

143. Type **MLEDIT** at the command prompt and press the Enter key. The

144. Multiline Edit Tools pop up for you to select an option.

145. Whenever you click on one of the Multiline in the edit Tools, a text explaining the type is listed below the OK button

146. The **Closed Tee** appears at the bottom of the OK button denoting that the Closed Tee is select for the drawing. Refer to the Figure 1.26 below

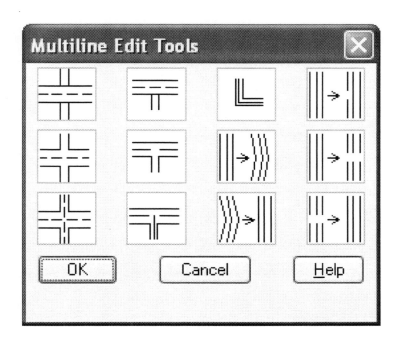

Figure 1.26

Rectangle:

Just as Line goes, Rectangles could be drawn through similar steps, with shortcuts, aliases, the Draw on the Menu Bar or using the Rectangular icon.

You can also right-click on any of the status bar icon to expand the Tool list to choose from.

Bring up editing Tools by Right-clicking on the Graphics area, whenever the need arises.

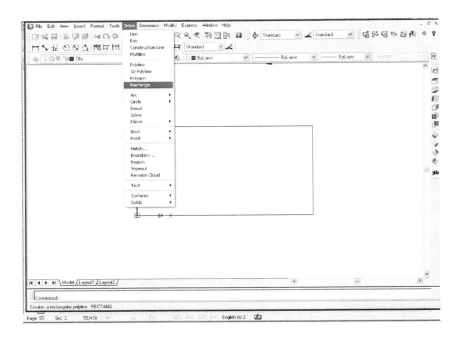

Figure 1.27

147. Click on Draw again and select **Rectangle** from the list of Tools.

148. Click on the Graphics area; release your finger from the left mouse button.

149. Drag the mouse away from the first point and click again on the graphics area to complete drawing the rectangle.

150. Repeat these steps until you are very comfortable in drawing a rectangle and move on to an Arc.

Figure 1.28

You will follow similar steps in drawing an Arc. There are different ways to draw an Arc depending on the point you are trying to convey. Arc comes in the following styles:

- 3 Points
- Start, Center, End
- Start, Center, Angle
- Start, Center, Length
- Start, End, Angle
- Start, End, Direction
- Start, End, Radius
- Center, Start, End
- Center, Start, Angle
- Center, Start, Length
- Continue

151. Click on the Draw from the Status Bar, scroll down to Arc and select 3 Points.
152. On the Graphics area, click on three separate locations to draw an Arc.
153. Try the other Options and find out how best you can draw an Arc.
154. Repeat this action until you are very good in drawing an Arc.

It is advisable to start each and every lesson by doing Revision, meaning going over prior things you have learned since everything is related one way or the other.

Tool Tips:

When you leave your pointer on any ICON for a few seconds, it will reveal the function of that particular icon in a Text format for you to read.

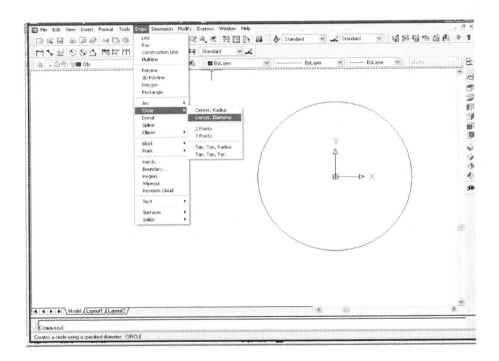

Figure 1.29

Figure 1.28 gives a list of different approach to drawing a circle. There is:

- Center, Radius
- Center Diameter
- 2 Points
- 3 Points
- Tan, Tan, Radius
- Tan, Tan, Tan

For now use **Center, Diameter** for drawing your first Circle until you become very good at drawing a circle. Others tools and techniques will be introduced in course of time and you will get to learn how to use these options.

<u>Circle:</u>

155.   Click on **Draw** on the Status Bar and select **Circle** to activate the tool command.

156.   Select Center, Diameter and move to the Graphics area

157.   On the Graphics area, click at a point and release your finger from the left button, move the mouse away from the first point and click again to complete the circle.

158.   Repeat this action several times to familiarize yourself with the art of drawing a circle.

Designing is like an art, you first learn how to speak its language; how to pick the right tools, then you apply them to particular instance until you get it right. The steps you are taking are helping you build your design skills as you learn this new language and vocabulary in order to use it correctly.

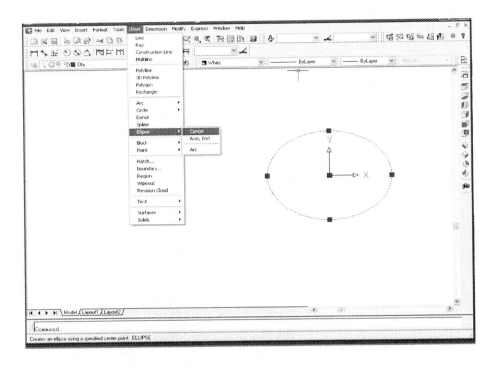

Figure 1.30

Ellipse:

Ellipse is like a circle viewed from an angle Refer to Figure 1.30. The following options will guide you in selecting a particular style for the ellipse.

- Center
- Axis, End
- Arc

159.   Select DRAW from the Status bar and click on Ellipse to bring up all the options.

160.   Use the Center to draw an Ellipse.

161.   To draw an Ellipse, make sure the **ORTHO** is on by pressing the F8 Function key.

162.   This will force our Lines to move, either in **Vertical** or **Horizontal** Axis.

163.   With the Center for Ellipse selected, click on the Graphics area and drag you mouse pointer **Vertically** upward and click again.

164.   Next move the mouse pointer **Horizontally** to the right or Left away from the origin and click again to complete drawing the Ellipse.

165.   Continue to draw several **Ellipses** until you are very good at it.

In Figure 1.30, you will notice **FIVE** squares also known as **GRIPS**.

These represent a true **Ellipse** since it has a **CENTER** and **QUADRANT** points. To activate the **Grips** move the mouse pointer to any sideline on the Ellipse and click on it, the whole figure lights up in five blue squares.

Click on one of the Squares, hold down the left button, and drag it to another location and click on the left button again to end the action. This will change the size and form of the Ellipse.

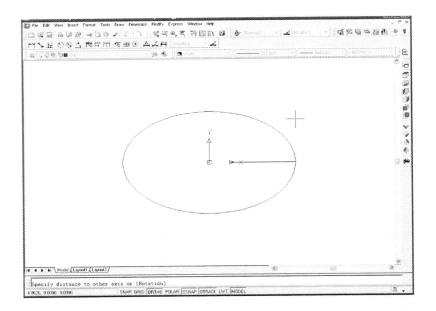

Figure 1.31

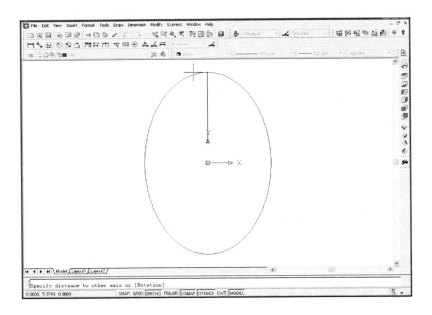

Figure 1.32

You have covered most of the basic steps in creating a drawing and the next lesson will cover **Absolute, Relative** and **Polar Coordinate System**. Knowing this essential Tool will aid you in making drawings easier and locating points in any quadrant to produce better results. In reality you will not have room for guesswork so as all drawings you do come out accurate.

Figure 1.33

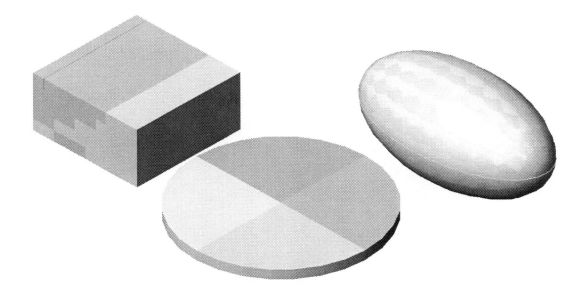

Figure 1.34

SUMMARY:

In this chapter, we learned how to open New from File, get familiar with some of the tools and draw a sketch using basic tools and saved it.

You were introduced to Basic AutoCAD from how to start and actually use different Drawing tools to draw sketches. You have so far covered contents of Table 1.03:

Table 1.03

Design Skills	Dialogue Boxes	Start Up Dialogue
Use a Wizard	Template Setup	Create New Folder
Open a Drawing	Save As	Customizing a Template
Limits	Upper Limits	Lower Limits
Full Scale	Sheet Layout	American Standards
International Standard	Creating Layers	Layer Properties Manager
Colors	Line Type	How to draw a Line
Draw Rectangle	Draw an Arc	Tool Tips
Draw a Circle	Draw Ellipse	Grips

Figure 1.33 shows drawings of 2D sketches while Figure 1.34 is demonstrating the uses of 3D Models for practical application using Lines, Circles and Ellipses.

There is a Stack of Lumber, a Pie Chart, and a Blimp.

This demonstrates the endless uses of AutoCAD. You will be introduced to the Editing drawings in the next chapter.

Complete the Exercises below to be able to have control of the software and know what move to make next.

Exercise:

1. Create a Template from scratch and give it a new name

2. Change the Limits to 15 x 12

3. Set up Layers with Object, Dims, Hatch, Centerline, Text and change the colors associated with them

4. Draw a Line, Circle, Arc, rectangle and an Ellipse.

5. Save all in a Folder as Project1 and exit AutoCAD.

The next lesson will cover **Editing tools**

YOU WANT TO KNOW HOW TO DO IT DON'T YOU? WELL LET'S DO IT!!!

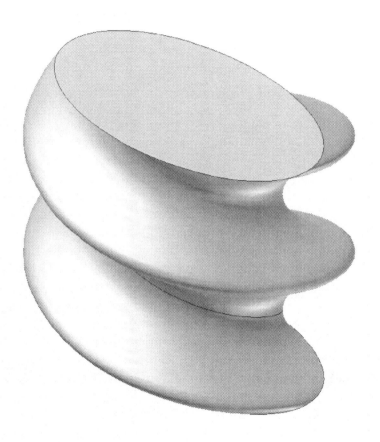

CHAPTER 2:

In this chapter you will explore many other functions to make your designing quicker and easier. You will be introduced to short cuts and basic designing tools in the exercises that would be covered.

After completing this Chapter, you will be able to:

    a. Use the Editing tools under the Modify tool bar

    b. Use Offset Object

    c. Know how to use Extend on Objects

    d. Learn about Drawing Lines

    e. Use Trim to remove unwanted lines

    f. Use the Move tool

    g. Use the Copy editing tool

    h. Use Erase for editing objects.

Figure 2.00

In Figure 2.00 is a **Modify Toolbar** with a list of different Editing tools including from the left to right of the screen, tools as listed in the Table below:

Table 2.00

Erase	Copy Object	Mirror	Offset	Array
Move	Rotate	Scale	Stretch	Trim
Extend	Break at Point	Break	Chamfer	Fillet & Explode

We will cover the tools as the need arises in subsequent chapters.

Editing:

(This will be explained in more detail later on in the chapter)

All designs, no matter how well planned, will be changed one way or the other during the course of the drawing. You will therefore be introduced to editing and Modifying tools, before creating your first drawing.

1. Start a new file by clicking on the **AutoCAD** icon from the desktop or click on **start** on the desktop, click on All Programs and select AutoCAD from the list of software.
2. Click on **open and select your Template** and click to open it.
3. Select the **Line** tool, click on the graphics area, release your finger from the left mouse button drag the mouse pointer away from the first point and click again to complete the operation. Hit the escape (**esc**) button
4. Click on the line just drawn and hit the **delete** button by the keypad, then click on the undo icon on the main menu and hit on the escape button (**esc**) to complete the first edit.

Offset:

This command is used to create parallel or concentric lines of objects at a specified distance. These include rectangles, circles, ellipse and different geometric shapes. Depending on the style you are aiming for, you can offset the object out or inside the original object. Follow these steps to create offset of different objects.

5. Click on Modify from the Main Menu, select **Offset** or type offset at the Command prompt and press the Enter key.

6. You will be asked to:

7. **Specify offset distance or [Through]**

8. Type **1.00** and press the Enter key, your pointer should turn into a **square box.**

9. Watch what message comes up in front of the Command.

10. **Select object to offset or <exit> appears** in front of the Command prompt

11. Click on the Line just drawn the pointer should now turn into a **crosshair.**

12. Move the pointer to another location and click on the Graphics area again, a

13. Copy of the line is placed a distance of 1.00 unit from the Original line. Refer to Figure 2.01.

14. Follow the procedure for drawing a Line above and draw a line perpendicular to the two lines as below.

15. Select the Line tool from Draw menu, at the Command prompt you will be asked to Specify first point

16. Click above the two lines and let go of your finger off the left mouse button

17. **Specify next point or [undo]** appears at the Command prompt

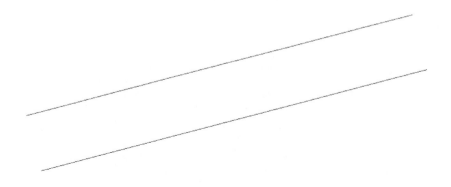

Figure 2.01

18. Type **'per' short** for **Perpendicular,** and press the Enter key.

19. Move the pointer closer to the parallel lines, and notice a perpendicular sign at the base of the pointer as you move it closer to the line.

20. Click to place the line on the first of two lines and click on 'esc' the escape key.

Offset command was used in creating the patterns in Figure 2.06; by invoking the Offset command after drawing each shape, specifying a distance and clicking on the lines and circles

Circle:

Follow these steps to draw a Circle

21. Click on draw from the Main Menu highlight, Circle and select Center, radius. A Message pops up requesting you to:

22. **Specify center point for circle or [3P / 2P / Ttr (Tan tan radius)]**

23. Click anywhere on the Graphics area, release your finger from the left mouse button and drag the Mouse pointer away from the original point and click again to place the circle.

Figure 2.02

Spline:

You will be guided to draw a Spline.

24. Click on Draw and select Spline from the list of tools. A Message pops up requesting you to:

25. **Specify first point or [Object]:**

26. Click close to the bottom of the screen. A Message pops up requesting you to:

27. **Specify the next point**

28. Release your finger from the Left mouse button, move the mouse pointer above the first point and click again. Continue to click up and down to follow a pattern. Hit the Enter key three times when finished to place the Spline.

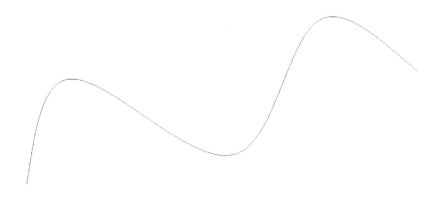

Figure 2.03

Rectangle:

29. Click on **Draw** from the Main Menu and select **Rectangle**. A Message pops up requesting you to:

30. **Specify first corner point or [Chamfer / Elevation / Fillet / Thickness / Width]:**

31. Click on the Graphics area. A Message pops up requesting you to:

32. **Specify other corner point or [Dimension]:**

33. Release your finger from the left mouse button, move the mouse pointer away from the first point and click again to place the rectangle.

Figure 2.04

Ellipse:

34. Click on Draw from the Main menu highlight **Ellipse** and select Center. A Message pops up requesting you to:

35. **Specify center of ellipse**

36. Press the Function key **'F2'** to turn the Ortho on. Ortho forces the objects to be drawn horizontally or vertically.

37. Click on the Graphics area, move the mouse pointer horizontally to the right and click at a distance.

38. **Specify distance to other axis or [Rotation]:**

39. Move the mouse pointer vertically upwards and click to place an Ellipse on the Graphics area

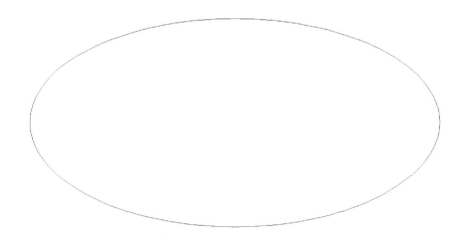

Figure 2.05

You should Notice by now that we use Draw to generate Geometric objects and Modify option to edit the sketches.

You are going to use these three lines for your Editing Lesson. First you will learn of a new tool called **Extend.**

Extend:

This command is used to lengthen or extend a line or an entity to another object; however you cannot extend a closed **Polyline**. This means if you draw a rectangle with the Rectangle tool, it automatically turns into one complete Polyline unlike drawing a rectangle using four separate lines

You have just used the **Offset** tool to make duplicate copies of **Geometrical objects**.

Next you will use Extend to extend object from one location, to the other and to do this

40. Click on **Modify** from the Main Menu and select **Extend**

41. **Select Objects** message appears at the Command:

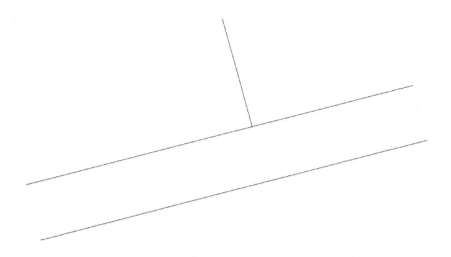

Figure 2.06

42. Click on the first line at the bottom and press the Enter key

43. **Select object to extend or shift select to trim or [Project / Edge / Undo]**

44. Click on the perpendicular line and watch the perpendicular line extend to the first line.

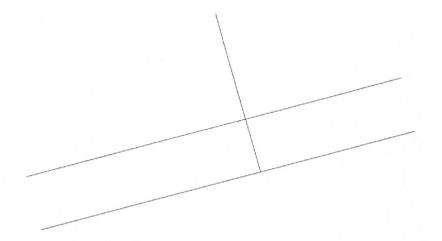

Figure 2.07

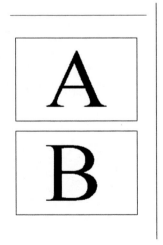

Figure 2.08

In Figure 2.04 **Rectangle A** was drawn with the rectangle tool from the **Draw** menu, as such it becomes one entity also known as a **Polyline.**

Rectangle B on the other hand was drawn with four different lines and it is not a Polyline.

This means you can use the move command to move **Rectangle A** all at once; but you can only move a Line when you try to move **Rectangle B.**

Alternatively, you cannot extend **Rectangle A** to the vertical Line since it is a Polyline, but the horizontal lines perpendicular to the vertical lines can be extended. Follow these steps for clarification of the above explanation.

45. Select Rectangle from the Draw menu, you will be asked at the Command prompt to:

46. **Specify first corner point or [Chamfer / Elevation / Fillet / Thickness / Width]:**

47. Type **0, 0** and press the Enter key. You will be asked again to:

48. **Specify other corner point or [Dimension]:**

49. Type **6.0, 4.0** and press the Enter key, a Rectangle is drawn. To see the rectangle, type Zoom at the Command prompt and the following message comes up

50. **[All / Center / Dynamic / Extents / Previous / Scale / Window]<real time>:**

51. Type **A** for all and press the Enter key. Next click **Pan** from the **View** menu and select **Realtime**, your pointer should turn into a **hand**.

52. Click and hold down the Left button on your mouse and move the rectangle to position it in the center of the screen.

<u>Drawing a Line</u>

53. Select Line from the Draw menu and press the **F8** function key to force the line only to move horizontally and vertically.

54. Click directly below the UCS icon as in Figure 2.08, move the pointer horizontally to the right, type **6.00** and press the Enter key

55. Move the pointer vertically downwards and type **4.00** and press the Enter key. Your drawing should look like that in Figure 2.09

56. Move the pointer horizontally to the left of the screen and type **6.00** and finally

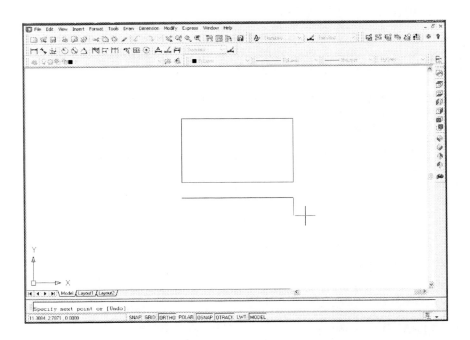

Figure 2.09

57. Move the pointer upwards and type **4.00** and press the Enter key two times to

exit the command.

58. Use the Line tool from the Draw Menu to sketch a vertical and horizontal lines as in Figure 2.10

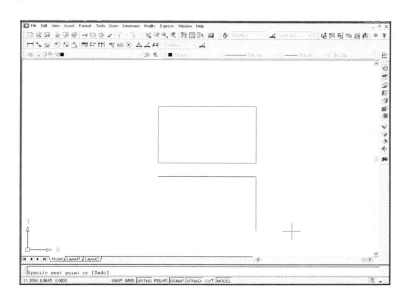

Figure 2.10

Figure 2.11

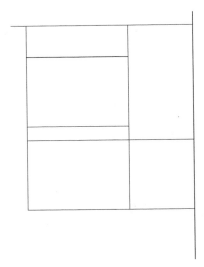

Figure 2.12

59. Click on Modify from the Main Menu and select Extend, you are then asked to:

60. **Select objects**: at the Command prompt

61. Click on the vertical line and press the Enter key. At the Command prompt you will be asked to:

62. **Select object to extend or shift-select to trim or [Project / Edge / Undo]**

63. When you click on the bottom Rectangle drawn with lines, the two horizontal lines will extend to meet the vertical line.

64. The upper Rectangle will not extend when you try to click on it to Extend. This is the reason why the Polyline cannot be used in Extend.

Trim:

Use the Trim command to remove unwanted objects in your drawing. However lines and other objects that do not cross each other cannot be trimmed. You will use delete in this case to remove such objects and lines that will not trim. To understand the concept of using the Trim to modify your sketches, follow these steps:

65. Select the Circle from the Draw Menu, or type circle at the Command prompt and click on the intersection of the first two lines, and release your finger from the left mouse button.

66. Move the pointer and click on the intersection of the second lines to place the circle as in Figure 2.13. You will use Trim tool to remove certain portions of the Lines.

Use the Trim tool to take off unwanted lines from the sketch.

67. Click on **Trim** from the **Modify** menu, **Select objects:** message appears up at the Command

68. Click once on the **Circle** and press the **Enter** key.

69. **Select object to trim or shift-select to extend or [Project / Edge / Undo]**

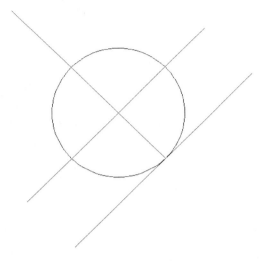

Figure 2.13

70. Click on the lines inside the Circle to remove all and press the Enter key

71. Click on **Undo on the Main Menu** several times after that, to restore the original drawing to use for the Move option.

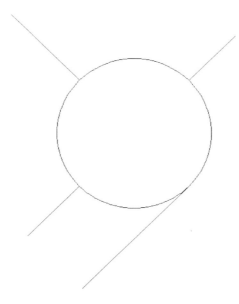

Figure 2.14

Move:

Use the Move command to relocate objects from one place to the other, if you are not satisfied with its present location. You can accomplish this with the Move command from the Modify Menu.

To move sketches do the following

72. Click outside the sketch in Figure 2.14, hold down the left button on the mouse and drag an invincible rectangle around the sketch. Release your finger.

73. All sketch should be highlighted as depicted in Figure 2.16

74. Click on **Move** from the Modify menu and you will be asked to:

75. **Specify base point or displacement:** click outside the sketch

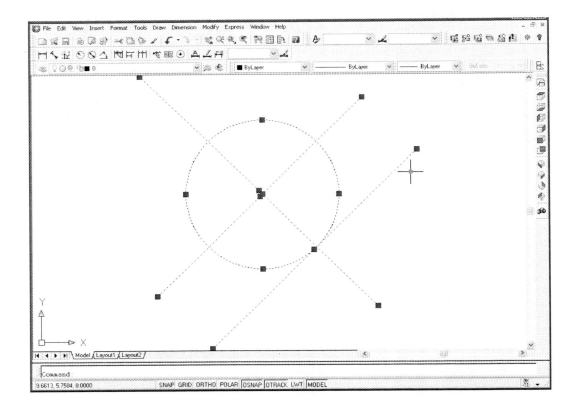

Figure 2.15

76. You are again asked at the Command prompt to:

77. **Specify second point of displacement or (Use first point as displacement)**

78. Release your finger from the left mouse button and move the mouse across the Graphics area.

79. When you are satisfied with its new location, click on the left mouse button to place the object.

Figure 2.16

Copy:

You will use the copy command to duplicate objects to avoid the need of redrawing it again.

The copied objects are then placed in a specified location.

The process of copying an object is very straightforward.

You first select the object to be copied, specify the destination and click to apply.

Follow these steps to copy the circle and lines just drawn.

80. Click on **Copy** from **Modify** on the Main Menu bar, you are asked to:

81. **Select objects:** at the Command prompt

82. Type '**All**' and press the Enter key two times. You will be asked to:

83. **Specify base point or displacement or [Multiple]:**

84. Click outside the sketch move the mouse across the graphics area and click to place the copy of the original object.

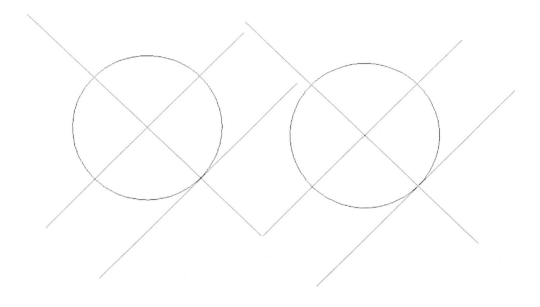

Figure 2.17

Erase:

To **erase** an object or Text from your drawing, you simply invoke the **Erase** editing tool from the **Modify** menu and click to erase the objects.

Alternatively you can locate the pencil icon on the toolbar as indicated below and follow the procedure for erasing the objects.

Figure 2.18

85. Click on Modify Erase, you will be asked at the Command prompt to:

86. **Select objects**: Click on all the objects you would like to erase and hit the Enter key.

87. Since we could not use the Trim option for the rest of the lines in Figure 2.14, use erase to remove the rest of the lines.

88. Click on the lines after invoking the erase command and when asked to:

89. **Select objects:** click on the lines and hit the Enter key.

This concludes the Editing processes to cover the needed options for most 2D Drawings. More Editing will be covered as and when they become necessary.

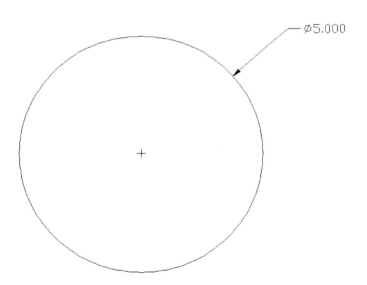

Figure 2.19

<u>Summary:</u>

- In this Exercise, you first learned how to draw a line, circle, Spline, rectangle and ellipse

- You used the **Offset** entity to make copy of the line

- Next you drew another line perpendicular to the two lines.

- With the aid of the **Extend** entity, you extended the perpendicular line to that of the double lines

- You then drew a circle from the center of all the intersecting lines.

- You were guided to use **Trim** to remove certain portions of the sketch

- The Undo button came in handy in restoring the sketch again

- You moved the whole sketch with the **Move** entity.

- Covered **Copy** option and finally

- Used the **Erase** option to remove other entities

Exercise:

Click on File, New from the Main Menu and go through all the steps we have just covered, from drawing a Line to editing it, without making references to any of the sketches and find out how much you have just learned.

The next Lesson will cover the **Coordinate System**

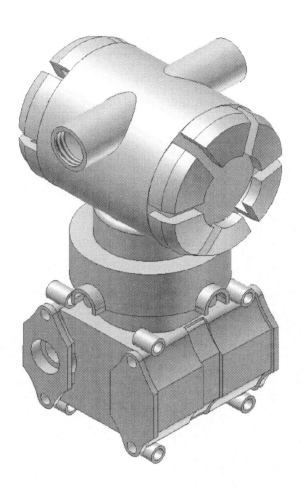

CHAPTER 3

In this chapter you will explore many other functions to make your designing quicker and easier. You will be introduced to short cuts and basic designing tools in the exercises that would be covered.

After completing this Chapter, you will be able to use:

- Absolute, Relative, Polar Coordinates, Offset, Origin
- The Object Selection
- Work with Crossing:
- Learn of what DDselect is used for
- The Noun /Verb selection
- Shift to Add to Selection
- Know of Drafting Settings
- Snap and Grid option
- The Rotate and Offset options
- The Trim and Dimensioning

Two perpendicular lines are used as reference to specify a particular location in XY plane. This crossing line, which is also known as the Cartesian coordinate system, is represented with three axes, X, Y, and Z. The Z plane is normally used in 3D models and would be covered in subsequent chapters.

On entering the coordinate values, you will be indicating intersections of distances from one point to the other in preferred units and its direction **+Ve** or **-Ve** along the X, Y, and Z axes relative to the coordinate system origin (0, 0, 0).

Intersections are specified in 2D on the XY plane, also called the construction plane. Consider a flat sheet of grid paper you work with daily that is represented by the Construction Plane.

The X value of a Cartesian coordinate specifies Horizontal distances are represented on the **+Ve** and **-Ve** X value on the Cartesian system and **+Ve** and **-Ve** Y value represent the vertical distances on the Cartesian system. The intersection of the two axes of X and Y is represented in AutoCAD as the **Origin (0, 0)**

Angles are measured counterclockwise from right to left and the system is divided into **Quadrants.**

Refer to Figure 3.00 below for the design of the Quadrants

Values entered **above** the **Horizontal Lines** are **positive** and that **below** the horizontal lines in the Coordinate system are **negative.**

Similarly, values entered to the right of the **Vertical** lines are **positive** and that to the left of the vertical central line is **negative.**

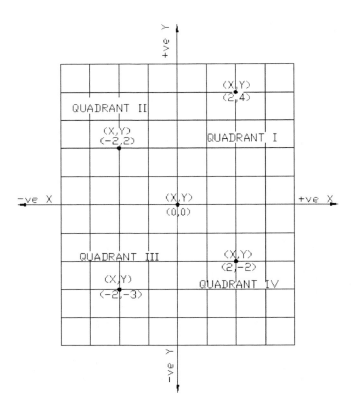

Figure 3.00

Absolute Coordinate System:

Intersection of the two axes of X and Y, are located in relation to the Origin. In AutoCAD the Origin is located at the bottom left of the graphic screen as the default.

The UCS **(User Coordinate System),** which is also the Origin, can be moved to any location of your choice, making that intersection the **Origin (0, 0)**

This will become very handy when working in 3D modeling environment and will be explained in detail when 3D is covered in subsequent chapters.

For now let us concern ourselves with the uses of the Coordinate system.

In Absolute coordinate, horizontal units increase in the positive X direction from the origin and decrease in negative X direction. Refer to Figure 3.00.

For further explanation follow this example for better understanding of the Absolute coordinate system

Absolute requires that all coordinates entered be made with reference to the **Origin.** For an example to draw a polygon **2 X 2**, you will first pick up the line tool from the Draw option, start from **0,0 2,0 2,2 0,2** then **0,0** again to complete the square. To visualize this follow the stapes below

Type **Line** at the **Command prompt** and press the **Enter key**, you will be asked to:

1. **Line Specify first point**: type **0,0** at the Command Prompt and press the Enter key

2. **Specify next point or [Undo]:** type **2,0** at the Command prompt and press the Enter key

3. **Specify next point or [Close / Undo]:** type **2,2** and press the Enter key

4. **Specify next point or [Close / Undo]:** type **0,2** and press the Enter key

5. **Specify next point or [Close / Undo]:** press the Enter key to exit the Line command.

Remember all references are made in relation to the **Origin** in the **Absolute Coordinate System**

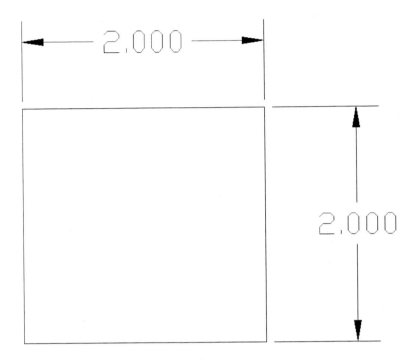

Figure 3.01

Relative Coordinate Systems:

The Relative Coordinate System is slightly different from that of the Absolute, in that the last intersection of the object will be marked as the reference point of the sketch rather than the Origin. The symbol also known as the **'at'** sign **'@'** is used in conjunction with unit entries to obtain the required sketch. In this example you will draw the same **2 X 2** square polygon but with Relative coordinates. To do this, type Line at the Command Prompt and press the Enter key to follow the steps.

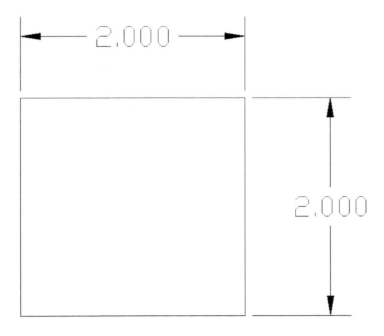

Figure 3.02

6. **Line Specify first point**: type **0,0** at the Command Prompt and press the Enter key

7. **Specify next point or [Close / Undo]:** type @ 2,0 at the Command Prompt and press the Enter key

8. **Specify next point or [Close / Undo]:** type @ 0,2 at the Command Prompt and press the Enter key

9. **Specify next point or [Close / Undo]:** type @ -2,0 at the Command Prompt and press the Enter key

10. **Specify next point or [Close / Undo]:** type @ 0, -2 at the Command Prompt and press the Enter key

11. **Specify next point or [Close / Undo]:** press the Enter key

12. This will produce same results but with a different approach

Polar Coordinate Systems:

The final approach will be to use the **Polar Coordinate System**. The Polar Coordinate System combines the **Absolute, Relative** and **Angles** using the less than key '<' on the keyboard to draw sketches. To understand its workings, follow these steps to make your sketches type **Line** at the Command Prompt and press the **Enter** key to follow the steps.

13. **Line Specify first point**: type **0,0** at the Command Prompt and press the Enter key

14. **Specify next point or [Close / Undo]:** type **@ 2,0** at the Command Prompt and press the Enter key

15. **Specify next point or [Close / Undo]:** type **@ 2<90** at the Command Prompt and press the Enter key

16. **Specify next point or [Close / Undo]:** type **@ 2<180** at the Command Prompt and press the Enter key

17. **Specify next point or [Close / Undo]:** type **@ 2<270** at the Command Prompt and press the Enter key

18. **Specify next point or [Close / Undo]:** press the Enter key to exit the line command

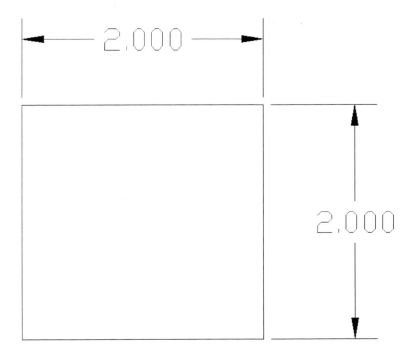

Figure 3.03

Object Selection

Selecting an object is a very essential part of drawing in AutoCAD. With Object Selection, you can go through the entire editing process one step at a time. This includes Move, Erase, Copy, Mirror, Offset Array, Move, Rotate, Scale, Stretch, Trim, Extend, Break, Chamfer and Fillet.

Figure 3.04

There is **Crossing** where an invincible window is drawn around an object to edit a particular line or entire drawing. Crossing is also used to stretch a sketch or an object from one point to the other. This form of Object selection makes it easier to keep the required parts and eliminate the unwanted ones. It will be further demonstrated in subsequent chapters other forms of Object Selection as and when it becomes necessary. For now follow these steps to learn how Object selection works.

19. Start AutoCAD and bring up your Template. Click on Save AS and give it a name like **Obj Sel – Project**.

20. Select Rectangle from the Draw option on the Main Menu or type Rectangle at the Command prompt to invoke the rectangle tool.

21. **Specify other corner point or [Chamfer / Elevation / Fillet / Thickness / Width]:** comes up at the Command prompt.

22. Click anywhere on the Graphics area.

23. **Specify other corner point or [Dimension]:**

24. Move the pointer away from the first point and click on the Graphics area again to complete the Rectangular object.

25. Select a circle from the Draw Option or type circle at the Command prompt

26. **Specify Center point for Circle or [3P/2P/Ttr (tan tan radius)]:**

27. Click on the graphics area to place the first point and a message will pop up to

28. **Specify radius or circle [Diameter]:** drag the mouse pointer to a different location and click on the graphics area again.

29. Your drawing should look like the one in Figure 3.05

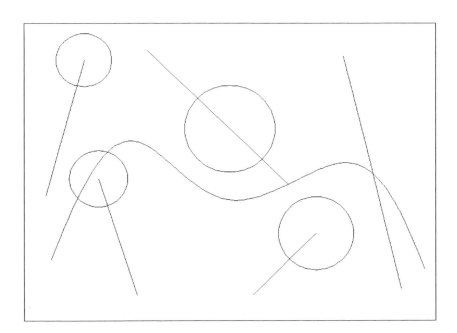

Figure 3.05

108

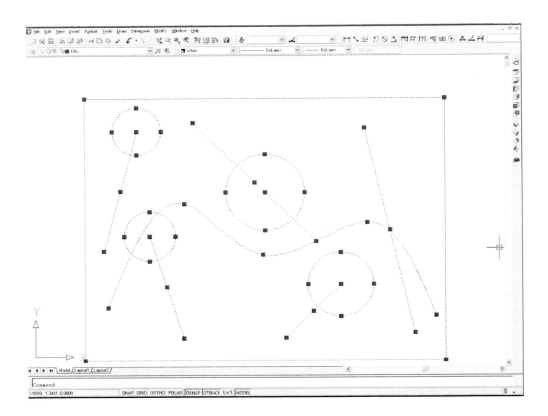

Figure 3.06

DDSelect:

Type DDSelect at the Command prompt or right-click in front of the Command prompt and click on OPTIONS.

Click on Selection in the Options dialogue box to bring up the, Object Selection Settings Dialogue box to activate the Object Selection Settings Dialogue box. In the

Dialogue box will be listed five different Selection Modes, starting with, **Noun/Verb** Selection, Use Shift to Add, Press and Drag, Implied Windowing, Object Grouping, and Associative Hatch.

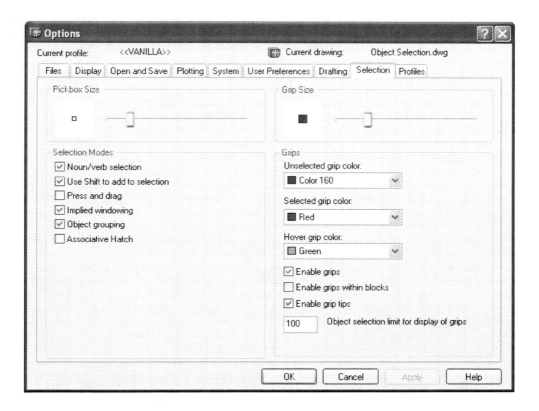

Figure 3.07

Noun/Verb Selection

Checking in the box by Noun/Verb Selection, will allow you to pick the Object (Noun) before using a tool like Move (Verb) or activate the Move (Verb) before selecting the Object (Noun) either way will work.

Deselecting the box by Noun/Verb Mode will only allow you to start the Move command before it will allow you to select the object.

This action will also not allow you to **Delete** the Object when it is selected. Follow these steps to understand the workings of the Noun/Verb Selection

30. Start AutoCAD, if it is not already opened and load the Drawing in Figure 3.05 You are going to use this drawing to go through above lesson.

31. Right-click in front of Command prompt and select **Option**

32. In the Options dialogue box, click on **Selection**

33. Place a check mark in the box by Noun/Verb selection and click Ok

34. Back on the Graphics area, click on one corner of Figure 3.05 and drag an invincible window around the rectangle.

35. The drawing should expose four **Blue Grips** at the corners of the rectangle and five grips each for a circle.

36. The lines will have three blue grips along its length with grips at all the points on the Spline. Refer to Figure 3.07

37. Hit the Delete key on the keyboard and everything goes away. Now click on the Undo command on the Main Menu to bring back all the objects.

Figure 3.08

38. Right-Click in front of the Command prompt again and select Options

39. Click on Selection from the Options dialogue box and uncheck the box by **Noun/Verb** selection and click on Ok.

40. Drag an invincible window around Figure 3.02 again and hit the delete key on the keyboard.

41. Notice that the objects would not delete, meaning the Noun/Verb selection is not active.

42. This is one of the many uses of the Noun/Verb selection. The next subject to cover is the Use Shift to add to selection

Use Shift to add to selection

If this option is checked, you will have to **Hold** down the Shift key to be able to make two or more selections. To demonstrate this,

43. Type **DDSELECT** at the Command prompt and press the Enter key and place a check mark in the box by **Use Shift to add to selection**

44. Using Figure 3.05 try clicking on one the objects. You will notice that only one of them gets selected at a time.

45. Uncheck the box by Shift to add to selection and try again. You will notice that the objects get select as it is clicked on.

46. This indicates the difference between activating the Use Shift to add to selection after it has been checked and unchecked.

Drafting Settings:

Drafting Settings allows you to choose the types of drawing aid are planning to use in sketching a drawing.

Type **DSettings** at the Command prompt and press the Enter key or right-click on one of the **Drawing aids** options at the bottom of the screen; **Snap, Grid, Ortho, or Polar** and select Settings.

This brings you to the Drafting Settings dialogue where three different categories of Snap and Grid, Polar Tracking, and Object snap are listed.

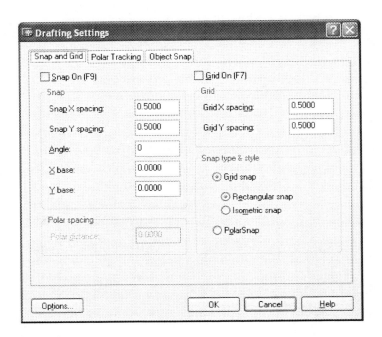

Figure 3.09

<u>Snap and Grid:</u>

Snap is used in conjunction with Grid to force the movements of the cursor to a specified distance. There is the positive X directional Snap and positive Y directional Snap.

For an example when you set the snap to 0.5 in and the Snap is turned on with the Grid loaded, you will be forced to snap **vertically** or **horizontally** from point A then point B a distance of 0.5 units. Turn the Snap on by simply clicking on snap or pressing the F9 functional key.

Changes can also be made with the Snap Mode system variable. In Figure 4.00 the

Default value for X and Y under Snap are set for 0.5000, which can be changed. Changing the value in X and clicking on OK will automatically force a change in the Y value to be the same 0.7500 for X will appear in the box by Y

Grid

The use of Grid is to visually aid you to position two points from the other either horizontally or vertically.

Grid is only for reference and will not appear on your Prints.

When **Grid** is turned on, a rectangular shaped object covered with Dots appears on the screen, which could be turned off by pressing the **F7** functional key Similarly, the Default values of 0.5000 assigned to X and Y in the Grid can also be changed. Changing one will affect the other. If you would like to have two different values for X and Y, you would need to type the different values in the box before clicking on OK to exit. Let us put the Snap and Grid into use to be able to understand all the theory above. Click in front of the Command and type Snap and press the Enter key

47. Command: **Snap** Press the Enter key, a message comes up
48. **Specify Snap spacing or [ON / OFF / Aspect / Rotate / Style / Type] <A>**
    Press the Enter key to accept Aspect option.
49. **Specify Horizontal Spacing <0.5000>** Enter to accept
50. **Specify Vertical spacing <1.000>:** type **2.000** and press the Enter key again.
51. Click on Draw, select Line tool and press the **F7** function key.

52. Click on the graphics area and move your mouse horizontally, the pointer Snaps to **0.50.**

53. Move the cursor vertically upwards and it will automatically snap to **2.00 units**. Notice how it snaps to the next point with a slight move of the mouse. You can use this to draw any shape in AutoCAD.

54. Go back the Settings and type **30** in the Angle Box

55. Click on Draw and select the Line tool again and watch how this one will draw

56. Make several different sketches to have the feel of the command.

57. To Exit the command when finished, right-click on snap and change angle **30** to **0** again

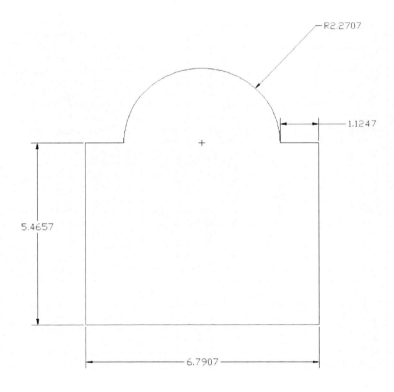

Figure 3.10

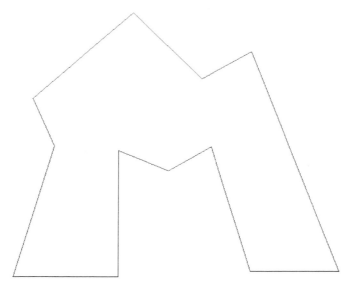

Figure 3.11

Drawing Sketches:

Now that you know most of the names of Tools and its commands, let us put

that into practical use. You will be guided in drawing different sketches and like

a new language the more you use it the better you become.

There are several ways to turn lines and circles into a complete drawing. There

are the icons which you can access with the mouse buttons, or type of tool, at the

Command Prompt.

You are going to use a combination of the Mouse and the keyboard to draw in

this lesson therefore **I would like you to follow attentively and do exactly as I**

ask you to, in order to obtain the end results.

You will be using **Rectangle, Polar Coordinate, Origin, Relative Coordinate, Offset, Fillet, Trim and Dimensioning.**

Start AutoCAD and bring up your Template1. For your information, the Template you created will be used to do all your projects in order not to set up any new layers. You will add more Layers to the Template as the need arises. The first thing you do when you load the Template is to save it as a project.

58. Click on File, Open and go to the **[C:]** drive and locate Mechanical-ACAD folder.

59. Double-click on Template1 to load it into AutoCAD graphics area

60. Click on File, Save as Project1 and click on the Save button

61. Project1 is now saved inside the folder, Mechanical-ACAD.

62. Click on Draw from the Main menu bar and select Rectangle and you will be asked to:

63. Specify first corner point or [Chamfer/Elevation/Fillet/Thickness/Width]:

64. Release your finger from the Mouse button and type **0, 0** and press the Enter key. You are asked to

65. **Specify other corner point or [Dimensions]:**

66. Type **4, 2** and press the Enter key again.

67. Next type Zoom, press the Enter key and a message comes up asking you to select one of the many options like:

68. **All/Center/Dynamic/Extends/Previous/Scale/Window]:**

69. Enter **E** short for **Extends** and press the Enter key, the drawing should fill the screen

70. Type Zoom and press the Enter key again, this time when you are asked for an option press the Enter key again, the pointer changes into a magnifying glass with a plus on the top of the magnifying glass and a minus sign at its base

71. **All/Center/Dynamic/Extends/Previous/Scale/Window]:**

72. Click on the middle of the graphics area; hold down on the left mouse button and drag the mouse downwards on the minus side to minimize your sketch.

73. You will have a better view this way to properly control your drawings refer to Figure 3.13

You are now going to use the keyboard to complete the rest of the sketch therefore takes your hands off the mouse and move your fingers unto the keyboard.

74. Type rectangle at the Command and press the Enter key

75. **Specify first corner point or**

   [Chamfer/Elevation/Fillet/Thickness/Width]:

76. Type **2,0** and press the Enter key and a message will pop up and ask you to

77. **Specify other corner point or [Dimensions]:**

78. Type **1.4142,1.4142** and press the enter key again

118

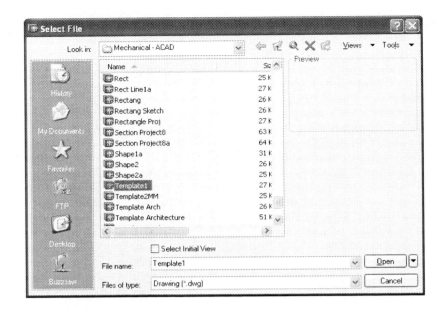

Figure 3.12

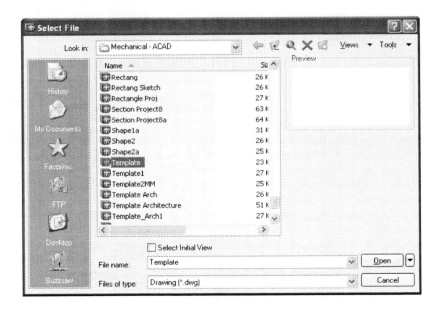

Figure 3.13

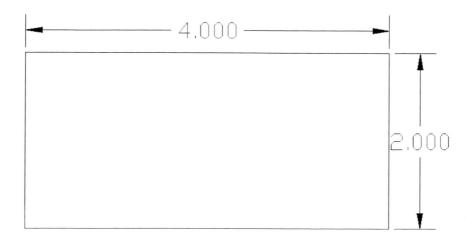

Figure 3.14

79. A Square is placed at the Midpoint of the larger rectangle.

Rotate

You will now use the Rotate option to rotate the rectangle **45**∘ using the midpoint as the base point.

80. Type Rotate at the Command prompt and you will be asked to: select object.

81. Click on one of the Lines of the Rectangle to highlight it and press the Enter key. You will then be asked to:

82. **Specify Base point:**

83. Click on the bottom left corner of the **Square** you just insert in the larger **Rectangle** and type **45°**. Your square should tilt towards **45°** as in Figure 3.16

You will have to know the diagonal distance to use it in drawing the inner rectangle. To obtain this value, we will do a little mathematics.

Half of the shorter side of the in Figure 3.13 is 1 inch and to find the inclined side we will use the **Sine rule** to calculate the distance '**x**' on Figure 3.14

$$\textbf{Sin 45 = 1/x}$$

$$\textbf{X = 1/Sin 45}$$

When you enter this value in a calculator, you will obtain:

$$\textbf{X = 1.4142}$$

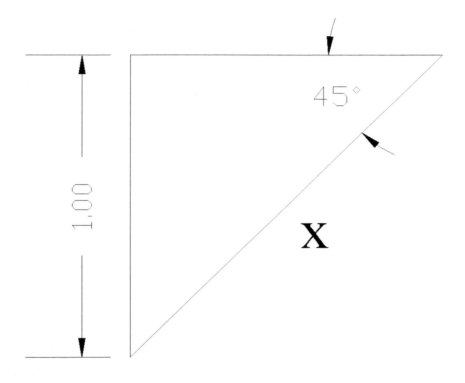

Figure 3.15

This value of **1.4142** will be the sides of the square in the diagram in Figure 3.16

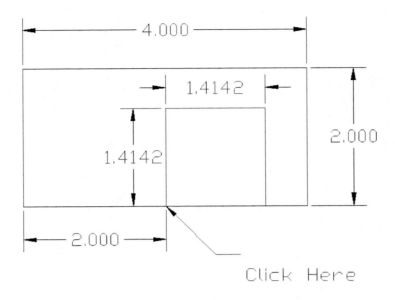

Figure 3.16

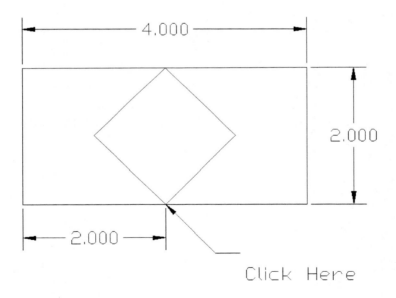

Figure 3.17

Offset:

Offset is used to create a copy of an original object to a given location

You are now going to use the **Offset** tool to make copies of the Original drawings.

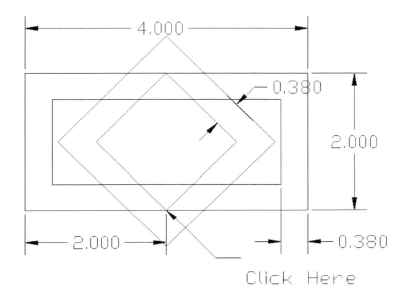

Figure 3.18

84. Click on Modify from the Main Menu and select Offset, you will be asked to:

85. **Specify offset distance or [Through]<1.0000>:**

86. Type **0.38** and click on one of the lines that bound the Square, **the pointer should turn into a square pick box.**

87. Click outside the Square, just drawn to add a larger copy of the square.

88. Click on one of the line that bound the larger Rectangle and click to place a copy inside the Rectangle. Refer to Figure 3.18

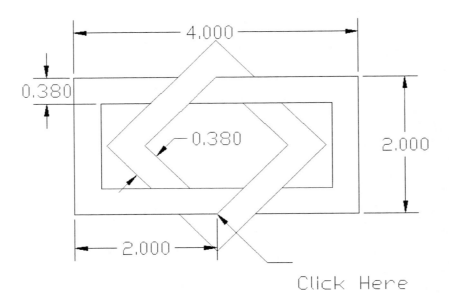

Figure 3.19

Dimensioning:

You will use Dimension Tool to place actual dimensions on the sketch

89. Click on the Dimension tool from the Main Menu tool bar and select Linear, you will be asked to:

90. **Specify first extension line origin or <Select objects>:**

91. Click on the letter **'A'** on the top left corner of the Rectangle. You will be asked to

92. **Specify second extension line origin:**

93. Move the mouse over to the right top corner of the rectangle and click on the letter **'B'** little pick box, which is also the endpoint. A message pops up:

94. **[Mtext/Text/Angle/Horizontal/Vertical/Rotated]:**

95. Move the mouse to the top of the rectangle and click again on the letter **'C'** to place the first Dimension

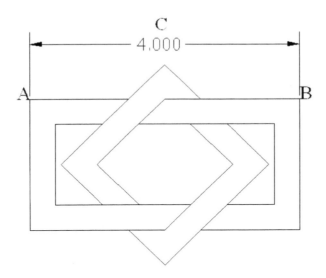

Figure 3.20

96.   Follow the steps above to place the rest of the dimensions as per Figure 3.19.

97.   To place the unit **0.38**, click on Dimensions from the Main menu and select **Aligned,** you will be asked to

98.   **Specify first extension line origin or <select object>:**

99.   Click on one of the lines on the square, you will be asked to:

100.   **Specify second extension line origin:**

101.   Type **per** short for perpendicular and press the Enter key

102.   Move to the opposite side of the line, the pointer changes into a perpendicular icon.

103.   Click on the opposite line to place the dimension

104.   The final design should look like that on Figure 3.19

TRIM:

Objects that cross each other can be edited with trim tool, to remove unwanted edges.

You are now going to use the Trim-editing tool to take off the unwanted lines in order for your drawing to look like the one in Figure 3.20

105.   Click on Modify and select Trim, you will be requested to

106.   **Select objects:**

107.   Press once on the **Enter key, a message pops up asking you to**

108.   **Select object to trim or shift-select to extend or [Project/Edge/Undo]:**

109.   Use the drawing of Figure 3.20 as a guide and click on the unwanted lines leaving the two objects intertwined with each other.

110.   Save your drawing as Project1

Summary:

In this exercise you covered topics that included:

- Absolute, Relative, Polar Coordinates, Offset, Origin
- The Object Selection
- Working with Crossing:
- Learning of what DDselect is used for
- The Noun /Verb selection
- Using Shift to Add to Selection
- Knowing of Drafting Settings
- Using Snap and Grid option
- The Rotate and Offset options
- The Trim and Dimensioning

Exercise

Look at the Final product and try to follow the steps just covered without opening the book. Good Luck!!!

The next Lesson will cover **Ellipse, Circle, and Polygon, F8 (Ortho), Offset, Fillet, Trim** and **Dimensioning.**

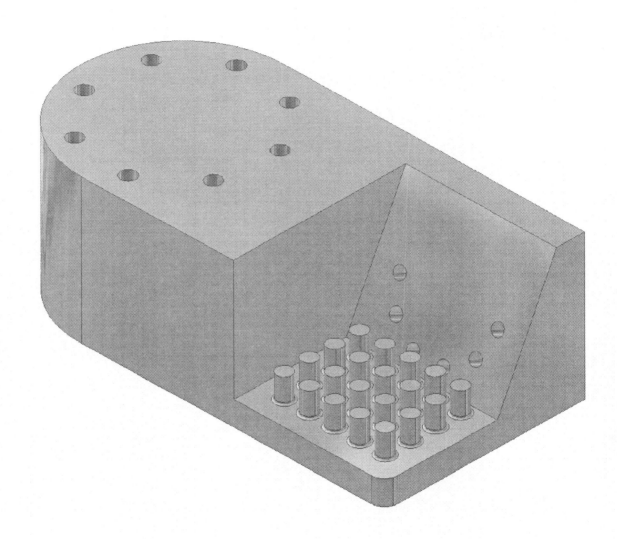

Chapter 4:

After completing this chapter, you will be able to:

- Create Polygons of with multiple sides
- Work with Ellipse
- Modify with offset
- Fillet Objects
- Trim Objects
- Learn to use the Zoom command
- Used the @ sign together with relative Coordinate
- Array objects
- Draw a pattern
- Use the Mirror option
- F8 Function key to generate ORTHO
- Generated Plate Drawings
- Created Array of objects
- Used Mirror editing tool

Circle and the Origin:

1. Type Circle at the Command prompt and press the Enter key, you will be asked to

2. **Specify center point for circle or [2P/ 3P/ Ttr (tan tan radius)]**

3. Type **0, 0** and press the Enter key. You will be asked to:

4. **Specify radius of circle or [Diameter]:**

5. Type the letter **'D'** on your keyboard, for the Diameter and press the Enter key

6. Type **2.75** and press the Enter key to place the Circle at the Origin

7. Type Zoom and press the Enter key. You will be asked to select:

8. **[All/Center/Dynamic/Extends/Previous/Scale/Window] <real time>:**

9. Type the letter **'E'** to choose Extends option

10. Type Zoom again and asked to select:

11. **[All/Center/Dynamic/Extends/Previous/Scale/Window] <real time>:**

12. Press the Enter key to accept <real time> and notice that the pointer has changed into a magnifying glass with a plus and minus signs by it.

Click on the center of the circle and drag the mouse down to minimize the circle.

13. Type Line at the Command prompt, you will be asked to:

14. **Specify first point**

15. Type **0,0** and press the Enter key You will be asked to specify next point or [Undo]

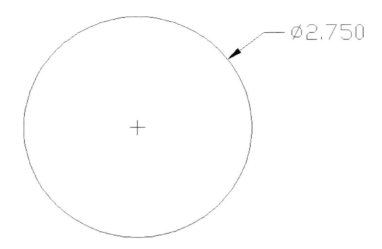

Figure 4.00

16. You will be asked to:

17. **Enter number of sides <4>**

18. Type **6** and press the Enter key, you will be asked to

19. **Specify Center of polygon or [Edge]:**

20. Type **0,0** and press the Enter key: you will be asked to

21. Enter an Option [Inscribed in Circle Circumscribed about circle] **<I>:**

22. Type **C** for **Circumscribed** and press the Enter key. You will be asked to

23. **Specify radius of circle:** Press the **F8** function key for Ortho move the pointer vertically downward.

24.   Type **0.75** and press the Enter key again to place the polygon Circumscribed inside the Circle.

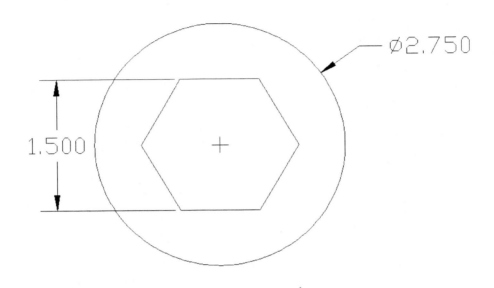

Figure 4.01

25.   Click on Draw from the main menu and select Line at the Command you are requested to

26.   **Specify first point**

27.   Type **0, 0** at the Command prompt and press the Enter key.

28.   **Specify next point or [Undo]:**

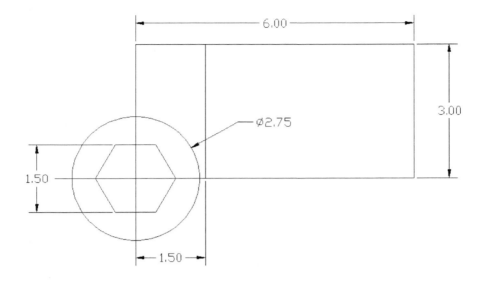

Figure 4.02

29.   Type Ellipse at the Command prompt and press the Enter key. You will be asked to:

30.   **Specify axis endpoint of ellipse or [Arc/Center]:**

31.   Type the alphabet '**C**'; short form for **Center** and press the Enter key. You will be asked to:

32.   **Specify center of ellipse.**

33.   Click on the intersection of the second **Vertical** line and the **Horizontal** line.

34.   Move the pointer vertically up, let go the mouse button and type **2.125** and press the Enter key. You will be asked again to:

35.   **Specify distance to other axis or [Rotation]:**

36.   Move the pointer **Horizontally** to the right, let go the mouse button and type 3.25. Press the Enter key to exit the Ellipse command.

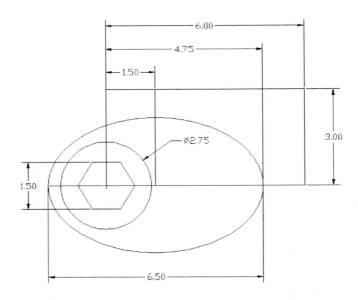

Figure 4.03

37.   Type Line at the Command prompt and press the Enter key. You will be asked to:

38.   **Specify first point**: Click on the Intersection of the Ellipse to the right and the Horizontal Line

39.   Move the pointer Vertically upwards and let go your finger off the mouse.

40.   Type **@ 0, 3** and press the Enter key 2X to exit the line command.

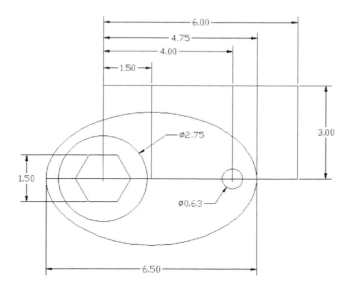

Figure 4.04

Offset:

You are going to use the Modify Option to offset the line **0.75**

41.   Click on Modify from the main Menu and select Offset you will be requested
      to:

42.   **Specify offset distance or [Through]<0.0000>:**

43.   Type **0.75** and press the Enter key, You will be asked to

44.   **Select object to offset or <exit>:**

45.   Click on the Vertical Line just drawn and click to the left of it to place a
      duplicate offset line.

46.   Type **Circle** at the Command prompt and press the Enter key. You will be
      asked to:

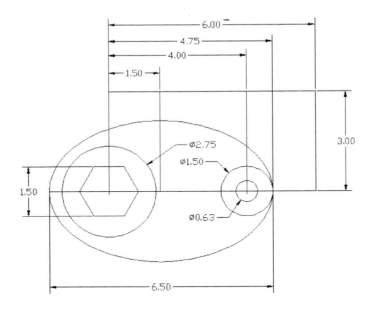

Figure 4.05

47.   **Specify center point for circle or [3p/2P/Ttr (tan tan radius)]:**

48.   Click on the **Intersection** of the offset line and the horizontal line, let go your finger off the mouse button.

49.   Type **'D'** short form for diameter and press the Enter key. You will be asked to:

50.   **Specify diameter of circle<0.000>** Type **0.63** and press the Enter key to place a circle at the intersection.

51.   Type Circle at the command prompt and when asked to

52.   **Specify center point for circle or [3P/2P/Ttr (tan tan radius)]:**

53. Click inside the smaller circle move the pointer to the edge of the Ellipse and click to place a circle outside the smaller circle. Refer to Figure 4.05

Offset

Use Offset to duplicate the Ellipse **0.75** units to create the outline for the next step of trimming the objects

54. Click on Modify from the Main Menu and select Offset. You will be asked to

55. **Specify offset distance or [Through] <0.750>:** This is the last entry and the value is retained until changed.

56. Press the Enter key to accept the **0.75** and press the Enter key. You are asked to:

57. **Select object to offset or <exit>:**

58. Click on one of the quadrants of the Ellipse and click inside the center of the sketch to place a smaller Ellipse as in Figure 4.04

Fillet:

You are now going to use Fillet to place Radius between the Ellipse and the circles to enable you to trim off the excess objects.

59. Click on modify and select Fillet from the lists of editing tools. You will be asked to:

60. **Select first object or [Polyline /Radius/Trim / mUltiple]:**

61. Type **'R'** short for Radius and Press the Enter key You will be asked to:

62. **Specify fillet radius<0.0000>:**

63. Type **0.50** and press the Enter key again. The pointer should turn into a little pick box and you will be asked to:

64.   **Select first object or [Polyline/Radius/trim/mUltiple]:**

65.   Click on the edge of the Inside ellipse and click on the larger circle and watch how the Geometry changes.

66.   **Press the Enter key** and repeat for the top portion of the ellipse and the larger circle. You will be asked to select the second circle.

67.   **Press the Enter key** again and this time use the edge of the ellipse and one the quadrants of the smaller circle and press the Enter key

68.   Click on the opposite quadrant of the Ellipse and the smaller circle to complete the Fillet. Your sketch should look like that of Figure 4.06

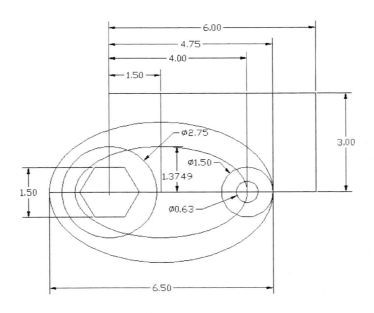

Figure 4.06

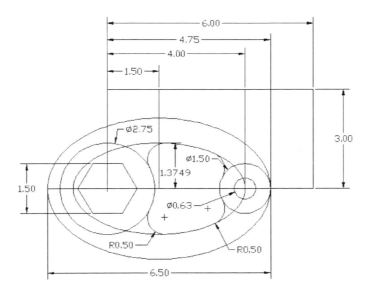

Figure 4.07

Trim:

You are going to use the Trim-editing tool to remove unwanted lines and arcs from the Geometry.

69.   Click on Modify from the main Manu and select the Trim option. You will be asked to:

70.   **Select objects:** Press the Enter key and start trimming away. You will be asked to:

71.   **Select object to trim or shift-select to extend or [Project/Edge/Undo]:**

72.   Click on the lines and Circles using the Geometry in Figure 4.07 as a guide. The objects that would not Trim, just click to highlight it and press the delete button on the keyboard.

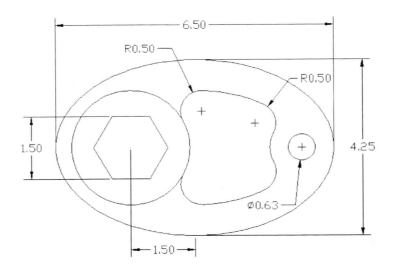

Figure 4.08

The next chapter will use **Array, Trim, Circles, and Lines, Offset, Dimensioning and Polar coordinates to generate a Geneva Cam drawing.**

73.   Type **Circle** at the Command prompt and press the Enter key. You will be asked to:

74.   **Specify center point for circle or [3P/2P/Ttr (tan tan radius)]:**

75.   Type **0,0** at the Command prompt and press the Enter key A message pops up asking you to:

76. **Specify radius of circle or [Diameter]:** Type '**D**' short for Diameter and press the Enter key and will be asked to:

77. **Specify Diameter of Circle:** Type **1.750** and press the Enter key again to place the Circle on the Origin

78. Type **Zoom** at the Command and press the Enter key. A message pops up asking for

79. **All/Center/Dynamic/Extends/Previous/Scale/Window]<real time>:**

80. Type '**E**' short for Extends and press the Enter key to enlarge the circle

81. Type Zoom at the Command prompt again and when asked to select

82. **All/Center/Dynamic/Extends/Previous/Scale/Window]<real time>:**

83. Press the Enter key to accept the **<real time>** your pointer should turn into a magnifying glass with a plus and minus sign attached to it.

84. Click in the center of the circle, hold down on the left mouse button and drag it downwards to minimize the circle.

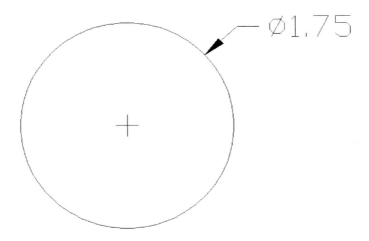

Figure 4.09

85. Draw another circle with center **0, 0** and make the diameter **1.00** instead of **1.750** whiles following the same steps from **#18.** See Figure 4.09

86. Type Line at the Command prompt, you will be asked to:

87. **Specify first point:**

88. Type **0,0** and press the Enter key You will be asked to specify next point or [Undo] A message pops up asking to:

89. **Specify next point or [Undo]:** Type **0,5** and press the Enter key **2Xs**

90. Type Line at the Command prompt, you will be asked to:

91. **Specify first point:**

92. Type **0,0** and press the Enter key You will be asked to specify next point or [Undo] A message pops up asking to:

93. **Specify next point or [Undo]:** Type **5,0** and press the Enter key **2Xs**

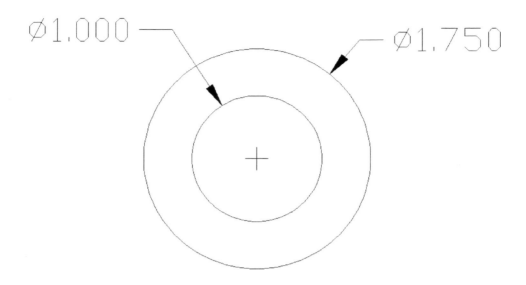

Figure 4.10

94. Click on Modify from the main Menu and select Offset, a message pops up asking you to:

95. **Specify offset distance [Through] <0.0000>:** type **0.125** and press the Enter key. A message requesting you to:

96. **Select object to offset or <exit>:**

97. Click on the Vertical line and first click to the right of the line

98. Next click on the Vertical line again and click to the left of it

99. This will place two lines on both sides the original Vertical line.

100. Press the Enter key again to activate Offset option and when asked to:

101. **Specify offset distance [Through] <0.1250>:**

102. Type **0.25** and press the Enter key, the pointer should turn into a square pick box and you will be asked to:

103. **Select object to offset or <exit>:**

104. Click on the Horizontal line and click above it to place the first copy of the line. A message pops up asking you to:

105. **Select object to offset or <exit>:**

106. Click on the original horizontal line again and this time click below it to place a copy and press the Enter key to exit the offset option. Refer to Figure 4.10

107. Click on Modify from the main Menu and select **Offset**, a message pops up asking you to:

108. **Specify offset distance [Through] <0.2500>:** type **1.625** and press the Enter key. A message requesting you to:

109. **Select object to offset or <exit>:**

110. Click on the Vertical line and click to place a construction line on the right, as an intersection for a circle.

111. Type **Circle** at the Command prompt and press the Enter key A message pops up requesting you to:

112. **Specify center point for circle or [3P/2P/Ttr (tan tan radius)]:**

113. Click on the intersection of the center line and the offset line of distance **1.625** and type the letter 'D' short for diameter. A message pops up requesting you to:

114. **Specify radius of circle or [Diameter]:**

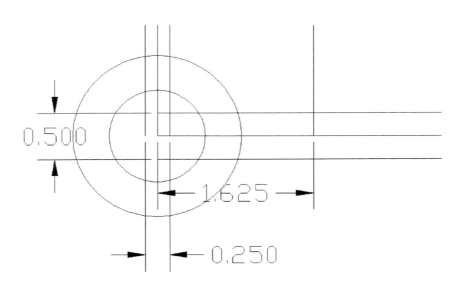

Figure 4.11

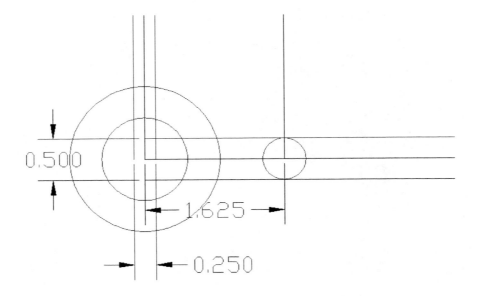

Figure 4.12

115. Type **0.50** and press the Enter key to place a circle at the intersection.

116. Type **Circle** at the Command prompt and press the Enter key. A message pops up requesting you to:

117. **Specify center point for circle or [3P/2P/Ttr (tan tan radius)]:**

118. Type **0, 0** and press the Enter key. You will be asked to:

119. **Specify radius of circle or [Diameter]:**

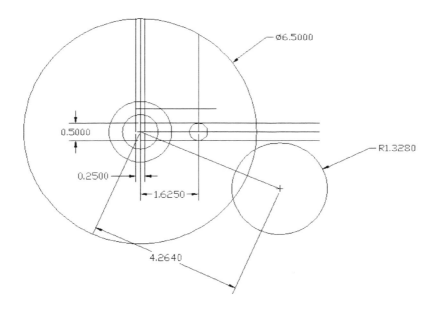

Figure 4.13

120.   Type **'R'** short for radius and press the enter key. A message pops up requesting you to:

121.   **Specify radius of circle or Diameter <0.25000>:**

122.   Type **4.228** and press the Enter key to place the radial circle.

123.   Type **Line** at the Command prompt and you will be asked to:

124.   **Specify first point:**

125.   Type **0, 0** and press the Enter key. You will be asked to:

126.   **Specify next point or [Undo]:**

127. Type **@4.228<337.5** and press the Enter key 2X

128. Type **Circle** at the Command prompt and press the Enter key and when asked to:

129. **Specify center point for circle or [3P/2P/Ttr (tan tan radius)]:**

130. Click on the intersection of the **22.5°** of the line just drawn with the outer circle. When asked to:

131. **Specify radius of circle or Diameter <4.2280>:**

132. Type **1.328** and press the Enter key to place the circle.

Trim:

133. Click on **Modify,** from the Main Menu, select **Trim.** A message pops up requesting you to:

134. **Select objects:**

135. Press the Enter key once. You are the requested to:

136. **Select objects to trim or shift-select to extend or [Project/Edge/Undo]:**

137. Use Figure 4.18 as a guide and trim away the unwanted objects

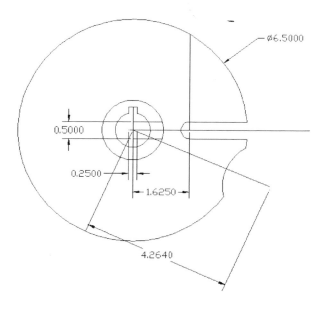

Figure 4.14

<u>Array:</u>

You are going to select certain objects to use for creating the array operation around the center point. Follow these steps carefully to complete editing the objects with the array command.

138. Click to select the following objects as shown in Figure 4.15 and

139. Click to select **Array** from the **Modify** editing tool and the Array dialogue box will be displayed.

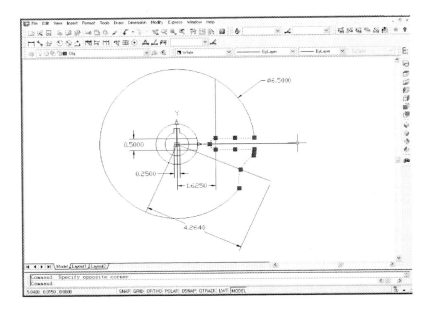

Figure 4.15

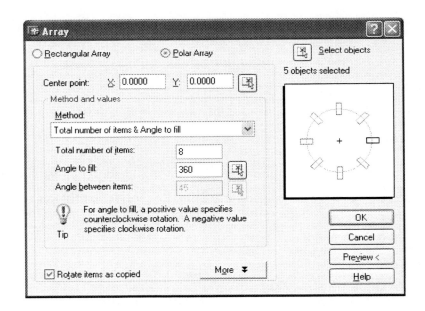

Figure 4.16

140. Click on Pick center and you will be asked to:

141. **Specify center point of array:**

142. Type **0, 0** at the command prompt and press the Enter key. This takes you back to the Dialogue box.

143. Click inside the Radio button by **Polar Array,** Type 8 in the box allotted for Total number of items, and click on OK to complete the array.

144. Your drawing should look like that of Figure 4.17

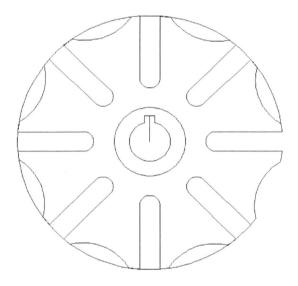

Figure 4.17

Trim:

The final step is to take away the unwanted objects with the aid of the Trim-editing tool. Follow these steps to complete the Trim.

145.　Click on Modify and select Trim from the list of editing tools and a message pops up requesting you to:

146.　**Select objects:**

147.　Press the Enter key once and you will be asked to:

148.　**Select objects to trim or shift-select to extend or [Project/Edge/Undo]:**

149.　Use the Figure 4.18 as a guide to remove the excess objects and press the Enter key to exit the Trim option

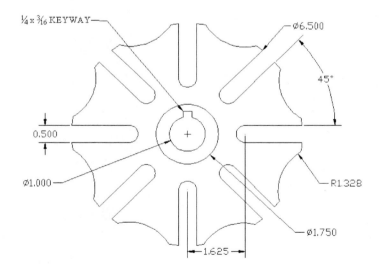

Figure 4.18

This concludes the design of the Geneva cam and hope you enjoyed drawing it as I enjoyed guiding you through the maze of steps.

The next Lesson will cover the uses of **Lines, Circles, Array, Offset, Donut, Trim, Mirror and Dimensioning**, in creating Patterns as used in the Graphics design, Interior Decoration as well as the Textile Industry with many more other applications.

Follow these steps to better understand the approach in Pattern design. Start AutoCAD if it not already running on your system, and load your Custom Template. Use the Object layer to start your drawing.

150. Click on Draw from the main Menu and select the Line tool. A message pops up asking you to:

151. **Specify first corner point or [Chamfer / Elevation / Fillet / Thickness / Width:**

152. Type **0, 0** at the Command prompt and press the Enter key. A message pops up asking you to:

153. **Specify other corner point or [Dimensions]:**

154. Type **2.5, 2.5** and press the Enter key

155. Next type Zoom and press the Enter key. A message pops up asking you to select:

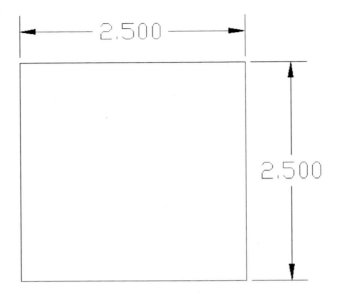

Figure 4.19

156. **[All/center/Dynamic/extends/Previous/scale/Window]<real time>**

157. Type the letter **'E'** short for Extends and press the Enter key again, the rectangle should enlarge to fill the screen.

158. Type Zoom and press the Enter key. A message pops up asking you to select:

159. **[All/center/Dynamic/extends/Previous/scale/Window]<real time>**

160. Press the Enter key again to accept real time, the pointer should turn into a Magnifying glass with a plus and minus on both sides.

161. Click on the center of the graphics area, press and hold down on the left mouse button and drag it downwards to minimize the rectangle.

162. Type **Circle** at the Command prompt and press the Enter key. A message pops up asking you to:

163. **Specify center point for circle or [(3P/2P/Ttr (tan tan radius)]**

164. Type **0, 0** and press the Enter key A message pops up asking you to:

165. **Specify radius of circle or [Diameter]:**

166. Type the letter **'R'** short for Radius and press the Enter key

167. **Specify radius of circle or [Diameter]:**

168. Type **1.00** and press the Enter key **2X**. A message pops up asking you to:

169. **Specify center point for circle or [(3P/2P/Ttr (tan tan radius)]**

170. Type **0, 0** and press the Enter key A message pops up asking you to:

171. **Specify radius of circle or [Diameter]:**

172. Type the letter **'R'** short for radius and press the Enter key

173. **Specify radius of circle or [Diameter]:**

174. Type **0.90** and press the Enter key

The next step is to offset the rectangle at a distance of **0.2** units

Offset:

175. Click on Modify from the Main Menu and select Offset. A message pops up asking you to:

176. **Specify offset distance or [Through] <Through>:**

177. Type **0.2** and press the Enter key

178. **Select object to offset or <exit>:**

179. Click on one of the lines that make up the rectangle to place a copy inside the larger one.

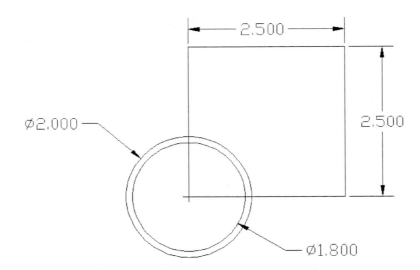

Figure 4.20

Your Sketch should look like that in Figure 4.21. You are now going to use the Trim-editing tool to remove certain portions of the objects.

180. Click on Modify from the Main Manu and select Trim from the list of items. A message pops up asking you to

181. **Select objects**:

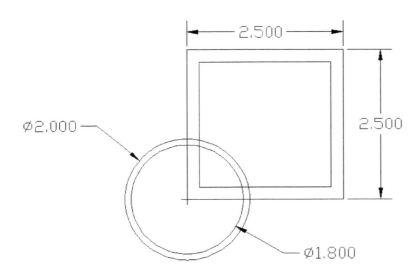

Figure 4.21

182. Press the Enter key once and click to delete the objects using Figure 4.21 as a guide. Line that could not be trimmed, click to select it and press the delete button

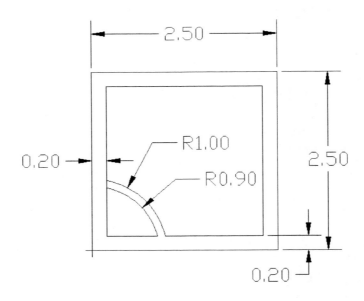

Figure 4.22

You are now going to place two construction lines on right and the topsides of the rectangle to be used to mirror the two objects drawn

183. Click on Draw from the Main Menu and select Line from the list of tools. A message pops up asking for you to:

184. **Specify first point:**

185. Type 'Mid' short for Middle and press the Enter key. A message asking to

186. **Specify first point: Mid of:**

187. Move the pointer, which is now turned, into a crosshair, closer to the Vertical Line and watch how it turns into a **Yellow Triangle.**

188. Click on the **Yellow triangle, press the F8 Ortho** key to turn it on and move horizontally to the right and click on a distance from the origin.

189. Click on **Mirror** from the Main Menu and select Mirror from the list of editing tools. You will be asked to

190. **Select objects:**

191. Click to select the **two arcs** at the bottom left corner of the square and press the Enter key. A message pops up asking you to:

192. **Specify first point of mirror line:**

193. Click on the endpoint of the Vertical line A message pops up asking you to:

194. **Specify second point of Mirror line.**

195. Click on the base of the Vertical line and you will be asked to:

196. **Delete source objects [Yes/No]<No>:**

197. Press the Enter key to accept 'No' and place a copy of the two arcs on the opposite side. Refer to Figure 4.23

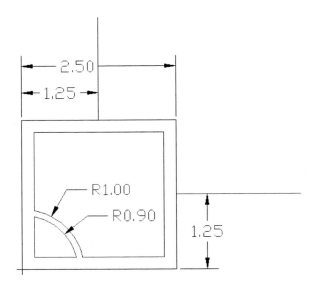

Figure 4.23

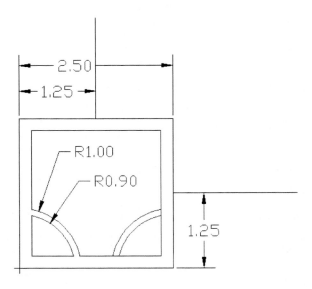

Figure 4.24

198. Click on Mirror from the Main Menu and select Mirror from the list of editing tools. You will be asked to:

199. **Select objects:**

200. Click to select the **four arcs** at the bottom corners of the square and press the Enter key. A message pops up asking you to:

201. **Specify first point of mirror line:**

202. Click on the endpoint of the Horizontal line A message pops up asking you to:

203. **Specify second point of Mirror line.**

204. Click on the base of the Horizontal line and you will be asked to:

205. **Delete source objects [Yes/No]<No>:**

206. Press the Enter key to accept '**No**' and place a copy of the four arcs on the opposite side. Refer to Figure 4.24

You will now have to take off the two construction lines.

207. Click on the two construction lines, the Vertical and horizontal and press the **delete** key

You are now going to learn of a new tool known as Donut. Donut is drawn using Polyline of wide arc segments. Follow these steps to draw a donut

208. Click on draw and select donut from the list of tools. You will be asked to

209. **Specify inside diameter of donut <0.5000>:**

210. Type **0.62** and press the Enter key and a message pops up

211. **Specify inside diameter of donut <1.0000>:**

212. Type **0.70** and press the Enter key. A message pops up asking you to

213. **Specify center of donut or <exit>:**

214. Type **1.25, 1.25** and press the Enter key and hit the **'esc'** short for escape key to exit the donut command.

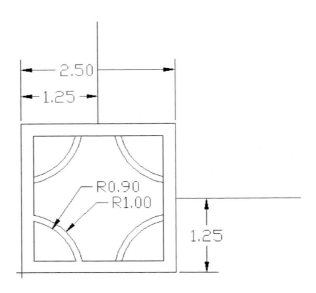

Figure 4.25

Now that the first Pattern is complete, you can use the Array editing tool to add several copies as needed. To do so, follow these steps to complete the rest of the Pattern.

215. Click on edit from the Main Menu and click on **select all** to highlight the entire drawing. Next

216. Click on Modify from the Main Menu and select **Array**

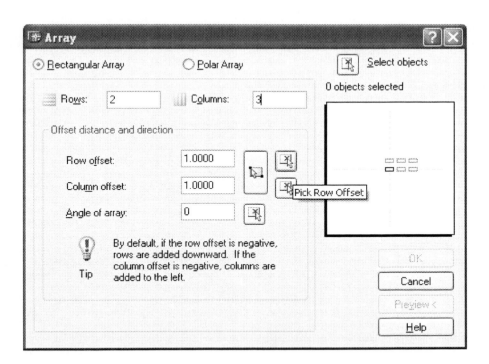

Figure 4.26

217.   The **Array** dialogue box pops up.

218.   Click in the Radio Button by **Rectangular Array**, enter **4** in the box by
        Rows: and **6** in the box by Columns and lick on **Pick Row Offse**t Button.

219.   Enter **2.650** in the Row and Column offset boxes and click on the OK button
        to complete the Array option.

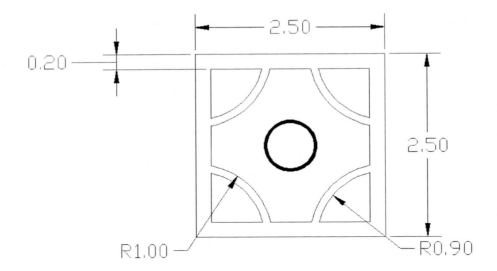

Figure 4.27

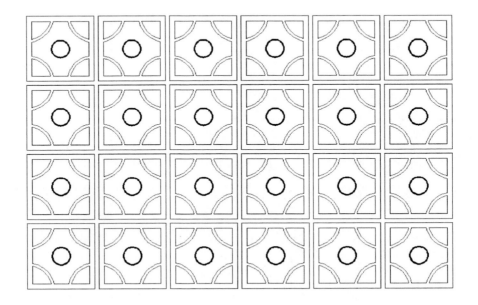

Figure 4.28

Summary:

You have really come a long way. All you have to do now is wrap your arms around yourself and give yourself a big hug for you have done it. You are on your way up and covered Mechanical design so far. You will be introduced to more Mechanical design when you cover Solid Modeling in subsequent Chapters. Like a new language, you learned about:

- Creating Polygons with multiple sides
- Working with Ellipse
- Modifying with offset
- Using Fillet Objects
- Using the Trim Objects
- Learning to use the Zoom command
- Using the @ sign together with relative Coordinate
- Using the Array objects
- Drawing a pattern
- Using the Mirror option
- Using the **F8** Function key to generate ORTHO
- Generating Plate Drawings
- Creating Array of objects
- Using Mirror editing tool

Exercise:

As usual, using the dimensions from Figure 4.18, generate a Geneva Cam making no references to the lesson just covered. Good Luck!!!

You will be introduced to Architectural design in the next Chapter and cover electrical before going back to Mechanical designing

The next Lesson will cover **Area, Distance, Status, List** and many more.

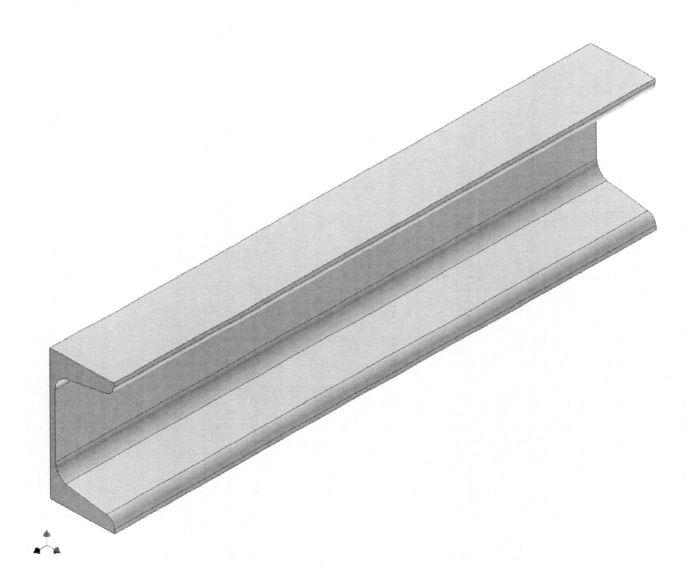

Chapter 5:

After completing this Chapter, you will be able to:

- Use the Area option to calculate area of irregular Shapes
- Use the Distance command to calculate values between two points
- Use ID to make certain Inquiries about a specific area of the entire drawing
- Use the Status for listing all related information about your drawing
- Get to know any and necessary inquiries you would need to find about your drawing
- Use Time to verify when a particular drawing was created as listed below
- Use Geometry for calculating angles

Current time: Tuesday, March 29 at 12:55:35:631 PM

Times for this drawing:

Created: Tuesday, February 08 at 8:01:45:921 AM

Last updated: Tuesday, March 29 at 12:39:39:609 PM

Total editing time: 0 day's 07:32:30.293

Elapsed timer (on): 0 day's 07:32:30.293

- **Region / Mass Properties** is a very useful tool, when used in 3D Modeling to calculate weights and volumes of solid bodies.

Figure 5.00

Inquiry:

Under Tools from the Main Menu are listed different options to help your design easier. One of these essential tools is the Inquiry dialogue box. Some the tools listed under Inquiry include, **Area, Region/Mass Properties, List, ID Point, Trim, Status and Set Variable.**

Area:

The correct value of Area of Certain complex shapes would be very difficult to calculate without the uses of the Area Tool.

The Area Tool is therefore used to calculate an enclosed polygon with or without other inserted figures, accurately as well as giving the results for the Perimeter.

You can Add or Subtract Objects from a particular enclosure with the aid of Area tool. To really understand its workings, follow the steps below to practically calculate the Area of a complex figure.

There are two ways you can choose to calculate the Area of an object. One when the Sketch is a complete polygon and classified as one entity, meaning whenever you click to select any one line of the polygon the entire figure is highlighted. An example is a rectangle drawn with the Rectangle tool.

The other choice is selecting different entities like lines to calculate the Area. An example is a rectangle drawn with ordinary Lines.

1. Start AutoCAD if it is not already loaded and bring in your Template.

2. Click on File, Save As **Area Calculations** under your personal folder that you set up at the beginning of Chapter 1

3. Select the Object tool from the Layer Properties Manager to make it current.

4. Click on **Draw** from the Main Menu and select **Line.** A message pops up at the Command prompt requesting you to:

5. **Specify first point:**

6. Type **0, 0** and press the Enter key to start from the Origin A message pops up at the Command prompt requesting you to:

7. **Specify the Next Point:** Use the Values in the Table below to create the Sketch in Figure 5.01 with the next entry being '**@1<45**'

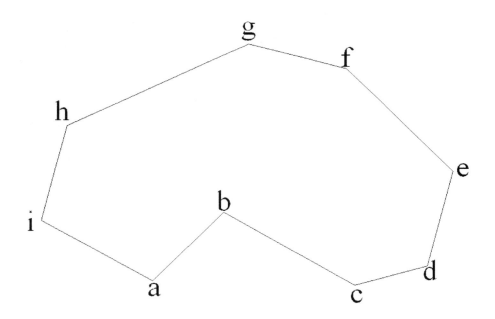

Figure 5.01

Table 5.00

0,0	@1<45	@1.5<330	@0.75<15
@1<75	@1.5<135	@1<165	@2<205
@1<255	C	Enter	Esc

8. For your information the sketch starts at the Origin which is '**A**' through the rest of the alphabets and terminates at the Origin

9. Click on **Tools** from the Main Menu, to see the list of other option, highlight **Inquiry** and select **Area**.

10. Alternatively you can type **AREA** at the Command prompt and press the Enter key. A message pops up at the Command prompt requesting you to:

11. **Specify first corner point or [Object/Add/Subtract]:**

12. Type **Add** and press the Enter key. **A message pops up at the Command prompt requesting you to:**

13. **Specify first corner point or [Object/Subtract]:**

14. Move to the Origin, your pointer should turn into a pick box, click on the Origin. A message pops up at the Command prompt requesting you to:

15. **Specify next corner point or press Enter for total (ADD mode):**

16. Continue from **B** and click on the Origin again to complete the cycle.

17. Press the Enter key **2X** after completing the cycle to get out of the Area command.

18. Press the **F2** function key to view and write down the results of the calculations. In the case of the above sketch, the results were listed as:

Area = 6.6820, Perimeter = 11.0229

19. Press the **F2** function key again to go back to the Graphics area.

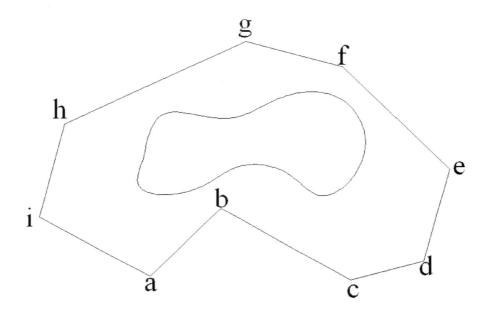

Figure 5.02

You are going to calculate a complex figure with an insert as in Figure 5.01, to find the total area covered.

Suppose you have a lake on your property and would like to know what the total area of the land is. Follow these steps to draw the profile of the **Lake.**

20. Click on Draw from the Main Menu, and select **Spline A message pops up at the Command prompt requesting you to:**

21. **Specify first point or object:**

22. Click inside the complex sketch **A** message pops up at the Command prompt requesting you to:

23. **Specify next point:**

24. Click away from the first point: A message pops up at the Command prompt requesting you to:

25. **Specify next point or [Close / Fit tolerance] start tangent**

26. Continue to create a Spline until you end up where you started to close the loop.

27. Press the Spacebar **3Xs** to exit the Spline command.

You are going to use area with **Add and Subtract** options to calculate the area of the land the lake sits on. To accomplish this start a new drawing and:

28. Click on Tool from the Main Menu, highlight Inquiry and click on Area. A message pops up at the Command prompt requesting you to:

29. **Specify first corner point or [Object/Add/Subtract]:**

30. Type the letter 'A' short for Add, and press the Enter key. A message pops up at the Command prompt requesting you to:

31. **Specify first corner point or [Object/Subtract]:**

32. Type **the** letter **O,** short for **Object**. A message pops up at the Command prompt requesting you that you are in Add mode and to:

33. **(ADD mode) Select objects:**

(ADD mode) Select objects: Your pointer should turn into a pick box

34. Click on the Complex sketch once and press the Enter key A message pops up at the Command prompt requesting you to:

35. **Specify first corner point or [Object/Subtract]:**

36. Type the letter **S**, short for **Subtract** and press the Enter key A message pops up at the Command prompt requesting you to:

37. **Specify first corner point or [Object/Add]:**

38. Type the letter **O** short for object and press the Enter key A message pops up at the Command prompt requesting you to:

39. **(SUBTRACT mode) Select objects:** Click on the lake once and press the Enter key 2Xs

This completes the calculations for the second step for the Area within an Area

Press the **F2** function key to view and copy or print the results of the calculations. Again find the results of my calculations below:

Area = 2.4458, Perimeter = 7.4275

Total area = 4.2363

The next exercise will cover a sketch drawn to scale so all of us will be on the same page. Start a new drawing and click on Draw from the main Menu and select Rectangle.

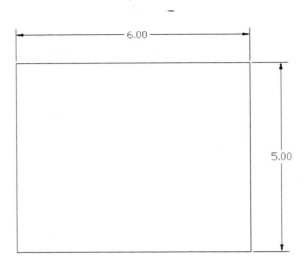

Figure 5.03

Start a new drawing and click on **Draw** from the Main Menu and select **Rectangle**. A message pops up at the Command prompt requesting you to:

40. **Specify first corner point or [Chamfer / Elevation /Fillet / Thickness / Width]:**

41. Type **0, 0** and press the Enter key A message pops up at the Command prompt requesting you to:

42. **Specify other corner point or [Dimension]:**

43. Type **6, 5** and press the Enter key. You should have a rectangle drawn from the Origin on the graphics area.

44. Click on **Tools** from the Main Menu, highlight **Inquiry** and select **Area**. A message pops up at the Command prompt requesting you to:

45. **Specify first corner point or [Object / Add / Subtract]:**

46. Type **O** short for **Object** and press the Enter key. Your pointer should turn into a pick box and A message pops up at the Command prompt requesting you to:

47. **Select objects:**

48. Click on one of the **lines** of the **Rectangle** and press the Enter key **2Xs**

49. Press the **F2** function key to view and copy or print the results

Area = 30.0000, Perimeter = 22.0000

If you were to mathematically calculate the area of the Rectangle in question you will multiply the lengths of the two sides to obtain the **Area**. Therefore **6 X 5 = 30** Next you will add up the sides to obtain the **Perimeter**. Therefore **6 + 6 + 5 + 5 = 22** this corresponds to the Area calculations with the Inquiry in AutoCAD

Figure 5.04

Irregular Objects:

Irregular objects have multiple sides, different lengths and angles. Refer to Figure 5.01. To be able to draw such objects, you may have to go back to your Geometry days to accomplish this feat.

You thought the Geometry was just for passing through with your education, it is in your life to stay. Let me refresh your memory on Geometry if you are rusty before we proceed on the irregular objects. You can skip this section if you are OK with basic Geometry.

Recall the following Geometric lesson?

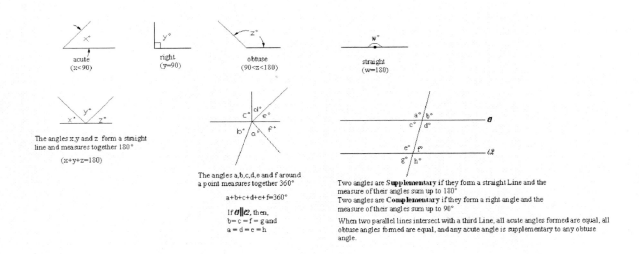

Figure 5.05

To be able to represent the Sketch in Figure 5.06, you should use Geometric calculations to know what angle to use to draw a particular Line. You will be guided through each step of the way to finish the drawing in Figure below.

Every intersection will be explained as you go along the line use Geometric calculations.

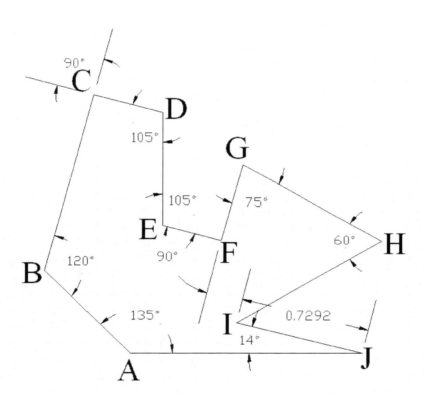

Figure 5.06

You will use Geometry to calculate the angles needed to draw each line of intersection and find the value of the missing angle and the length. Starting from 'A' and working clockwise the first Line drawn from 'A' to 'J' will be a horizontal length of **1.30** to form the base of the irregular object.

Start AutoCAD if it is not already running on your machine. At the Command prompt type the following lines:

50. Command: **Line** (Press the Enter key) A Message pops up requesting you to:

51. **Specify first point:**

52. Type 0,0 and press the Enter key, A Message pops up requesting you to:

53. **Specify next point or [Undo]:**

54. Type **1.30** and press the Enter key twice, to place a horizontal line from 'A' to 'J'.

The next Line will start from the endpoint of 'A', with a length of **0.58** at an angle of **135°** ending at 'B'

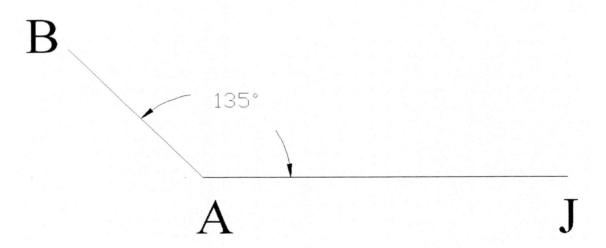

Figure 5.07

55. Type **Pline** short for Polyline and press the Enter key. A Message pops up requesting you to:

56. **Specify start point:**

57. Type **0,0** and press the Enter key. A Message pops up requesting you to:

58. **Specify next point or [Arc/Halfwidth/Length/Undo/Width]:**

59. Type **@58<135** and press the Enter key. A Message pops up requesting you to:

60. **Specify next point or [Arc/Close/Halfwidth/Length/Undo/Width]:**

61. Type **@1.06<75** and press the Enter key. A Message pops up requesting you to:

62. **Specify next point or [Arc/Close/Halfwidth/Length/Undo/Width]:**

63. Type **@0.40<345** and press the Enter key. A Message pops up requesting you to:

64. **Specify next point or [Arc/Close/Halfwidth/Length/Undo/Width]:**

65. Type **@0.66<-90** and press the Enter key. A Message pops up requesting you to:

66. **Specify next point or [Arc/Close/Halfwidth/Length/Undo/Width]:**

From **B**, a Line will be drawn with a length of **1.06** units. To calculate the angle to draw this Line, you should first extend the Horizontal Line 'AJ' and join it with another Line from the tip of the Line 'B' just drawn to form a Triangle. See Figure 5.08

The corresponding angle of **135°** and **45°** should form a **180°**.

The Upper angle is given, as **120°** therefore you will need a **60°** to make a total of **180°**. The only angle left to should have a value of **75°**. Therefore you will draw a Line of **1.06** units at an angle of **75°** for the next step. Refer to Figure 5.08. Thus **@1.06<75**

You will now move from Point **'C'** to Point **'D'** and the way to do that is to calculate the enclosed angle with which to draw the Line with.

67. Type **@0.34<345** and press the Enter key. A Message pops up requesting you:

68. **Specify next point or [Arc/Close/Halfwidth/Length/Undo/Width]:**

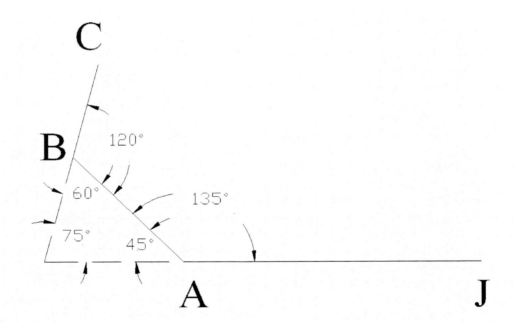

Figure 5.08

Since there is a **90°** angle at this point, a Line drawn Perpendicular to it will also form a **90°**. Subtracting this from the inclined angle of **105°** should give the difference of **15°**. Considering the fact that the angle is located in the **IV Quadrant**, **15°** should be deducted from **360°** to give us the needed angle of **345°** from point **'C'**. Thus, **@0.40<345. Refer to Figure 5.09**

The next line to be drawn is from the endpoint of '**D**'. It is already given as an angle **105°**. If we were to draw a **90°** to add to the inclined angle of **15°**, we will get a total of **105°**. Therefore let it be **@0.66<-90** since we are moving downwards from point '**C**' to point '**D**'.

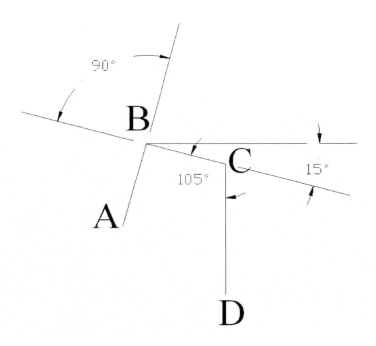

Figure 5.09

Since we used a **90°** to draw Line '**CD**' connecting the end point with a perpendicular Line will leave us with a **15°** angle. This **15°** angle is located in the **IV Quadrant** as such we will deduct it from **360°** to obtain the needed angle of **345°**. Hence type **@0.34<345**

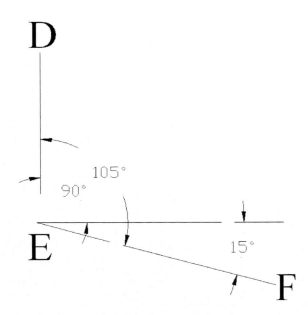

Figure 5.10

69. Type **@0.46<75** and press the Enter key. A Message pops up requesting you to:

From Point **'F'** you are going to draw a Line to Point **G**. To calculate the angle needed to draw the Line correctly, you will notice that it is already given that the angle at Point **'F'** is **90°**.

If you were to draw a perpendicular Line from Point 'E' to Line **'FG'**, you will form a triangle with a **90°** at **'F'** and **15°** at E. The remaining angle will be **75°** in order to have a complete triangle. Draw a line by typing **@0.46<75** Refer to Figure 5.11

70. Type **@0.90<330** and press the Enter key. A Message pops up requesting you to:

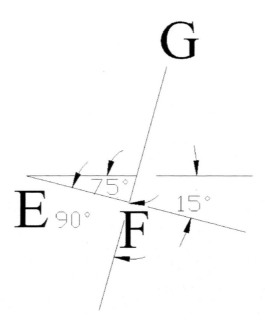

Figure 5.11

71. **Specify next point or [Arc/Close/Halfwidth/Length/Undo/Width]:**

72. Type **@0.94<210** and press the Enter key. A Message pops up requesting you to:

73. **Specify next point or [Arc/Close/Halfwidth/Length/Undo/Width]:**

74. Click on point **'J'** to complete the drawing and press the **'Esc'** key on the keyboard to end the operation.

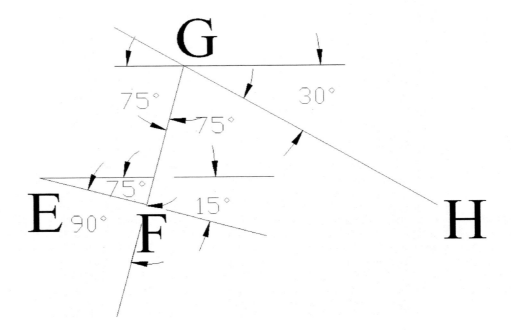

Figure 5.12

Follow these steps to calculate what angle will be needed to draw the next line '**GH**'

75. Draw a Horizontal Line from the endpoint of '**G**' and extend '**GH**' and '**FG**'. Refer to Figure 5.13.

76. This will result in the formation of two **75°** angles at each intersection.

77. Adding all the angles from **0°** counterclockwise up to the **75°** angle will sum up to a Total of **330°**. 0 + 180 + 75 + 75 = **330**

78. Use angle **330°** together with a distance of **0.90** to draw the line from point '**G**' to point '**H**'. Thus the entry will be **@0.90<330**

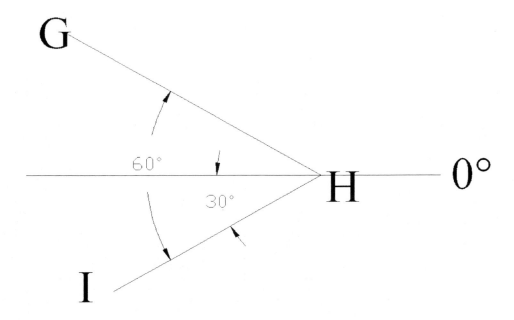

Figure 5.13

79. Draw a Horizontal Line to bisect the angle 60° at '**H**' in two halves. Refer to Figure 5.13

80. Extend the Line to cross the Horizontal Line to form a 30° angle

81. Sum up all the angles fro zero up to the bottom line of '**HI**', to obtain **210** ° total. 0 + 180 + 30 = **210**.

82. Use **210°** together with 0.94 to draw line '**HI**'. Type **@0.94<210**

83. Move the mouse pointer to the endpoint of '**J**' click and hit the '**Esc**' key to complete drawing the irregular shape as in Figure 5.06. Add all necessary dimensions and save your drawing.

Make the following entries in AutoCAD using the Line tool

Command: **L** enter 0, 0 enter twice. Follow the steps below.

Command: **PL** and press the Enter key and continue to enter the rest of the DATA to complete the irregular Object.

0, 0 enter @0.68<135 enter @1.06<75 enter @0.4<345 enter @0.66<-90 enter @0.34<345 enter @0.46<75 enter @0.9<330 enter @0.94<210 enter finally click on the end of the Horizontal Line at '**J**' to complete the drawing.

Add all necessary dimensions as in Figure below.

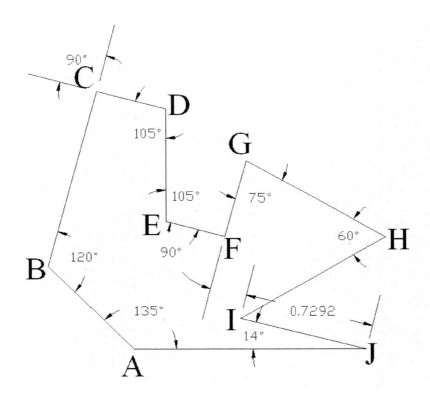

Figure 5.14

Distance:

Use Distance to determine the value of one point from a location to the other. Angles enclosed in selected points on the XY plane, are also displayed. Units currently in use will be displayed along with the measured value. A change in X is known as Horizontal **Delta X** and a change in Y, is known as Vertical **Delta Y.** To understand the steps taken to compute the Distance, follow these simple steps.

84. Start a new drawing and click to select the **Line** tool from **Draw** on the Main Menu. A message pops up at the Command prompt requesting you to:

85. **Specify first point:**

86. Type **0, 0** at the Command and press the Enter key A message pops up at the Command prompt requesting you to:

87. **Specify the next point.**

88. Type **@8< 26** and press the Enter key **2X** to exit the Line command

89. Type Zoom and press the Enter key. A message pops up at the Command prompt requesting you to select:

90. **[All / Center / Dynamic / Extends / Previous / Scale / Window] <real time>:**

91. Enter the letter **E,** short for Extends and press the Enter key

92. Type **Zoom** and press the Enter key again A message pops up at the Command prompt requesting you to select:

93. **[All / Center / Dynamic / Extends / Previous / Scale / Window] <real time>:**

94. Press Enter to accept the real time option, your pointer should turn into a **magnifying glass** with a plus and minus sign at both sides

95. Click on the middle of the screen, press and hold down the left mouse button and drag it downwards to minimize the line just drawn.

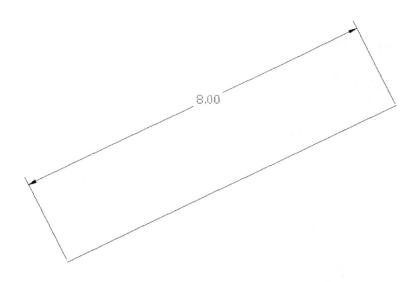

Figure 5.15

Distance:

You are now going to calculate the distance of the Line just drawn.

96. Click on **Tools** from the Main Menu, highlight **Inquiry** and select **Distance**
    A message pops up at the Command prompt requesting you to
97. **Specify first point**
98. Type **0,0** and press the Enter key, the pointer automatically anchors to the Origin and A message pops up at the Command prompt requesting you to
99. **Specify second point:**

100. Move the pointer to the end of the Line and click on it

101. Press the **F2** function key to view copy or print the results. Listed below is the results obtained in the exercise, your values should read the same.

Distance = 8.0000, Angle in XY Plane = 26, Angle from XY Plane = 0

Delta X = 7.1904, Delta Y = 3.5070, Delta Z = 0.0000

List:

    ✦ List will calculate and display the Center point, radius, Circumference and area of a **CIRCLE** in X Y and Z coordinates.

    ✦ Calculate the Constant width, area, perimeter and point to point from X Y and Z coordinates, of a **RECTANGLE**

    ✦ Calculate Point to point from X Y and Z coordinates of a **COMPLEX** object,

    ✦ Calculate the **LENGHT** and the Delta X Delta Y and Delta Z

    ✦ Display the **LAYER** used to draw the Sketch

    ✦ Calculate the Circumference as well as the Number of Control points of X Y and Z coordinates of an enclosed **SPLINE.** The following lesson will guide you through the LIST option

102. Start a new drawing and type Circle at the Command prompt A message pops up at the Command prompt requesting you to:

103. Specify center point for circle or [3P / 2P /Ttr] (tan tan Radius)]

104. Type **0, 0** and press the Enter key

105. Specify radius of circle or [Diameter]

106. Type the letter '**D**' short for Diameter and press the Enter key A message pops up at the Command prompt requesting you to:

107. Specify diameter of circle:

108. Type **5.000** and press the Enter key

List:

To List the parameters of the circle just drawn,

109. Type **LIST** at the Command and press the enter key. A message pops up at the Command prompt requesting you to:

110. Select Objects:

111. Click on the **TANGENT** or a **QUADRANT** of the circle and press the Enter key. The text Editor Automatically opens to List all the parameters of the Circle drawn.

Center point, X= 0.0000 Y= 0.0000 Z= 0.0000

Radius 2.5000

Circumference   15.7080

Area 19.6350

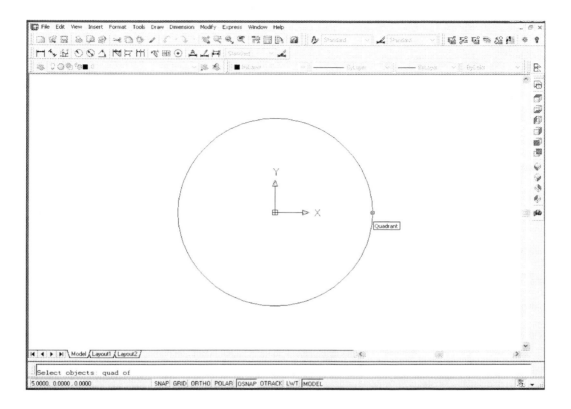

Figure 5.16

The next lesson will utilize the power of **Polyline** together with using the keyboard in combination with the mouse, to draw columns and arches for the front of a building. Imagine a long rope that has been bent into a shape of a Rectangle compared to four equal lengths of sticks that has also been placed head to tail to form a Rectangle.

The rope-Shaped Rectangle will be considered as a Polyline, since **it forms one entity when stretch**, whiles the sticks become separate entities when moved apart from each other.

192

Summary:

In this Chapter:

- ♣ You learned how to use the Area option to calculate area of irregular shapes

- ♣ Used the Distance command to calculate values between two points

- ♣ Used ID to make certain Inquiries about a specific area of the entire drawing

- ♣ Used the Status for listing all related information about your drawing

- ♣ Covered the Region

- ♣ Learned about Object / Subtract

- ♣ Learned about Object / Add

- ♣ Got to know List, Delta X and calculate Perimeter of an Object.

- ♣ Use Geometric calculations to draw Irregular Shapes

Exercise:

- • Draw the Sketch in Figure 5.17 and calculate the area of the shaded area below.

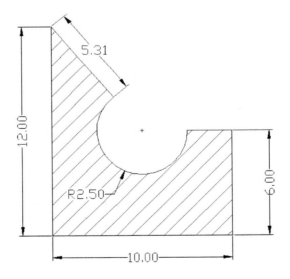

Figure 5.17

- Use the Spline Tool to draw an outline of a Topographic Map and calculate the Area and Perimeter. Specify first corner point or [Object/Add/Subtract]: o

Select objects: Area = 464.4111, Perimeter = 93.8540

The Area and Perimeter calculated for the Shape in Figure 5.18 is recorded above.

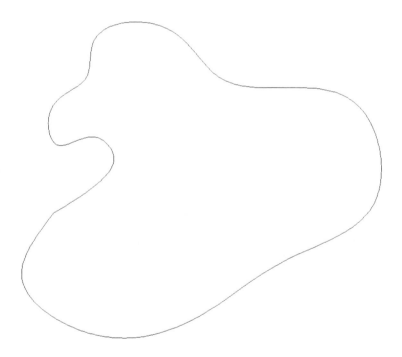

Figure 5.18

- Calculate the Area and Perimeter of the Irregular object in Figure 5.14

- Change the Units to Metric and Using Geometric calculations as explained in this Chapter, draw the Irregular Shape in Figure 5.19 and find its Area and Perimeter. Take into account the Holes on the plate.

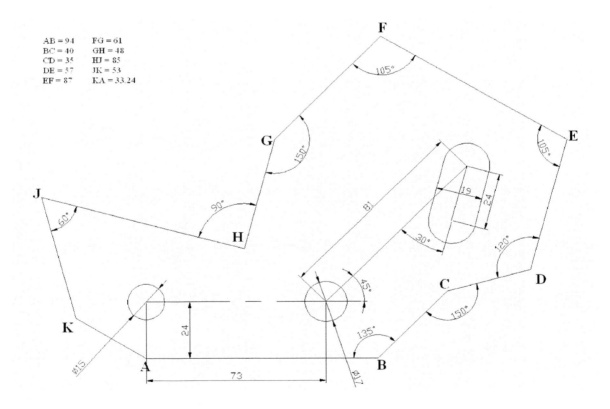

Figure 5.19

The next couple of chapters will cover **Intermediate AutoCAD**. You will be building on what you have learned so far.

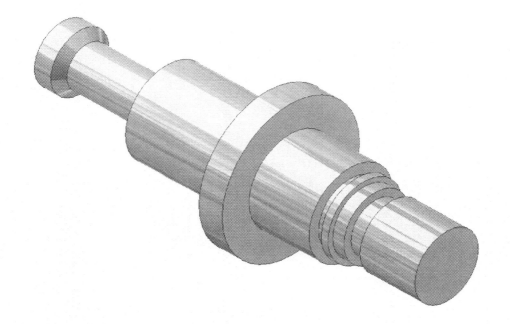

Chapter 6:

Intermediate AutoCAD

Topics shall include but not limited to Creating sorting and retrieving predefined components, Polyline construction and editing, modifying and printing or plotting drawings.

You will learn to use Donut, and its applications. You will also build layouts and be introduced to Architectural drawings.

After completing this chapter, you will be able to:

- Plot drawings that you create.
- Learn to use the Editing tools to modify Polyline and other objects.
- Know how Donuts are drawn and its applications.
- Build Layouts and be introduced to Architectural drawings
- Retrieve predefined components together with its applications.
- Manipulate the Fillmode for a better design.
- Know what Boundary Hatch is and its applications.
- Learn about Pen Up and Pen Down for freehand sketching

Donut:

Donut in AutoCAD is nothing but two concentric circles placed inside the other. There is a command known as **Fillmode** that controls how the circle would be presented.

When the Fillmode is turned OFF the two circles appears without any solid filling inside. On the other hand with the Fillmode turned ON values entered will show how the Donut will come out.

The value of the inside Diameter also controls if the Donut will appear with an inside hole or without a hole.

You will learn how to set the values with Fillmode, draw Donut with Fillmode set to **On** and with Fillmode set to **OFF** and know the difference. Follow these steps to draw a donut:

1. Start AutoCAD and open a new file. Save it as **Donut project**
2. Type **Fill** at the Command prompt and press the Enter key. A message pops up requesting you to:
3. **Enter mode [ON / OFF] <ON>:**
4. Type **OFF** and press the Enter key.
5. Type **Donut** at the Command prompt and press the Enter key. A message pops up requesting you to:
6. **Specify inside diameter of donut <0.0000>:**
7. Type **1.000** and press the Enter key. A message pops up requesting you to:
8. **Specify outside diameter of donut. <1.0000>:**
9. Type **1.500** and press the Enter key. A message pops up requesting you to:
10. **Specify Center of donut or <exit>:**

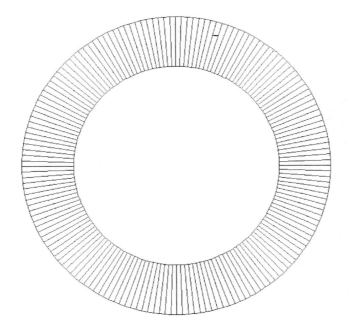

Figure 6.00

11. Type **5, 5** and press the Enter key to place the Donut. Refer to Figure 6.00

You will now turn the **Fillmode ON** and go through the same steps above to see the difference. Start a new file.

12. Type **Fill** at the Command prompt and press the Enter key. A message pops up requesting you to:

13. **Enter mode [ON / OFF] <OFF>:**

14. Type **ON** and press the Enter key.

15. Type **Donut** at the Command prompt and press the Enter key. A message pops up requesting you to:

16. **Specify inside diameter of donut <0.0000>:**

17. Type **1.000** and press the Enter key. A message pops up requesting you to:

18. **Specify outside diameter of donut. <1.0000>:**

19. Type **1.500** and press the Enter key. A message pops up requesting you to:

20. **Specify Center of donut or <exit>:**

21. Type **5, 5** and press the Enter key to place the Donut. Refer to Figure 6.01

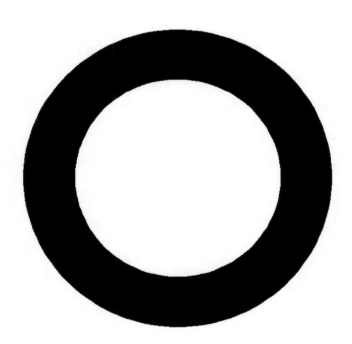

Figure 6.01

200

You will now turn the **Fillmode ON** and change the inside **Diameter** of the Donut to **ZERO**. Go through the same steps above to see the difference. Start a new file in AutoCAD and Save as Solid Donut

22. Type Fill at the Command prompt and press the Enter key. A message pops up requesting you to:

23. **Enter mode [ON / OFF] <OFF>:**

24. Type **ON** and press the Enter key.

25. Type **Donut** at the Command prompt and press the Enter key. A message pops up requesting you to:

26. **Specify inside diameter of donut <0.0000>:**

27. Type **0.000** and press the Enter key. A message pops up requesting you to:

28. **Specify outside diameter of donut. <1.0000>:**

29. Type **1.500** and press the Enter key. A message pops up requesting you to:

30. **Specify Center of donut or <exit>:**

31. Type **5, 5** and press the Enter key to place the Donut. Refer to Figure 6.00

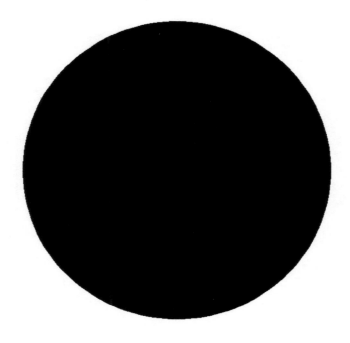

Figure 6.02

<u>BOUNDARY HATCH and FILL:</u>

In AutoCAD, **patterns** are used to distinguish between different objects such as
Sections of Solids and other components.

These patterns, otherwise known as Hatching, help identify the differences between
parts. Objects that completely enclose an area make up the properties for hatching.
To be able to properly create a hatch, multiple objects should have their endpoints
coincide with each other to form an enclosed object.

Exceptions are Hatch patterns created using the **Select Object** option. The Polyline
tool can be utilized to change ordinary lines into enclosed figure ready for Hatching

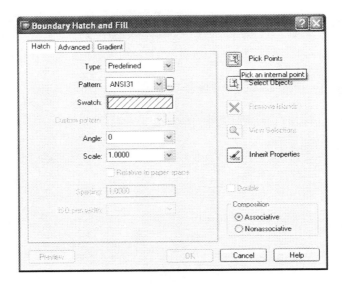

Figure 6.03

You are going to learn how to use the Hatching tool but first you should be well versed in certain terminology.

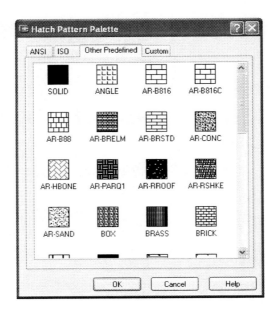

Figure 6.04

Creating Hatch:

To properly create a Hatch Pattern, you first have to define the area you will like to place the hatch pattern. You do this with the aid of Polyline or generating a region of selected objects.

These selected boundaries are then filled with a hatch pattern, different colors and or a gradient.

Hatch patterns can always be edited and their angular orientation changed or different ones selected. The Scale of the spacing can also be changed through the hatch editing option.

Follow these steps to create a hatch pattern. Start AutoCAD if it is not already running and open a new file

32. Click on Draw from the Main Menu and select the rectangle tool. A message pops up requesting you to:

33. **Specify first corner point or [Chamfer / Elevation / Fillet / Thickness / Width]:**

34. Type **0, 0** and press the Enter key. A message pops up requesting you to:

35. **Specify other corner point or [Dimension]:**

36. Type **6, 5** and press the Enter key.

Click to select the Line tool from Draw on the Main Menu and draw the two lines as in Figure. Refer Line drawing in previous Chapters if you are having difficulty in drawing a line.

37. Type **Bhatch** at the command and press the Enter key.
38. The Boundary Hatch and Fill dialogue box opens up.

39. **Click on Pick points:** A message pops up requesting you to:

40. **Select Internal point:**

41. Click inside the first of three boxes with designation 'A' and press the Enter key

This action takes you back to the Boundary Hatch and Fill dialogue box again for your next action

42. Change the Angle from **0 to 90** and the Scale **2.500**

43. Click OK to place a new Hatch in the selected box.

44. Press the Enter key again to activate the Bhatch command

45. Back in the Boundary Hatch and Fill dialogue box, change the Angle to zero and Scale to **1.500.**

46. Click on Pick points.

47. This action returns you to the Graphics area.

48. Click inside the next box designated with letter **'B'** and press the Enter key. Back in the Boundary Hatch and Fill dialogue box

49. Click on OK to complete creating the Hatch pattern.

50. Go through the above procedure, change the Angle to **Zero (0)** and Scale to **3.00** select the Internal portion of the box and click on OK

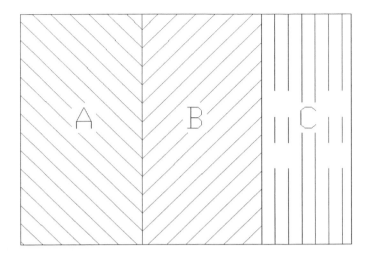

Figure 6.05

Editing a Hatch Pattern:

To edit a hatch Pattern just double-click on a pattern just created, this opens up the Boundary Hatch and Fill dialogue box. Click to make changes to the Angle as well as the Scale and click on Ok to accept the changes.

Open Hatch Patterns:

Draw a polygon as in Figure and click to delete certain portions of the lines as indicated. You are going to use this object for your next lesson.

Figure 6.06

51. Type Bhatch at the Command prompt and press the Enter key. The Boundary Hatch and Fill dialogue box opens up.

52. Click on **Select Objects**

53. Back on the Graphics area, you are asked at the Command prompt to select objects.

54. Type **'ALL'** at the Command prompt and press the Enter key **2Xs**

55. This brings you back to the **Boundary Hatch and Fill dialogue box.**

56. **Click on Ok to complete the Hatch pattern. Refer to Figure 6.08**

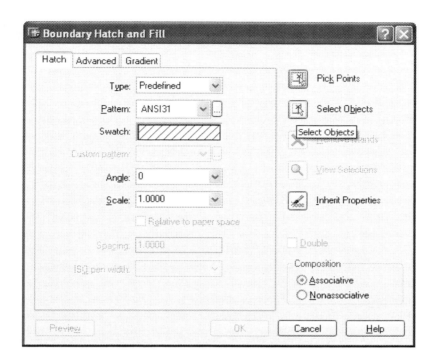

Figure 6.07

Sketch

166. Type Sketch at the Command prompt and press the Enter key. A message pops up requesting you to:

167. **Sketch record increment <0.1000>:**

208

Figure 6.08

168. Type **0.5** and press the Enter key A message pops up requesting you asking for different options including:

169. Pen eXit Quit Record Erase Connect:

170. Click on the screen and move the pointer upward, a trail of a sketch line will follow the pointer.

This operation is known as **Pen Down,** when you click on the screen again the sketch tool will stop the trail; this is known as **Pen Up.** Click on the screen again; complete drawing the letter '**A**'.

Repeat for the letters '**B**' and '**C**' and press the Enter key to exit the Sketch command. Refer to Figure 6.09

171. **Specify second point**

172. Move the pointer up to a vertex and bring it down again to form the Alphabet '**A**'

Figure 6.09

The top **'ABC'** has sketch increment of **1.000** and the bottom **'ABC'** has a sketch increment of **0.500**

Summary:

This Chapter began with the introduction to Intermediate AutoCAD that covered topics that include how to:

- Plot drawings that you create.
- Use the Editing tools to modify Polyline and other objects.
- Draw Donuts apply it to other objects
- Retrieve predefined components together with its applications.
- Use the Fillmode in designing Donuts
- Create Boundary Hatch in 2D sketches.
- Use Pen Up and Pen Down for freehand sketching

Exercise

Go through all the topics just covered in this chapter. Draw couple of sketches and use the Hatching tool to add Hatch to the sketch.

Change the Fillmode and draw different types of donuts.

The next lesson will cover **Blocks**

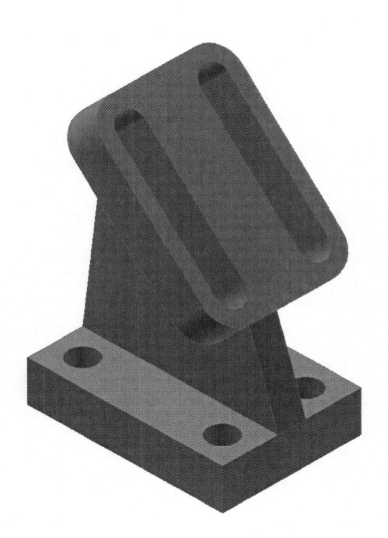

Chapter 7:

After completing this lesson you will be able to:

♣ Use the Block Command to create Blocks

♣ Learn how to Insert Blocks into your drawing to avoid redrawing of parts

♣ Edit Blocks by renaming and deleting not currently used Blocks

♣ Learn the uses of the Explode command in splitting a Block

♣ Learn to create Wblock and know the differences between Blocks and Wblock

To better understand the uses of Blocks let us begin by creating a Block for illustration purposes.

By so doing you will learn how to create a block as well as find out its uses in a drawing.

The example to use is a 40 amp Fuse being fitted into a Ladder diagram. You will start by drawing a part and using it to create the block.

Open AutoCAD if it is not already loaded on your system and start a new file.

1. Type **Rectangle** at the Command prompt and press the Enter key. A message requesting you to

2. **Specify first corner point or [Chamfer / Elevation / Fillet / Thickness / Width]:**

3. Type **0, 0** and press the Enter key. A message requesting you to

4. **Specify other corner point or [Dimension]:**

5. Type **0.5, 0.375** and press the Enter key again to exit the rectangle command.

6. Click on Draw select the Line tool and add two vertical lines as in

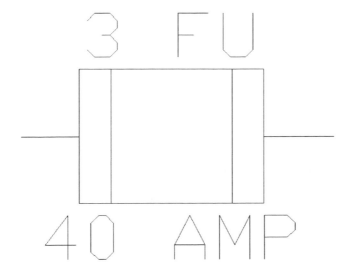

Figure 7.00

7. Click on Draw, Text and select Multiline text

8. A crosshair with **'abc'** at its base appears on the screen with a message requesting you to:

9. **Specify first corner:**

10. Click anywhere on the graphics area A message requesting you to:

11. **Specify opposite corner or [Height / Justify / Line Spacing/ Rotation / Style / Width]:**

12. Hold down the left mouse button, click and drag to create a rectangular box in which to enter the text.

13. Type **'3 FU'** and click on Ok. Use the Move command to place the text above the rectangle.

14. Repeat the Multiline text option and type **40 AMP**.

15. Place it at the bottom of the Fuse box. Refer to Figure 7.01

You are now going to use the **40AMP Fuse** just drawn to create your BLOCK. Follow these steps to draw the Block

16. Type **BLOCK** at the Command prompt and press the Enter key. The Block definition dialogue box pops up for your next entry.

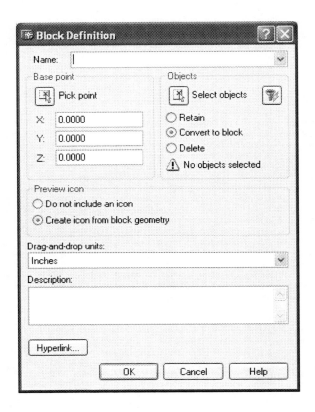

Figure 7.01

17. Enter **40AMP FUSE** in the box allotted by Name:

18. Notice that the radio buttons by, **Convert to block** and **Create icon from block geometry** are already selected.

19. You have the option of changing the required units under, **Drag-and-drop units:** Use **inches** for this lesson

20. Type 40 AMP Fuse to be used in a Ladder Diagram under Description

21. Click on **Select Objects:** button, A message pops up requesting you to:

22. **Select objects:**

23. Type '**ALL**' and press the Enter key 2Xs to go back to the Block Definition

24. : You will be notified of number of objects selected; in this case seven objects were found and selected.

25. A picture of the Block appears on the Block Definition.

26. Click on Pick Point A message pops up requesting you to:

27. **Specify Insertion base point**

28. Click on the bottom left corner of the Fuse. You are again brought back to the Block Definition dialogue box.

29. Everything is selected and you are ready to create your first block.

30. When you click on the OK button, a copy of the Block will be saved for reuse in your drawing.

To test the uses of the Block do the following:

31. Delete the current sketch of the Fuse drawing you just made from the graphics area.

32. Type 'I' short for insert and press the Enter key

33. Insert Block dialogue box opens up with the name of the current block highlighted

34. Click on Ok, A message pops up asking you to:

35. **Specify Insertion point or [Scale / X / Y / Z / Rotate /PScale / PX / PY / PZ / PRotate]:**

36. Click anywhere on the Graphics area to insert the Block.

37. When you click on any of the lines that make up the block everything will be highlighted meaning it is one entity also known as a BLOCK.

This is for tutorials, if the Block were to be inserted in a real file, it will be placed at a particular point in the drawing.

Now that you know how to create one, **what is a BLOCK?**

Block:

Blocks are parts and objects, Drawn and specifically saved into a folder, where it can be retrieved and used in the same drawing or another drawing, in order not to redraw same objects or parts over and over again.

Blocks are inserted into drawings when needed in a particular location and scaled to fit the purpose intended for.

The first thing you did when the Block Definition dialogue box opened up was to enter a name. This name will refer to a particular name when inserting a block into your drawing. After inserting a block you will notice that objects that go to make up the Block are treated as one. In other sense, when you click on a line of a Block, the entire block will be selected as one piece.

Blocks can be edited by using the move, scale, erase and the list command. The WBLOCK is like a Global tool that can be inserted and used in all drawings, while as the Block is used as a local tool in that it is only inserted in a particular drawing, in which it was created.

WBLOCK:

You will now be guided through the steps in creating a Wblock. A detailed explanation of writing blocks together with Attributes will be given in Chapter 12. You will use the Block Fuse you created earlier in this lesson. (Refer to Figure 7.02) Start AutoCAD and click on open and load the Block Fuse as indicated below. Type Wblock at the Command Prompt and press the Enter key.

38. Command: Wblock. After pressing the Enter key, the Write Block dialogue box appears on the Graphics area

39. Click on Browse at the end of the box under Filename and path and save it in a known location. Refer to Figure 7.03

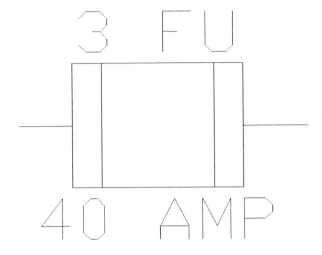

Figure 7.02

♣ Click on Save to return to the **Write Block** dialogue box

♣ Click on the **Select Object** option, located at the top right of the Write Block dialogue box. The pointer should turn into a Pickbox.

You are requested to select objects at the Command Prompt.

♣ Type **ALL** and press the Enter key **2x's** (Twice)

♣ Back in the Write Block dialogue box, you will move the pointer to the far top left and click on Pick point.

♣ Click on one of the endpoints of the Fuse and this action returns you to the Write Block.

♣ This final action will take a snap shot of the object on the screen.

♣ Look at the top left corner of the screen and click on OK to complete the creation of the Wblock of the Fuse.

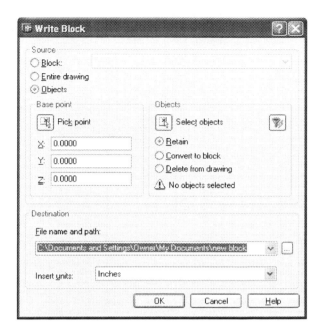

Figure 7.03

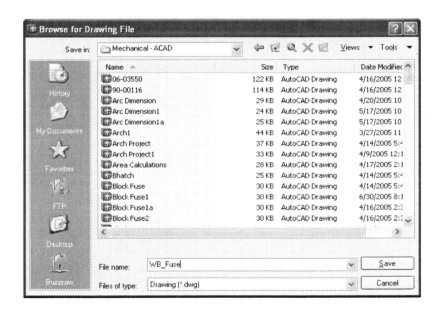

Figure 7.04

RENAME:

Rename is used to change names of Linetypes, Layers, and Blocks otherwise known as objects, which are stored in particular files under name in certain areas of your Folder.

Other uses of RENAME is to enable you view items in a list of contents when it is not to be edited. To understand the uses of RENAME, use the following steps as a tutorial guide to accomplish renaming different items for the Layer.

Start AutoCAD and Open the Template you created in Chapter 1. AutoCAD creates a special layer when you first start a new drawing. This Layer is also known as **Layer 0** and is assigned the **color 7** by default, with a **Continuous Linetype** and a **Lightweight** of **0.01 inch** or **0.254 mm**.

This Layer by default **CANNOT** be **ALTERED**, **RENAMED** or **DELETED**.

40. Type **RENAME** at the command prompt and press the Enter key.

The **Rename** dialogue box pops up, as in Figure 7.05. Click on the first item, listed under **Named Objects**; the **Bhatch**. Old Name will immediately register it inside the box:

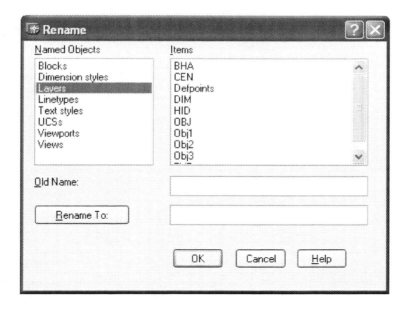

Figure 7.05

41. Click inside the box by **Rename To:** type **BH** and click on **Rename To:**

42. The name changes from **Bhatch** to **BH** under **Items:**

43. Follow the steps above and change the rest of the items and click **OK** button when finished.

Table 1

Bhatch	BH
BLOCK	BLK
CenterLN	CLN
Dimension	DIM1
Dims	OBJ1
OBj	OBJ2
Text	TXT

44. When you next type **Layer** at the command prompt, the list of items in the
Layer Property Manager should reflect the change.

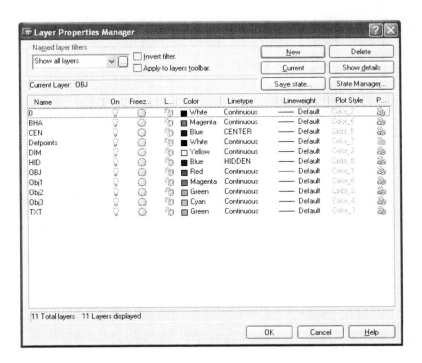

Figure 7.06

PURGE:

Items, such as layers and block definitions, which are not used in a drawing, are
removed with the aid of the Purge command.

Figure 7.07

PURGE removes only one level of reference. Repeat **-PURGE** until there are no unreferenced named objects. You can use **PURGE** or **-PURGE** at any time during a drawing session.

<u>Summary:</u>

You covered Topics that included:

♣ Using the Block Command to create Blocks

♣ Learning how to Insert Blocks into your drawing to avoid redrawing of parts

♣ Editing Blocks by renaming and deleting not currently used Blocks

♣ Learning the uses of the Explode command in splitting a Block

♣ Learning to create Wblock and know the differences between Blocks and Wblock

Exercise

- Create different drawings and make one into a Block and the other a WBlock and save your drawing.

- Edit the Block as well as the WBlock and add different items to the list created.

The next lesson will cover **Sketch Tools**

Chapter 8:

In this lesson you will use the Drawing tools as well as the Modify editing tool to generate a **Broken-Out-Section** drawing of Part.

You will cover **Offset, Circle, Line, and Radius, Diameter, Dimensioning, Threads, Chamfer, Fillet, Mirror, Array and Boundary Hatch**.

You are given a sketch of the Top view of a part together with certain values to be used in generating a Front view section of the Main part.

After completing this lesson you will be able to:

♣ Draw Circles and Lines

♣ Use the Offset on objects

♣ Assign Radius and Diameter to your drawings

♣ Cover Tangent and use the Mirror tool

♣ Learn the uses of Extend and Projection

♣ Learn to use Trim.

♣ Know how to use the Chamfer and Fillet Tools

♣ Learn to hatch a Sketch

Given:

Table 8.00

Flange OD	6.500
Flange Thickness	0.500
Groove Thickness	0.250
Raised Face Ø	2.500
OAL Height	2.500
Chamfer	0.125 X 45°
Fillet Radius	0.125
Thread Size	2.25-12-UNC-2
Bore Hole Ø	Ø5.00
Hole Size	0.602

You are going use the sketch of the top view together with all the values given in Table to generate the section view from the Front. Start AutoCAD if it is not already loaded and open your Template. Save the File as Section Project

Circles and Lines

1. Type **Circle** at the Command prompt and press the Enter key. A message pops up requesting you to:

2. **Specify Center point for circle or [3P / 2P / Ttr (tan tan radius)]**

3. Type **0, 0** and press the Enter key. A message pops up requesting you to:

4. **Specify radius of circle or [Diameter]:**

5. Type **'R'** short for Radius, press the Enter key and type 1.50 and press the Enter key again.

6. Type **Zoom** and press the Enter key. A message pops up requesting you to select:

7. **[All / Center / Dynamic / Extents / Previous / Scale / Window] <real time>:**

8. Type **'E'** short for Extents and press the Enter key again, the circle should fill the screen.

9. Type **Zoom** and press the Enter key. A message pops up requesting you to select:

10. Press the Enter key again to accept <real time>. Your pointer turns into a **magnifying glass** with a plus and minus signs at the end.

11. Click on the center of the circle, hold down on the left mouse key and drag the pointer down to minimize the circle

12. Refer to # **1** and draw another circle from **0, 0** and a diameter of **2.50** inches

OFFSET

13. Draw a vertical and horizontal Construction lines from the origin to be used as for the Offset.

14. Click on **Modify** and select **Offset** from the list of editing tools A message pops up requesting you to:

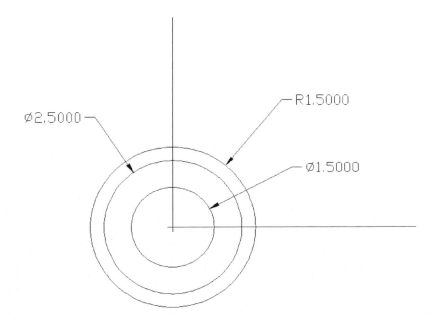

Figure 8.00

15. **Specify offset distance or [Through] <Through>:**

16. Type **2.50** and press the Enter key. A message pops up requesting you to:

17. **Select object to offset or <exit>:**

18. Click on the Vertical line and click to the right away from the Origin. A copy of the line will be placed at a distance of **2.50** from the Origin.

Radius and Diameter

19. Type circle at the Command prompt and place a circle at the intersection of the second vertical line and the horizontal line. Give it a **Diameter** of 0.575

20. Repeat # **19** and give it a **Radius** of 0.75. Refer to Figure 8.02

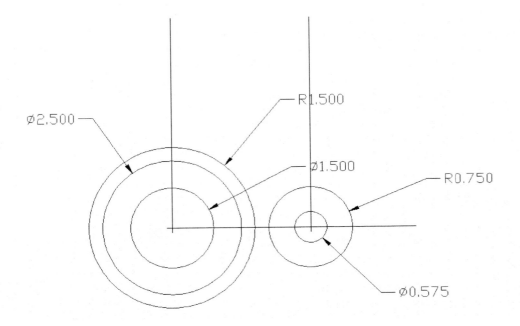

Figure 8.01

Tangent

21. Type **Line** at the Command prompt and press the Enter key. A message pops up requesting you to:

22. **Specify first point:**

23. Type **'Tan'** short for tangent, and press the Enter key. A message pops up requesting you to place the line Tangent to

24. Move the pointer closer to the first larger **Circle,** the pointer turns into a tangent sign, and click on the circle to place the first line.

25. Type **'tan'** again and move the pointer to the next circle and click to place the next line on the circle.

26. Hit the **'Esc'** key once to exit the line command.

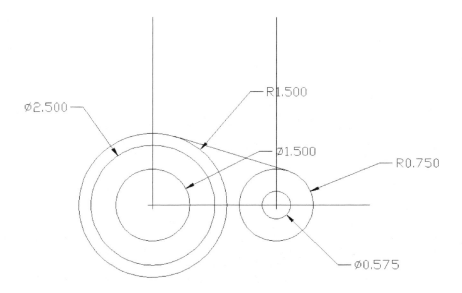

Figure 8.02

MIRROR:

You are now going to use the **Mirror** editing tool to make copies of the object just drawn.

27. **Click on Modify and select Mirror**. A message pops up requesting you to:

28. Select objects and the pointer turns into a pick box.

29. Click on the line object just created on top of the two circles and press the Enter key. . A message pops up requesting you to:

30. **Specify first point or mirror line.**

31. Move the pointer to the top of the Origin and click on the end on A message pops up requesting you to:

32. **Specify Second point or mirror line.**

33. Move it to the right and click on the end of the horizontal line, placed in the Center of both circles and press the Enter key. A message pops up requesting you to:

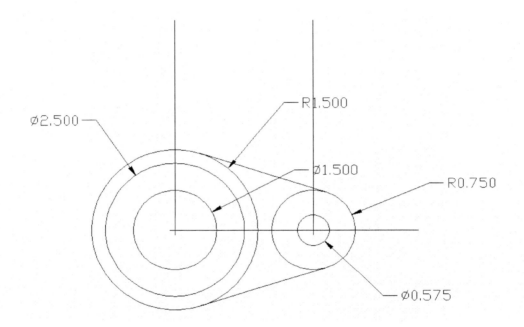

Figure 8.03

34. **Delete source object [Yes / No]: <N>**

35. Press the Enter key again to accept the **NO** option to complete the Mirror command.

36. **Click on Modify and select Mirror.** A message pops up requesting you to:

37. **Select objects** and the pointer turns into a pick box.

38. Click on the two Tangent line objects just created, and click to select the two circles with Radius **0.75** and **Ø0.575**. A message pops up requesting you to:

39. **Specify first point or mirror line.**

40. Move the pointer to the top of the Vertical line in the middle of the Origin and click on the end. A message pops up requesting you to:

41. **Specify Second point or mirror line.**

42. Move it to the base and click on the end of the Vertical line, and press the Enter key. A message pops up requesting you to:

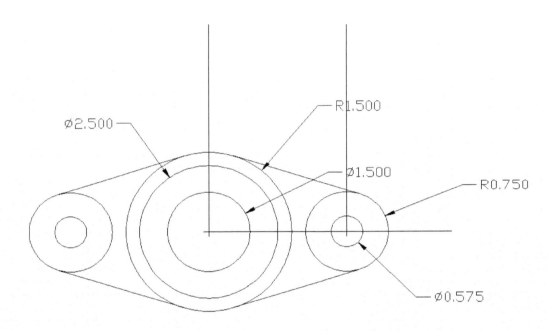

Figure 8.04

43. **Delete source object [Yes / No]: <N>**

44. Press the Enter key again to accept the **NO** option to complete the Mirror command. Refer to Figure 8.05

Extend and Projection:

You are now going to draw lines to project the outlines of the Object just completed unto the Front view as a section.

Use the Line Command to draw Vertical Lines at the intersection of the **Quadrants** of the Circles and the Horizontal Line and use the Mirror editing tool to make copies of all the Lines. Follow these steps:

45. Type Line at the Command prompt and press the Enter key. A message pops up requesting you to

46. **Specify first point:**

47. Click on the intersection of the Quadrants and the Centerline to draw vertical lines. Refer to Figure 8.06

Mirror:

Using the Mirror Command, click to select all the Vertical lines just drawn and make copies to the other side of the Origin

48. **Click on Modify and select Mirror.** A message pops up requesting you to:

49. Select objects and the pointer turns into a pick box.

50. Click on the line objects just created at the intersections of the Centerline and the quadrants of the circles and press the Enter key. A message pops up requesting you to:

51. **Specify first point or mirror line.**

52. Move the pointer to the top of the Origin and click on the end on A message pops up requesting you to:

53. **Specify Second point or mirror line.**

54. Move it to down and click on the end of the Vertical line, placed in the Center of the Origin and press the Enter key. A message pops up requesting you to:

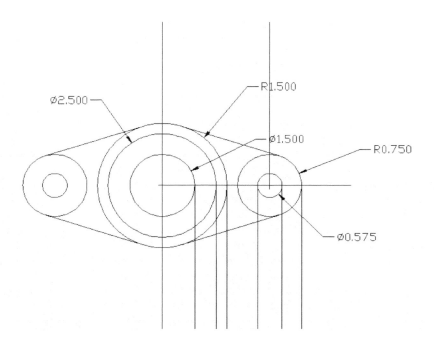

Figure 8.05

55. **Delete source object [Yes / No]: <N>**

56. Press the Enter key again to accept the **NO** option to complete the Mirror command. Refer to Figure 8.07

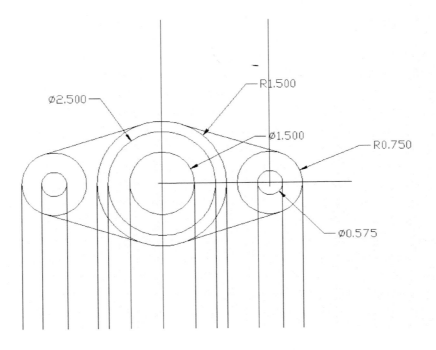

Figure 8.06

OFFSET:

You are going to draw a Horizontal Line from one end of the projected Lines to the other and use the Offset and Extend options to complete the second object

57. Type **Line** at the Command prompt and press the Enter key. A message pops up requesting you to:

58. **Specify the first point:**

59. Click on the Bottom left end of the Line in Figure 8.07. A message pops up requesting you to:

60. **Specify next point or [Undo]:**

61. Click on the Bottom right end of the Line in Figure 8.07 and hit the **'Esc'** button

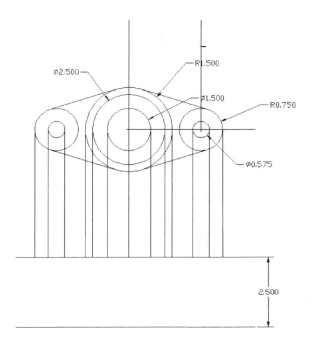

Figure 8.07

Offset the Horizontal line just drawn at a distance of **2.50** inches downwards.

62. Type **Offset** at the Command prompt and press the Enter key. A message pops up requesting you to:

63. **Specify offset distance or [Through]: 2.500**

64. Press the Enter key to accept **2.500** inches. A message pops up requesting you to

65. **Select the object to offset**

66. Click on the Horizontal line just drawn and click below it to place the copy of the Line and hit the 'Esc' short for escape to exit the offset command.

67. Repeat **#63** but this time; make the offset value to **0.25** inches and another one **0.50** inches

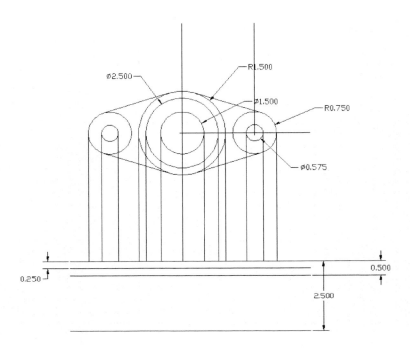

Figure 8.08

EXTEND:

You are now going to use the Extend command to extend the Vertical Lines to coincide with the Horizontal Line.

68. Click on Modify and select Extend. A message pops up requesting you to

69. **Select objects**: the pointer should turn into a pick box.

70. **Click on the last horizontal line and press the Enter key** A message pops up requesting you to

71. **Select objects to extend or shift-select to trim or [Project / edge / Undo]:**

72. Click on the Projected Vertical Lines, one at a time to extend all the lines to the base line and hit the **'Esc'** button when finished. Refer to Figure 8.10

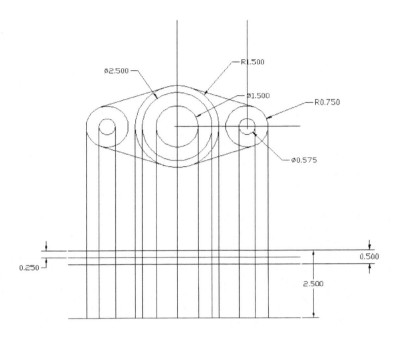

Figure 8.09

TRIM:

You are now going to use the TRIM command to take away unwanted lines in the drawing.

73. Click on Modify and select Trim from the list of options. A message pops up requesting you to

74. **Select objects:**

75. Press the Enter key once A message pops up requesting you to

76. **Select object to trim or shift-select to extend or [Project / Edge / Undo]:**

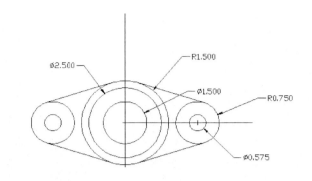

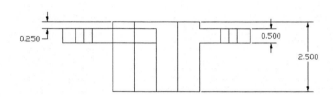

Figure 8.10

CHAMFER:

You are now going to use the Chamfer command to add a **0.125" X 45°** at the base edge

77. Click on **Modify** and select **Chamfer** from the list of items A message pops up requesting you to

78. **Select first line or [Polyline / Distance / Angle / Trim / Method / mUltiple]:**

79. Type the letter '**A**' short for **Angle** and press the Enter key.

80. **Specify chamfer length of the first line <0.0000>:**

81. Type **0.125** and press the Enter key

82. **Specify Chamfer angle from the first line<0>:**

83. Type **45** and press the Enter key. A message pops up requesting you to

84. **Select first line or [Polyline / Distance / Angle / Trim / Method / mUltiple]:**

85. Click on the outer Vertical line

86. Select second line

87. Click on the Horizontal base line to complete the chamfer. Repeat for the rest of the edges always pressing the Enter key to activate the chamfer command. Refer to Figure 8.12

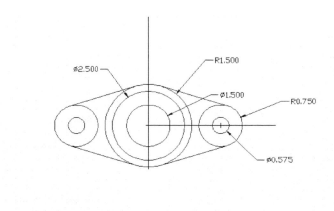

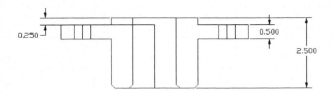

Figure 8.11

FILLET:

You are now going to use the **Fillet** command to add a **0.125"** Radius to the corners of the Flange and the body.

88. Click on **Modify** and select **Fillet** from the list of items A message pops up requesting you to

89. **Select first object or [Polyline / Radius / Trim / mUltiple]:**

90. Type the letter **'R'** short for **Radius** and press the Enter key.

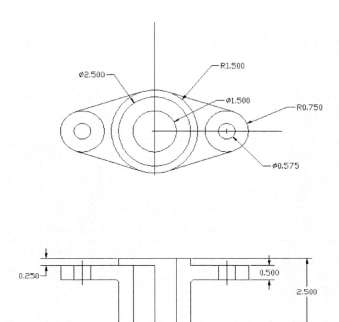

Figure 8.12

91. **Specify fillet radius <0.0000>:**

92. Type **0.125** and press the Enter key

93. **Select first object or [Polyline / Radius / Trim / mUltiple]:**

94. Click on the outer vertical line of the body and the horizontal line of the flange to place the first fillet.

95. Press the Enter key again to reactivate the fillet command.

96. Click on the outer vertical line of the body and the horizontal line of the flange to place the second fillet.

97. Refer to Figure 8.13

Dimensioning:

You are now going to add two Dimensions to be used in calculating how many instances to Array the object as well as the Row distance for the threads. Refer to Figure 8.14.

The values obtained from dimensioning the top of the first thread and the base of the Fillet is **1.3750"**. Divide **1.3750** by **0.1250** to obtain **11** instances. This will be the number of instances to apply to the **Row**, to cover the threads needed for this part.

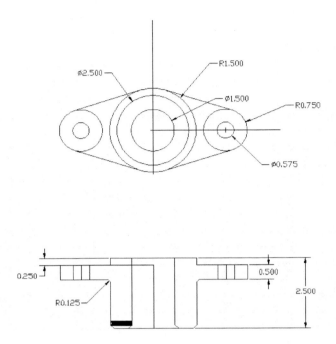

Figure 8.13

ARRAY:

You are now going to use the **Array** command to create a thread profile of **2.25-12 UNC – 2.** When setting up the Array, you will need a **Row of 11** instances with a distance of **0.125** and **1 Column** using the Rectangular array.

98. Click on Modify and select Array from the list of items. The Array dialogue box pops up with the default settings.

99. The Radio button by the Rectangular is activated.

100. Click inside the box by Rows and change the value to **11**

101. Click inside the box by Row offset and change the value to **0.125**

102. Click on <u>S</u>elect objects, which you bring you to the Graphics area.

103. Click to select the three lines that represent the threads and press the Enter key.

104. Click on the OK button to complete the Array command and your drawing should reflect on that of Figure 8.16

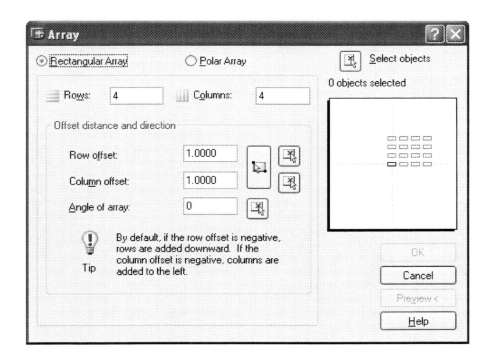

Figure 8.14

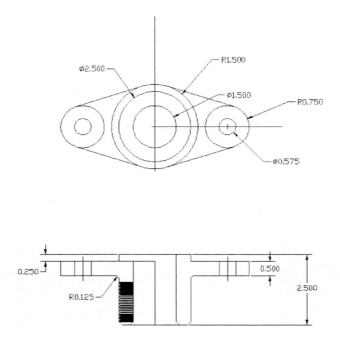

Figure 8.15

Boundary Hatch:

You will finish the drawing with a Hatch pattern. Refer to Chapter 6 to refresh your memory on how to use the Bhatch. For now type Bhatch at the Command prompt to bring in the Boundary Hatch dialogue box up.

105. Type **BH** at the Command prompt and press the Enter key. The Boundary Hatch and Fill dialogue box pops up

106. Click **Pick Points,** which will bring you, back to the graphics area.

107. Click inside the allotted area to select it as in Figure and press the Enter again. This action will send you

108. Back to the **Boundary Hatch and Fill** dialogue box

109. Change **1.000** in the box by Scale into **5.000** and press the **OK** button to complete the hatch. Figure 8.17

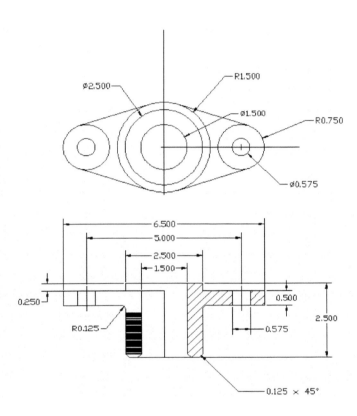

Figure 8.16

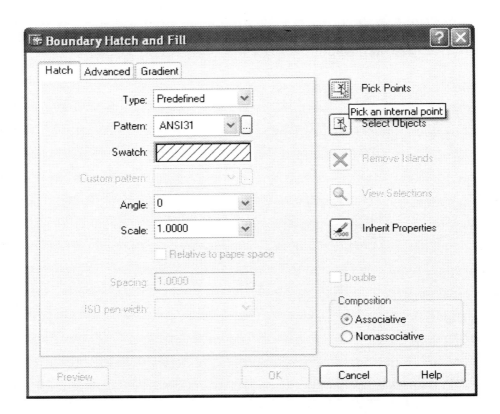

Figure 8.17

Summary:

You covered several tools and its usage in this chapter, used the edit command for certain changes and drew different sketches. Things covered included:
Boundary Hatch. You also learned how to:

♣ Draw Circles and Lines

♣ Use the Offset on objects

♣ Assign Radius and Diameter to your drawings

♣ Cover Tangent and use the Mirror tool

♣ Learn the uses of Extend and Projection

♣ Learn to use Trim.

♣ Use the Chamfer and Fillet Tools

♣ Learn to hatch a Sketch

Exercise

- Open a technical drawing or an engineering book and pick out drawings randomly and sketch these drawings.

- Apply all topics covered in this chapter to your sketches, and find out how much knowledge acquired.

The next lesson covers **Architectural** design

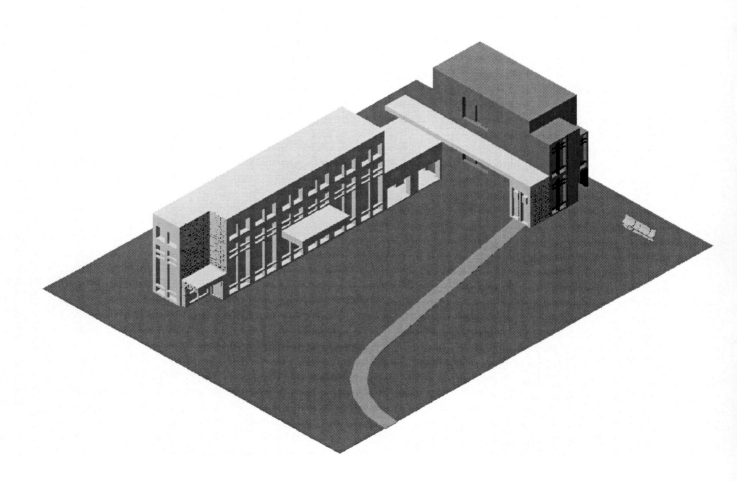

Chapter 9:

Most of the drawings you have covered so far, dealt with Mechanical designs and everything that goes to make a better part. You will now be introduced to Architectural design and the different symbols that go to make up your design easier and faster.

You will first learn how to set up the units and dimensions of your design and make basic Architectural design. 3D Architectural design will be covered in the Advanced AutoCAD section. You will be guided through step-by-step approach to design until you are comfortable in doing it yourself. Follow these steps for the Setup.

After completing this lesson you will be able to:

♣ Define the Architectural Setup

♣ Make a Layer Setup

♣ Make a Units Setup

♣ Learn about DDunits Setup

♣ Cover Dimension Style

♣ Cover Dimension Style Setup

♣ Learn about Block Definition

♣ Design a Door in Architectural style.

Architectural Setup:

1. Double-click on the AutoCAD icon on the Graphics area to start AutoCAD program or click on Start from the Graphics area. Select Programs and click on AutoCAD to open the program.

2. Create New Drawing dialogue box pops up.

3. Click inside the Start from Scratch Folder.

4. At the Start from Scratch Dialog box, click inside the Radio Button by **Imperial (feet and inches)** to activate it and click OK. Refer to Figure 9.00

5. A Blank Drawing Sheet opens up, ready for you to draw on.

Layer Setup:

6. Type Layer at the Command prompt and press the Enter key 2Xs.

7. The Layer Properties Manager opens up with Layer1 loaded

8. Type **Obj** and hit the Enter key 2Xs for a new layer, make the necessary

Entries each time pressing the Enter key for the next Layer. Refer to Figure 9.01

9. Starting from the Last Layer Dims, click inside the black square under color to activate the Select Color palette.

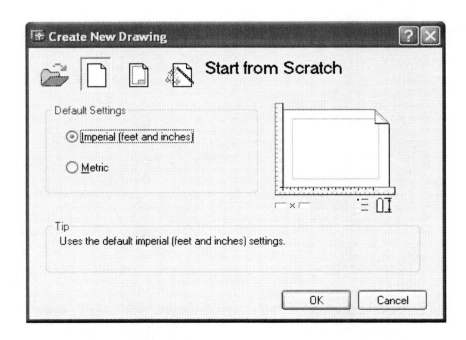

Figure 9.00

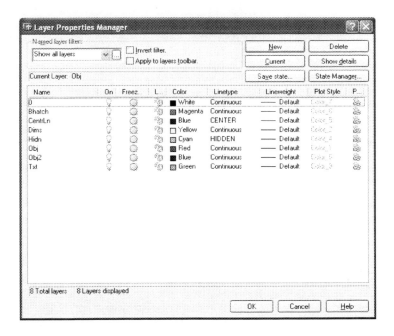

Figure 9.01

10. Click on Magenta and click on Ok.

11. Follow the same steps to fill in the rest of the colors. Refer to Figure 9.02

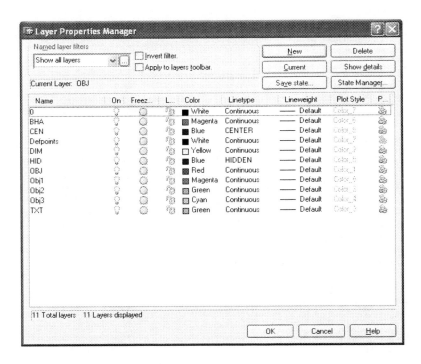

Figure 9.02

12. Click on **Continuous** on the **Hidn** line under Linetype

13. **Select Linetype** dialogue box opens up. Refer to Figure 9.03

14. Click on Load to open the **Load or Reload Linetypes**, dialogue box.

15. Scroll down to **Hidden** in the list of Linetype.

16. Click to highlight it and click **Ok** to load it

17. Back in the **Select Linetype** dialogue box, click on **Hidden** to highlight it and click on **OK** to load it into your **Layers**.

18. Click on **Continuous** on the **Centr** line under Linetype

19. **Select Linetype** dialogue box opens up. Refer to Figure 9.03

20. Click on Load to open the **Load or Reload Linetypes**, dialogue box.

21. Scroll down to **Center** in the list of Linetype.

22. Click to highlight it and click **Ok** to load it

23. Back in the **Select Linetype** dialogue box, click on **Center** to highlight it and click on **OK** to load it into your **Layers**.

24. Refer to Figure 9.04

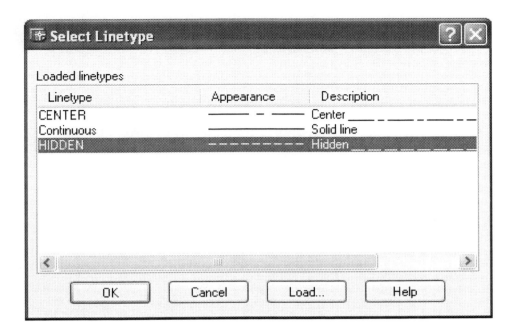

Figure 9.03

25. Click on **Save**, the **Save Drawing As** dialogue box opens up.

26. Click on the arrow by **Save in,** locate your Folder under C: drive and save as **Template Arch**

Units Setup:

There are several ways of setting up the Architectural units. This includes, **Units, DDunits** and **Dimension Style.** You will be introduced to all the three options and go into details on the **Dimension Units.**

Dimension Style covers customized setup of the **Arrow size, Text Height** as well as **Units and Precision**. Follow these steps to setup the units. Angular and Linear units are changed in this dialogue box.

27. Type **Units** at the Command prompt and press the Enter key.
28. Drawing Units dialogue box pops up. Refer to Figure 9.05

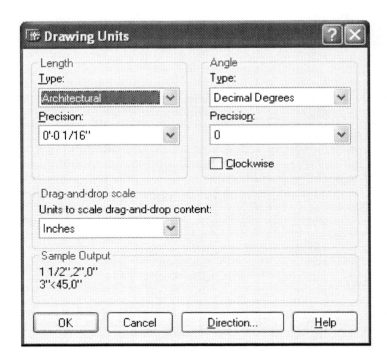

Figure 9.04

29. Click on the arrow under Type and select **Architectural.** This format represents each drawing unit as 1 inch

30. A length of **100 feet** can be represented in Architectural units as **100'** since **1 unit** is equal to **1 inch.**

31. When you enter **100'** to represent the length of a line, it will be measured as **1,200.00"**

DDunits Setup:

Another format to set the Units with is the **DDunits**. When you type **DDunits** at the Command prompt, it will invoke the Drawing Units Dialogue box for you to enter the required units to use for your drawing.

Dimension Style:

To invoke the **Dimension Style Manager** Dialogue box, type **Dimstyle** at the Command Prompt. Alternatively, you can click on **Dimension** on the Main Menu and select **Style** from the list of options. The Dimension Style Manager Dialogue box opens up on the Graphics area. Follow these steps to setup all the necessary units to be used in the Template just created.

Dimension Style Setup:

32. Click on Dimension and select Style, Dimension Style Manager Dialogue box opens up. Refer to Figure 9.06

33. Click on **New** and type Architecture in the allotted box. Figure 9.07

34. Click on Continue to open the **New Dimension Style: Architecture**

35. Click on Lines and Arrows move to the Arrowheads and click on the arrow besides Closed filled.

36. Select **Architectural tick** from the list of items, for **1st** and **2nd**

37. Next Click on Leader and change it to **Architectural tick**

38. Click on the browser button to the right of Text Style and select New under Style Name

39. Enter Vertical in the box by Style Name and click OK

40. Click on the Arrow by Font name and change it to **Times New Roman** or whatever Font Style is used in your company

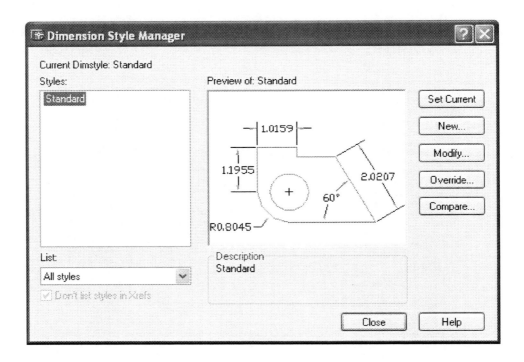

Figure 9.05

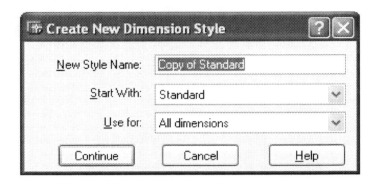

Figure 9.06

41. Other titles can be added on as the need arises.

42. Click on Close to exit the Text Style dialogue box

43. Click on Fit and place a mark in the Radio button by **Either the Text or the arrows, whichever fits best**

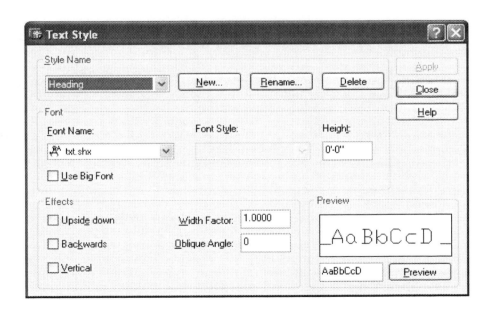

Figure 9.07

44. Click on the **Primary Units** and move to **Linear Dimension**

45. Click to expand the arrow by unit format and select **Architectural**

Use the contents of the **Table** below to fill in the values in the Dimension Style.

Table 9.00

Lines and Arrows	Baseline	2"
	Extend Beyond dim Lines	2"
	Offset from Origin	2"
	Arrowheads	Architectural tick
	Center Mark for Circles	2"
Text	Text Height	2"
	Offset from dim line	2"
Fit	Either the text or the arrow Whichever fits best	
Primary Units	Unit Format	Architectural
	Precision	0'- 0 1/16"

46. Click on Close to exit the Dimension Style Manager and Save the **Template. Arch**

Now that you have finished setting up the Dimension Style, you can use it to start drawing. You will use it for basic Architectural drawings. You will learn to draw layouts, doors, Tables and chairs and add dimensions. You will use the Rectangle tool to draw a chair and save it as a block to be used in other drawings. You will use one drawing file to do all your basic drawings and create individual Block to insert it later in your drawing.

47. Click on Draw and select Rectangle from the list of tools. A message pops up, requesting you to:

48. **Specify corner point or [Chamfer / Elevation / Fillet / Thickness / Width]:**

49. Type **0,0** and press the Enter key A message pops up, requesting you to:

50. **Specify other corner point or [Dimensions]:**

51. Type **6, 6** and press the Enter key.

52. Click on Draw from the Main Menu and select **Arc** then select **Start, End, and Radius.** A message pops up, requesting you to:

53. **Specify start point of arc or [Center]:**

54. Click on the corner at **A** then **B** A message pops up, requesting you to:

55. **Specify center point of arc or [Angle / Direction / radius]:**

56. Type **3** to place the arc and press the Enter key to exit.

57. Use **Trim** to remove the Line between A and B.

Block:

Create blocks to be used later in your drawing. You are going to use the **Absolute Coordinate** together with your **Architectural Template**, to draw an open object and add an arc to the top. Follow these steps:

58. Click on **Draw** from the Main Menu and select the **Line** tool. A message pops up requesting you to:

59. **Specify first point:**

60. Type **0, 6** at the command prompt and press the Enter key. A message pops up requesting you to:

61. **Specify the next point:**

62. Type **0, 0** and press the Enter key again. A message pops up requesting you to:

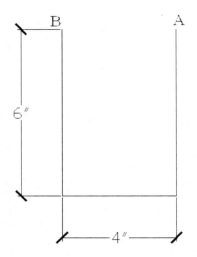

Figure 9.08

63. **Specify next point or [Undo]:**

64. Type **4, 0** and press the Enter key. A message pops up requesting you to:

65. **Specify next point or [Close / Undo]:**

66. Type **6, 6** and press the Enter key 2xs to complete the sketch. Refer to Figure 9.09

You are now going to add an arc to the sketch

67. Click on **Draw** from the Main Menu, highlight **Arc** and select **Start, End, and Radius.** A message pops up requesting you to:

68. **Specify start point of Arc or [Center]:**

69. Click on the endpoint, designated by the letter '**A**'. A message pops up requesting you to:

70. **Specify end point of arc.**

71. Click on the endpoint designated by the letter '**B**'. A message pops up

requesting you to:

72. **Specify center point of arc or [Angle / Direction / Radius]:**

73. Move the point up above the letters '**A**' and '**B**', let go your finger off the left mouse button, type **2** and press the Enter key. To complete the Arc. Refer to Figure 9.09

You are now going to use this object to create a Block. Follow these steps.

74. Click on Draw and highlight **Block** then select **Make**, a **Block Definition** dialogue box pops up

75. Enter **Chair** in the box allotted for **Name** and click on **Select objects**

76. The graphics area opens up and A message pops up, requesting you to:

77. **Select objects:**

78. Type **All** and press the Enter key

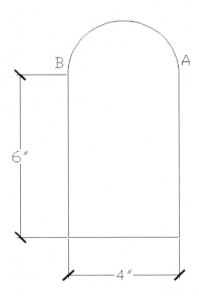

Figure 9.09

79. Back in the **Block Definition** dialogue box,

80. Click on **Pick point** to go back to the graphics area and click on the Origin.

81. Click on **OK** in the Block Definition dialogue box to turn the sketch into a **Block.**

This Block created can only be used in the current drawing. When you save your drawing and close the File, the Block is save together with the File. Anytime that you open this particular file, the said Block could be inserted in any location of the drawing.

No other file will be allowed to use this block because it is Local.

The next Block to cover will be **Wblock** also known as **Write Block** type. This Block is Global, in that; it can be inserted and used in all other drawings regardless of their shape or form.

Figure 9.10

You are now going to use the basic tools to design a Conference Room in an office building. You will learn how to draw Chairs, Tables, Projector Screen, Door and other furniture that go to make up a Conference room.

82. Click on Draw from the main Menu and select rectangle. A message pops up requesting you to:

83. **Specify first corner point or [Chamfer / Elevation / Fillet / Thickness/ Width]:**

84. Type **0, 0** and press the Enter key. A message pops up requesting you to:

85. **Specify other corner point or [Dimensions]:**

86. Type **190, 250** and press the Enter key to complete the rectangular sketch.

87. Type **Zoom** and press the Enter key. A message pops up requesting you to Select:

88. **All / Center / Dynamic / Extents / Previous / Scale / Window] <real time>:**

89. Enter the letter '**E**' short for Extents and press the Enter key.

90. Click on Modify from the Main Menu and select Offset. A message pops up requesting you to:

91. **Specify offset distance or [Through] <Through>:**

92. Type **5** and press the Enter key. A message pops up requesting you to:

93. **Select objects to offset or <exit>:**

94. Click on '**A**' of the rectangle and click on '**B**' inside the Rectangle to place an offset copy.

95. Draw a Construction Line at the edge of the outer rectangle and offset it **36" 2Xs.** Figure 9.11

96. Extend the last two lines of the offset to the inner rectangle and trim it. Refer to Figure 9.13

97. Draw a line from the edge of the first Wall 36' from '**C**' to '**D**' inside the rectangle. Refer to Figure 9.14

You will use these steps to draw a door to the Conference room.

Door:

Designing a door in AutoCAD Architecture is like an art. You will use **SCE** form of the Arc option to generate the Door. In Arc you can use different options including **SCE (Start Center End)** option. Follow these steps in drawing a door to the conference room.

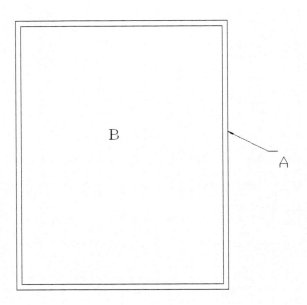

Figure 9.11

98. Click on Draw from the main Menu and select **SCE** from the list of items. A message pops up requesting you to:

99. **Specify start point of arc or [Center]:**

101. Click on **D**. Refer to Figure 9.15. A message pops up requesting you to:

102. **Specify second point of arc or [Center / End]:**

103.Click on **C**. refer to Figure 9.15. A message pops up requesting you to:

104.**Specify end point of arc or [Angle / cord Length]:**

105.Click on **E** to place the **Door** at the Entrance.

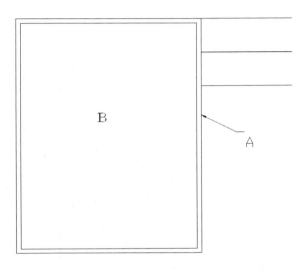

Figure 9.12

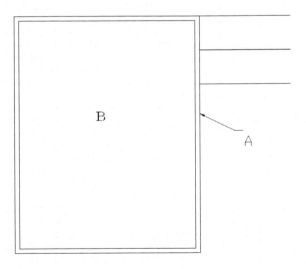

Figure 9.13

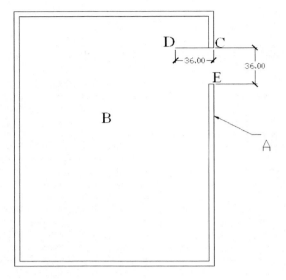

Figure 9.14

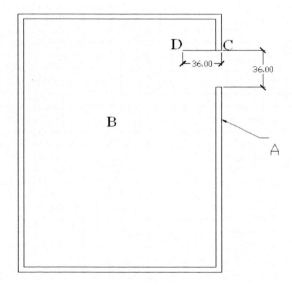

Figure 9.15

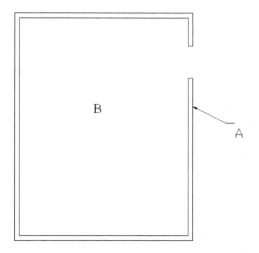

Figure 9.16

Draw two Construction lines on the top and side of the Rectangle to be used for offset. Refer to Figure 9.16

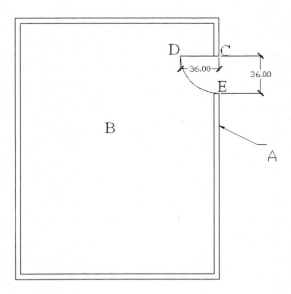

Figure 9.17

104. Click on Modify from the Main Menu and select Offset from the list of items. A message pops up requesting you to:

105. **Specify offset distance or [Through] <0.0000>:**

106. Type **18** and press the Enter key, the pointer turns in a pick box and A message pops up requesting you to:

107. **Select objects to offset or <exit>:**

108. Click on the Vertical construction line and click away from it. Repeat for the opposite side. Refer to Figure 9.18

109. Press the Enter key again to activate the Offset command and type **60** and press the Enter key. A message pops up requesting you to:

110. **Select objects to offset or <exit>:**

111. Click on the Horizontal line on the side of the rectangle to place two offset lines opposite each other. Refer to Figure 9.19

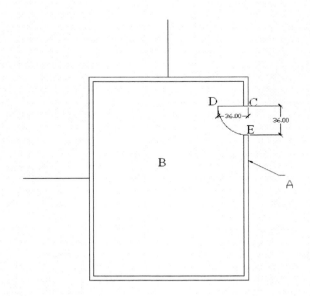

Figure 9.18

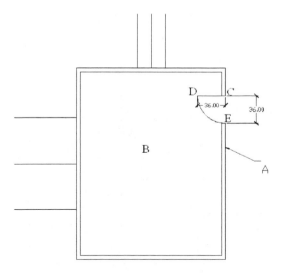

Figure 9.19

112. Use **Extend** edit tool to extend the lines to cross each other. Refer to Figure 9.19

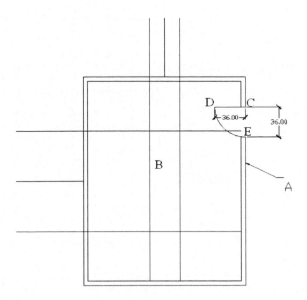

Figure 9.20

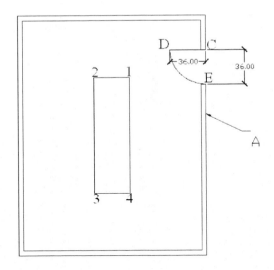

Figure 9.21

113. Use the Trim edit tool to trim the excess lines. Refer to Figure 9.20

You are now going to place an arc on the top and bottom of the Conference table. There are different options to use in drawing an arc. In this lesson you will use the **(SER)** Start End Radius option. Follow these steps to place the arc on the rectangle.

114. Click on Draw from the Main Menu and highlight Arc, and select Start, End, Radius A message pops up requesting you to:

115. **Specify start point of arc or [Center]:**

116. Click on '**1**' at the top edge of the rectangle. A message pops up requesting you to:

117. **Specify end point of arc:**

118. Click on '**2**' at the top edge of the rectangle. A message pops up requesting you to:

119. **Specify center point of arc or [Angle / Direction / Radius]:**

120. Move the pointer **vertically upwards**, type **18** and press the Enter key to place the first arc.

121. Click on Draw from the Main Menu and highlight **Arc**, and select **Start, End, Radius** A message pops up requesting you to:

122. **Specify start point of arc or [Center]:**

123. Click on '**3**' at the bottom edge of the rectangle. A message pops up requesting you to:

124. **Specify end point of arc:**

125. Click on '**4**' at the bottom edge of the rectangle. A message pops up requesting you to:

126. **Specify center point of arc or [Angle / Direction / Radius]:**

127. Move the pointer **vertically downwards**, type **18** and press the Enter key to place the second arc. Refer to Figure 9.21

Use the **Trim**-editing tool to remove the two horizontal lines inside the two arcs. Refer to Figure 9.22. The next design will cover drawing a **Chair** and using the **Rectangular Array** to add more copies around the Conference Table.

128. Click on Modify and select Offset. A message pops up requesting you to:

129. **Select offset distance or [Through] <Through>:**

130. Type **6** and press the Enter key.

131. Click on Rectangle from the Draw Menu and A message pops up requesting you to:

132. **Specify first corner point or [Chamfer / Elevation / Fillet / Thickness / Width]:**

133. Click on the end of the offset vertical line

134. Type **@-12, 12** and press the Enter key.

274

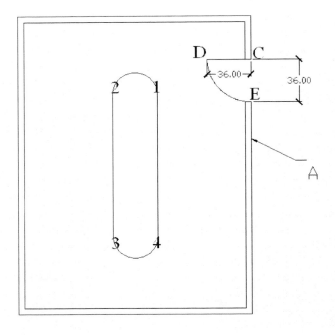

Figure 9.22

Array:

You are going to use the Rectangular Array command to add copies of the chair by the Conference table. Click on the Vertical offset line and hit the delete key.

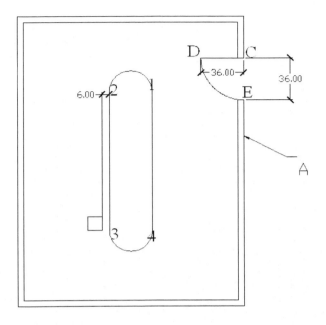

Figure 9.23

135. Type Array at the Command prompt or select Array from the list under Modify edit tool. The array dialogue box pops up, refer to Figure 9.23

136. Make the necessary entries to reflect that of Figure 9.23 and click on Select Objects button

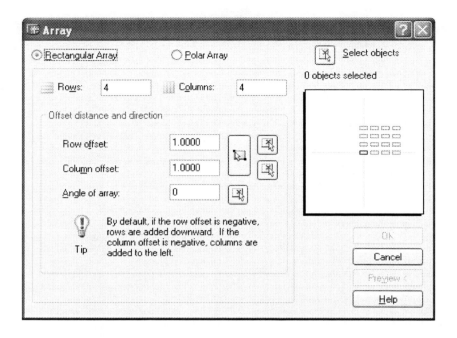

Figure 9.24

137. Back on the Graphics area A message pops up requesting you to:

138. Select objects:

139. Click on the small rectangle just drawn and press the Enter key. This will put you again on the Array Dialogue box

140. Click on OK to complete the Array

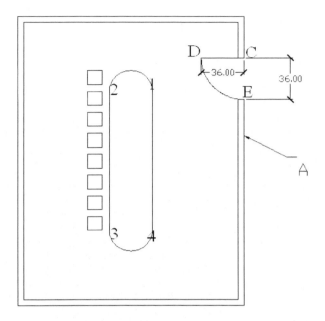

Figure 9.25

Mirror:

You are going to use the Mirror editing tool to add a mirror image of the chairs from one side to the other.

141.   Use the Line tool to place a construction line in the center of the conference table.

142.   Click on Modify and select Mirror editing tool. A message pops up requesting you to:

143.   **Select objects:**

144.   Click just bellow the 'x' mark, hold down the left mouse button, drag it down and click at the base of the first chair closer to **'Y'** to place a window around the chairs.

145. Press the Enter key A message pops up requesting you to:

146. **Specify first point of Mirror Line:**

147. Click on 'a' by the base of the Vertical Line. A message pop up requesting you to: Refer to Figure 9.25

148. **Specify second point of Mirror line:**

149. Click on the top end of the Vertical Line by '**b**' and press the Enter key.

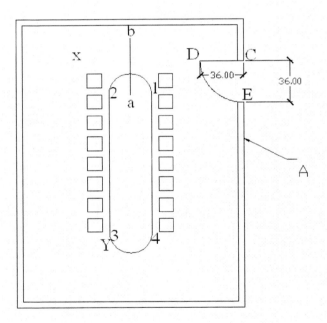

Figure 9.26

You may need to import certain drawings into your current drawing from another source.

You do so by using the **External Reference** option, also known as **Xref**. Xref allows you to reference another drawing without making it permanent part of the current drawing.

One way to understand External Reference properly before we actually put it in use is to imagine putting parts from different locations together through the Internet.

 A drawing is created in one office in a different location and you are to retrieve a part and add to your drawing in an assembly.

With external reference this part can be updated when changes are made and this will automatically reflect in the final part and not affect its manufacture.

Summary:

In this exercise you were introduced to Architectural design and setup and also covered topics like

♣ Making a Layer Setup

♣ Designing a Units Setup

♣ Working with DDunits Setup

♣ Creating Dimension Style

♣ Creating Dimension Style Setup

♣ Designing a Door in Architectural design

Exercise

• Start a new Folder and build it up from Template setup to adding Units and create Dimension Style adding different Layers to your Template.

The next lesson will cover **Xref**

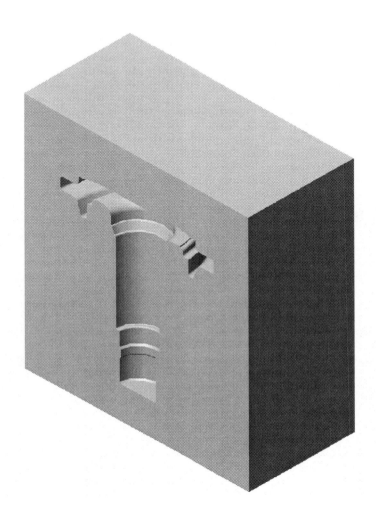

Chapter 10:

Xref:

After completing this lesson you will be able to:

♣ Import Objects with Xref

♣ Edit Xref

♣ Use the detach option in Xref

♣ Use Reload to update the Xref

♣ Learn to use Unload

♣ Use the Xref Manager

Follow these steps to add an Xref part to the current drawing.

1. Using the Line Tool, Draw a cylinder with a hole in it as in Figure 10.00

2. Add all the necessary dimensions and save it as **Waste Tank**.

3. Draw another part as in Figure 10.01 and Save as a Pin. Add all dimensions.

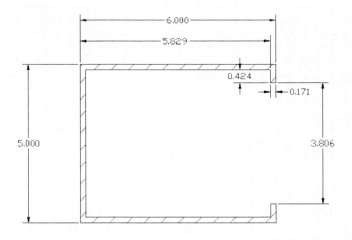

Figure 10.00

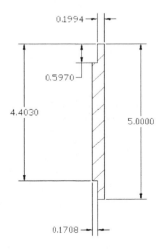

Figure 10.01

4. Make the Waste Tank the current drawing on your screen and bring in the Cover as an Xref to be attached to the Waste Tank.

5. Click on **Insert** from the Main Menu and select External Reference.

6. The **Select Reference Manager** Dialogue box pops up on the screen. Refer to Figure 10.03. Do not panic you are doing just fine.

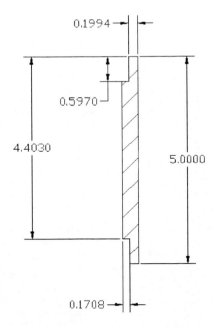

Figure 10.02

7. Click on the arrow besides **Look in** and search for the Folder you saved the **Cover** in.

8. Click to highlight the **Cover** and click on Open

9. **External Reference** dialogue box opens with different options including: Click on Ok. A Message pops up requesting you to:

Table 10.00

Attachment	Overlay	Path Type
Insertion Point	Scale	Rotation

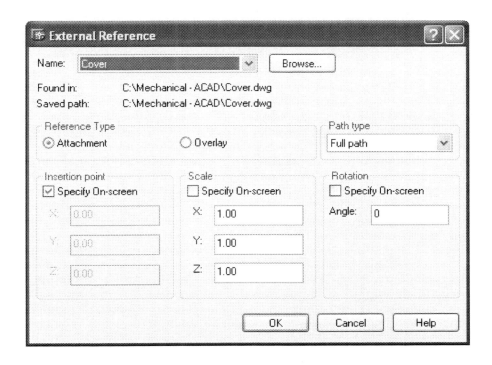

Figure 10.03

10. **Specify insertion point or [Scale / X/Y/Z/Rotate/ PScale /PX /PY/ PZ/ PRotate]:**

11. Click any where on the screen to Insert the **Cover** Part:

12. Use the Move command to insert the Cover from '**a**' to '**b**'

13. Click on Modify from the Main Menu and select **Move** from the list of items. A Message pops up requesting you to:

14. **Select objects:**

15. Click on the **Cover** and press the Enter key. A message pops up requesting you to:

16. **Specify base point or displacement:**

17. Click on the corner designated by '**a**'. A Message pops up requesting you to:

18. **Specify second point or displacement or use first point as displacement:**

286

19. Click on the corner designate by the letter '**b**' on the waste Tank to Insert the Cover.

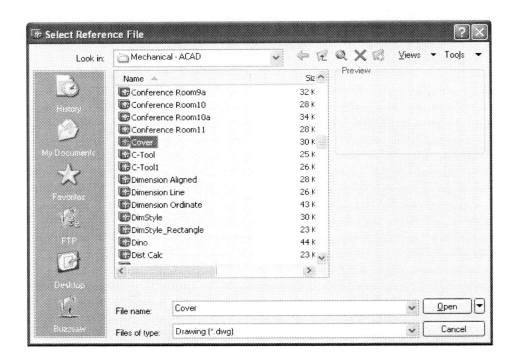

Figure 10.04

Editing the Xref:

You will make changes to the Cover Plate, and Reload it into the Waste Tank file and notice how the changes are automatically updated.

20. Click to open the Cover Plate and make the following changes.
21. Add a thickness of **0.125"** to the Cover plate and save it again.
22. Open the Assembled parts of the waste Tank and the Cover Plate.

23. Click on Insert from the Main Menu and select **Xref Manager**.

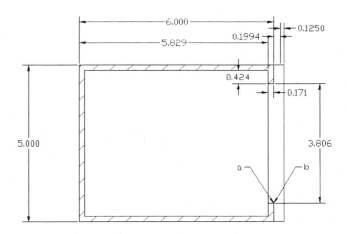

Figure 10.05

24. Notice that a check mark has been placed by the Cover and also showing the **Status, Size, Type, Date and Saved Path.**

25. **Detach, Reload, Unload, Bind, Open, Browse and Save** will all be grayed out.

26. Click to highlight the **Cover** and all these options will be activated.

27. Select Reload, click on **OK** and watch what happens to the Cover plate.

28. The Cover Plate is automatically updated.

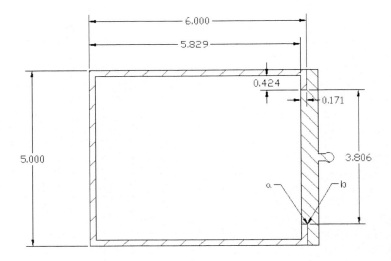

Figure 10.06

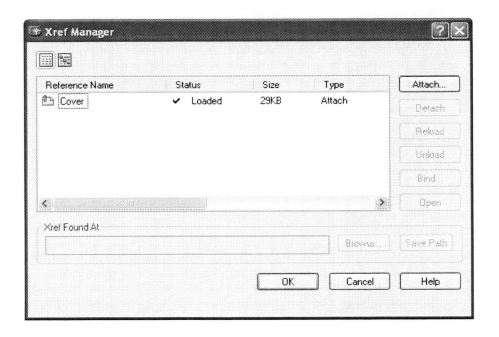

Figure 10.07

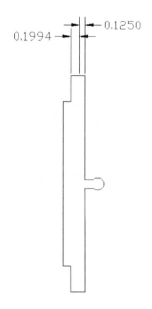

Figure 10.08

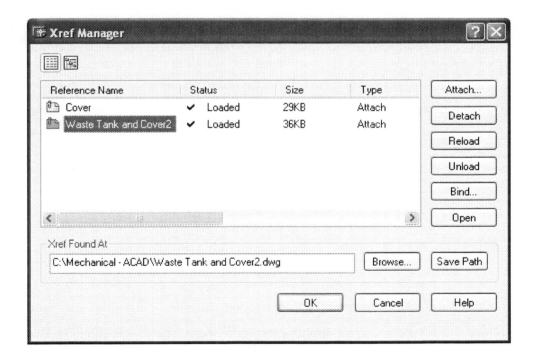

Figure 10.09

Figure 10.08

Figure 10.09

Detach:

Detach is used to completely remove an Xref from your drawings. Unlike the Erase and Delete Edit options, layer definitions associated with Xref will not go away when deleted or erased

You will need Detach tool, to completely remove all dependent objects of an Xref from your drawing.

To Detach an Xref,

29. Click on **Insert** from the Main Menu and select the **Xref Manager.**

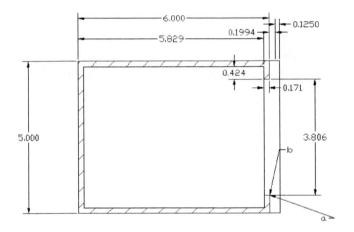

Figure 10.10

30. Click to highlight the Waste Tank and Cover

31. Click on Detach to completely remove the Waste Tank and the Cover from the Drawing after clicking on OK

<u>Reload:</u>

Reload enables the latest Xref of drawings as well as any changes made to a drawing to be updated.

AutoCAD will reload each Xref the moment you open your drawing making sure the latest version reflects that of the referenced drawing.

Other employees in the company can access externally saved files through the network environment immediately, by reloading the Xref.

To Reload an Xref

32. Click on **Insert** from the Main Menu and select the **Xref Manager.**

33. Click to highlight the Waste Tank and Cover

34. Highlight the waste Tank and Cover and click OK to Reload.

All changes made in the Drawing ever since opened the first time, will be Reloaded in the Xref.

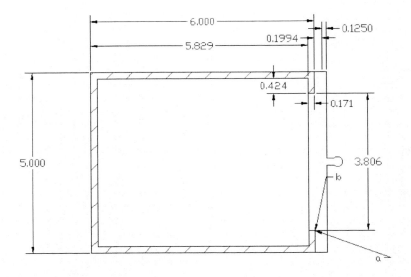

Figure 10.11

35. From the Insert menu, choose **Xref Manager.**

36. In the **Xref Manager**, select an external reference and then select Detach.

37. Choose OK.

Unload:

You will be using the Cover in this exercise. The first thing to do is to open the Cover to the Waste Tank and add a handle to it.

38. Start AutoCAD and click on File, Open
39. From the Select File, highlight Cover and click on open to place the Part on the Graphics area.
40. Draw a handle on the top of the Cover and click on Save

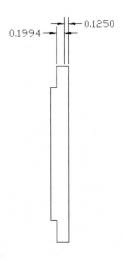

Figure 10.12

41. Click on Insert from the Main Menu and click and select External Reference.
42. Highlight Cover and click Open to place it on the Graphics area.
43. Click on Insert from the Main Menu, select Xref Manager
44. Click to highlight Cover in the Xref Manger.

45. Click on Reload and OK, the Xref Cover gets updated with the handle now attached to the Cover.

<u>Summary</u>:

You were introduced to Xref (External Reference in this Chapter and covered all aspects of the Xref tool. Topics that you learned included:

* Learning of Xref and its many uses

* Editing Xref

* Using Detach in Xref

* Using the detach option in Xref

* Using Reload to update the Xref

* Learning to use Unload

Exercise

You and another user use the Xref to exchange Files and go through the Attach, Detach and Reload options.

The next exercise will cover **Dimensioning and Tolerance**

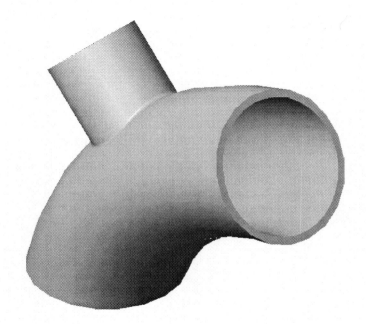

Chapter 11:

Dimensioning:

Figure 11.00

After completing this lesson you will be able to:

♣ Use Tolerance and Dimensioning properly on sketches

♣ Use Quick Dimensioning

♣ Use Linear Dimensioning

♣ Use Aligned dimension

♣ Use Ordinate Dimension

♣ Create Baseline Dimensioning

♣ Know what DIMDLI stands for and its uses

♣ Create Dimension with Continue

♣ Know of what Actual size means

♣ Know what Allowance means in dimensioning

♣ Cover Basic Size

♣ Cover Fits in Dimensioning

♣ Cover Clearance, Line and Interference Fit

♣ What Geometric Tolerance is used for?

AutoCAD is loaded with all aspects of Dimension Style ranging from Quick Dimension to Continue Dimension. We will cover all the Dimensions, starting with the Quick Dimension. Below is a Table of contents, listing Dimensioning incorporated with AutoCAD. You will now be introduced to Dimensioning with AutoCAD, starting with **Quick Dimension**

Table 11.00

Quick	Linear	Aligned
Ordinate	Radius	Diameter
Angular	Baseline	Continue

Dimensioning is a very essential part of design, in that properly dimensioned drawings will generate the right manufactured parts.

Many a part has been scrapped due to improper dimensioning or tolerance.

Care should be taken in placing the right dimensioning at the right places and checked and rechecked.

It is also helpful to have another person go over the final drawing to ascertain that everything is correct.

You are going to be introduced to Dimensioning as carried out in most of the industries and the Pressure Vessels in particular.

Below is an example of a drawing of a Nozzle that will be used on a Shell, for a Pressure Vessel. There should not be room for guessing.

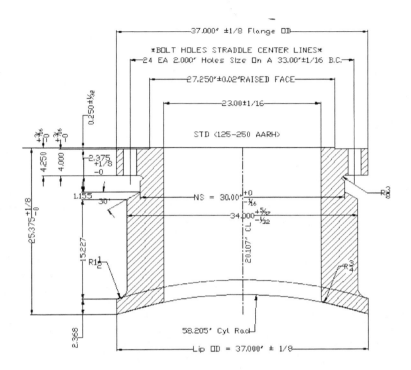

Figure 11.01

This will include; the length, width and height, diameter, radius, angle and its actual location.

The Architect, Engineer and the designer need this information as well as the Machinist, to make their work easier and worthwhile.

AutoCAD offer a broad range of dimensioning which include; Ordinate, Linear, Geometric, Angular and even Tolerances to name a few.

You will be guided through each and every type of dimensioning to create well-organized and properly dimensioned parts and drawings.

Scaling also play an important part in dimensioning when small parts are drawn larger than it is physically built.

This generates the options of using the **1:4. 2:1**, type of identifying measured parts and other scaling conversions, to represent how the actual part is built.

A production drawing must contain all necessary information for the machinist to be able to mill, drill or turn the part to specification and not to make any mistake.

When designing the part, the Designer and Engineer should have a good knowledge of the mindset of the Machinist.

The drawing in Figure 11.06 for an example, contain all the necessary information needed by the machinist to create a functional part.

 Let us use this drawing as an example to add all the necessary dimensions needed to make the part accurately. Refer to Figure 11.06.

Notice that the drawing has the following dimensions added as well as Tolerances and Notes.

Table 11.01

Material	SA182F11
FACING	STANDARD
QUANTITY	1
CLASS	600
TYPE	V-NOZZLE ON A SHELL
SIZE	24"
TYPE	NUT STOP
TYPE	V1
ANGLE	30°
CYLINDRICAL RADIUS	58.205R
SHELL THICKNESS	2.25"
LIP OD	37.00"
OAL	25.375"
LIP TYPE	WITH NO BEVEL
ID	23.000"

For more on Dimensioning, refer to **(ANSI / ASME Y14.5M – 1994)** that covers Dimensions in all aspect of every Industry.

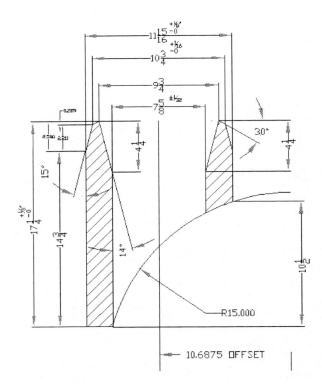

Figure 11.02

1. Start AutoCAD if it is not already loaded on your System

2. Type **'LINE'** at the Command prompt and press the Enter key. A Message pops up requesting you to:

3. **Specify the first point:**

4. Click on **'A'.** A Message pops up requesting you to:

5. **Specify next point or [Undo]:**

6. Click on **'B'** to place a Line on the Graphics area and hit the **'Esc'** key on the keyboard. Refer to Figure 11.00

Quick Dimension:

When asked to type something that is in quotes, you do not have to make the entries starting with the quotes. Just enter the value inside the quotes. For an example, when asked to type **'C'**, just enter the letter **C**.

You will learn how to use the Quick option, to add dimensions to the Line

7. Click on Dimension from the Main Menu and select Quick Dimension, the pointer should turn into a Pickbox. A message pops up requesting you to:

8. **Select geometry to dimension:**

9. Click on the Line to select it and it should turn into broken lines.

10. Press the Enter key and a Message pops up requesting you to:

11. **Specify dimension line position, or [Continuous / Staggered / Baseline / Ordinate / Radius / Diameter / datumPoint / Edit / seTtings]<Continuous>:**

12. Click on the letter 'C' to place the dimension of the line.

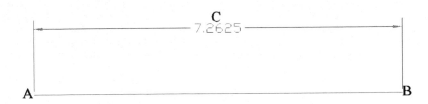

A————————————————————————————B

Figure 11.03

Linear Dimension:

Linear dimension unlike Quick dimension will let you pick two points to place the dimension text as well as use the Mtext command to override the original text or add text to the dimension. To understand the Linear Dimension option, follow these steps. You will use the same steps above to draw the Line.

13. Type **'LINE'** at the Command prompt and press the Enter key. A Message pops up requesting you to:

14. **Specify the first point:**

15. Click on **'A'.** A Message pops up requesting you to:

16. **Specify next point or [Undo]:**

17. Click on **'B'** to place a Line on the Graphics area and hit the **'Esc'** key on the keyboard. Refer to Figure 11.02

A ——— **B**

Figure 11.04

18. Click on **Dimension** from the Main Menu and select **Linear.** A Message pops up requesting you to:

19. **Specify first extension line origin or <select object>:**

20. Click on the endpoint by the letter '**A**'. A Message pops up requesting you to:

21. **Specify second extension line origin:**

22. Click on the endpoint by the letter '**B**'. A Message pops up requesting you to select:

23. **[Mtext / Text / Angle / Horizontal / Vertical / Rotated]:**

You have the option of clicking on the Graphics area to place the Dimension Text or select any of the options listed above. Let us type the letter '**M**' and press the Enter key. The **Text Formatting** dialogue box opens up as in Figure 11.05. You can choose to delete the closed less and more that brackets and type any text in place of that or add text to the brackets to describe the dimension style. Let us see how it works in both ways.

24. Hit the delete key on the keyboard several times to get rid of the brackets. Type **Quick Dimension,** and click on OK. A message pops up again requesting you to select:

25. **[Mtext / Text / Angle / Horizontal / Vertical / Rotated]:**

26. Click on the Graphics area below the Line just drawn, to place the dimension.

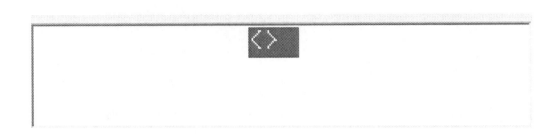

Figure 11.05

You are now going to use both options to place dimension and text in your drawing.

27. Click on File, Open and locate and load the Line just drawn.

A——————————————————————————————————————B

Figure 11.06

28. Click on **Dimension** from the Main Menu and select **Linear.** A Message pops up requesting you to:

29. **Specify first extension line origin or <select object>:**

30. Click on the endpoint by the letter '**A**'. A Message pops up requesting you to:

31. **Specify second extension line origin:**

32. Click on the endpoint by the letter '**B**'. A Message pops up requesting you to select:

33. **[Mtext / Text / Angle / Horizontal / Vertical / Rotated]:**

34. Type '**M**' and press the Enter key to open the **Text Formatting** dialogue box.

35. Type Quick Dimension and click OK to place the dimension and text on the Graphics area. You will be requested to select:

36. **[Mtext / Text / Angle / Horizontal / Vertical / Rotated]:**

37. Click below the line drawn to place the Line and Text.

Figure 11.07

Another very important aspect of using the Linear and Mtext is the ability to place Tolerances by the dimension. Let us use the same process in placing the dimension on the Line using Tolerance.

38. Click on **Dimension** from the Main Menu and select **Linear.** A Message pops up requesting you to:

39. **Specify first extension line origin or <select object>:**

40. Click on the endpoint by the letter '**A**'. A Message pops up requesting you to:

41. **Specify second extension line origin:**

42. Click on the endpoint by the letter '**B**'. A Message pops up requesting you to select:

43. **[Mtext / Text / Angle / Horizontal / Vertical / Rotated]:**

Figure 11.08

44. Type '**M**' and press the Enter key to open the **Text Formatting** dialogue box.

45. Press the Horizontal arrow by the keypad to move the cursor to the right of the Brackets.

46. Type '<>%%P1/16' and press the Enter key. This will place a Tolerance of plus or minus **1/16"** by the dimension text.

47. Quick Dimension and click OK to place the dimension and text on the Graphics area. You will be requested to select:

48. **[Mtext / Text / Angle / Horizontal / Vertical / Rotated]:**

49. Click below the line drawn to place the Dimension and Text together with the **1/16** Tolerance.

Start AutoCAD, if it is not already running on your system and invoke the Line tool. You are going to use the Line tool to draw a sketch and add dimensions to the sketch.

50. Click on Draw from the Main Menu and select the Line tool. A message pops up requesting you to:

51. **Specify first point:**

52. Click on the letter '**A**'

53. **Specify next point:**

54. Click on the letter '**B**' and hit the 'esc' key on the keyboard.

55. Click on **Dimension** from the Main Menu and select **Linear.**

56. Click on the end of the line by letter '**A**' then '**B**' and hit the **'esc'** key on the keyboard to place the Linear Dimension of the Line.

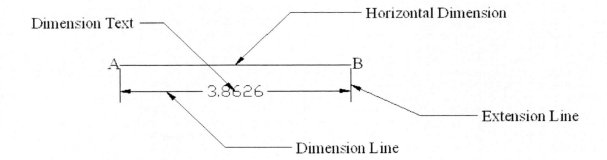

Figure 11.09

Aligned Dimension

57. Click on Draw from the Main Menu and select the **Line** tool. A message pops up requesting you to:

58. **Specify first point:**

59. Type **0, 0** and press the Enter key. A message pops up requesting you to:

60. **Specify next point:**

61. Type **@2<30** press the Enter key and hit the 'esc' key on the keyboard.

62. Click on Dimension and select Aligned. A message pops up requesting you to:

63. **Specify first extension line origin or <select object>:** A message pops up requesting you to:

64. **Click on the letter 'A'**

65. **Specify second extension line:**

66. Click on the endpoint by the letter **'B'** and hit the 'esc' key.

You are now going to add Aligned dimension to the Line

67. Click on **Dimension** from the Main Menu and select Aligned. A message pops up requesting you to:

68. **Specify first extension line origin or <select object>:**

69. Click on the endpoint by the letter **'A'.** A message pops up requesting you to:

70. **Specify second extension line origin:**

71. Click on the endpoint by the letter **'B'** then a point by the letter **'C'** to place the aligned dimension on the line. Refer to Figure 11.11

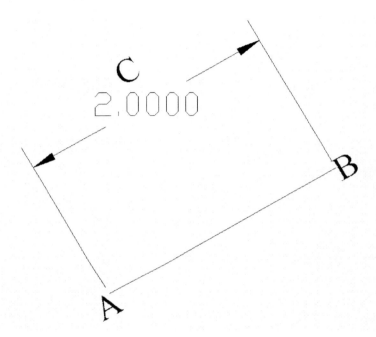

Figure 11.10

Figure 11.11

Ordinate Dimension:

The ordinate dimensioning is like utilizing the Absolute Coordinate system. All references are made to the origin and the dimension will be placed a distance of X or Y from **0, 0** to the next point. Dimensions placed with the ORTHO on will have a straight line with the dimension placed at its end.

Dimensions placed with the ORTHO off, will have a bend automatically placed in the leader line.

These bends help you manage your dimension line to avoid clutter when there are dimensions placed closer to each other.

A very important factor to remember is to start all your drawings from the origin of the UCS or **0, 0** in order for the dimensions to come out right.

Follow these steps to place Ordinate dimensions on a sketch.

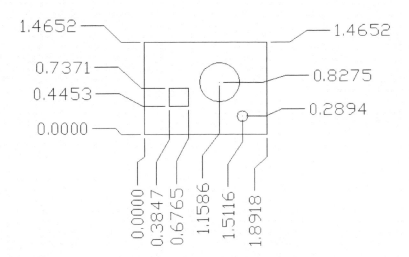

Figure 11.12

DIMENSIONING:

Baseline Dimension:

The Baseline dimension also known as the **Parallel Dimensioning** is used to create multiple dimensions with reference to a **Base Point**.

In essence, a dimension must first be placed on an object before invoking the baseline command to measure from. The baseline dimension is another useful tool in arranging the dimensional text without clogging the drawing.

The dimensions are placed in such a way, in order not to overlap each other, hence the name Parallel Dimensioning.

You will be guided to place baseline dimension on a simple sketch. Start AutoCAD and open a new file or load the Template.

72. Type **'PLINE'** at the Command prompt and press the Enter key. A Message pops up requesting you to:

73. **Specify the first point:**

74. Type **0, 0** and press the Enter key. A Message pops up requesting you to:

75. **Specify next point or [Undo]:**

76. Type **5, 0** and press the Enter key A Message pops up requesting you to:

77. **Specify next point or [Undo]:**

78. Use the values in the Table below to draw the sketch.

Table 11.02

0,0	@5,0	@0,2	@1.5,0	@0,-2
@4,0	@0,2	@-1.5,0	@0,3	@-3,0
@0,-1	@-1.5,0	@0,1	@-1,0	@0,-3
@-2,0	@0,2	@-1.5,0	C	Enter 2Xs

a. Your sketch should look like the one in Figure without the letters A B and C

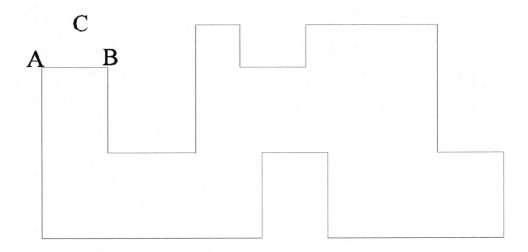

Figure 11.13

79. Click on Dimension from the Main Menu and select the Linear Dimension. The pointer turns into a crosshair and A Message pops up requesting you to:

80. **Specify first extension line origin or <select objects>:**

81. Click on the endpoint by the letter 'A' A Message pops up requesting you to

82. **Specify second extension line origin:**

83. Click on the endpoint by the letter 'B'. A Message pops up requesting you to

84. **Specify dimension arc line or [Mtext / Text / Angle]:**

85. Click on the Graphics area closer to the letter 'C' to place the Linear Dimension.

You are now going to add Baseline Dimension to the two Lines. Refer to Figure 11.14

86. Click on Dimension from the Main Menu and select Baseline. The pointer turns into a Pick Box and A Message pops up requesting you to

87. **Select base dimension:**

88. **Click on the 1.5000 linear dimension just placed on the Graphics area by the letter 'C'.** A Message pops up requesting you to

89. **Specify a second extension line origin or [Undo / Select] <Select>:**

90. Click on the endpoint by the letter 'D' and continue on to the letter 'F' and press the Enter key **2Xs** when finished to exit the Baseline Dimension. Refer to Figure 11.14

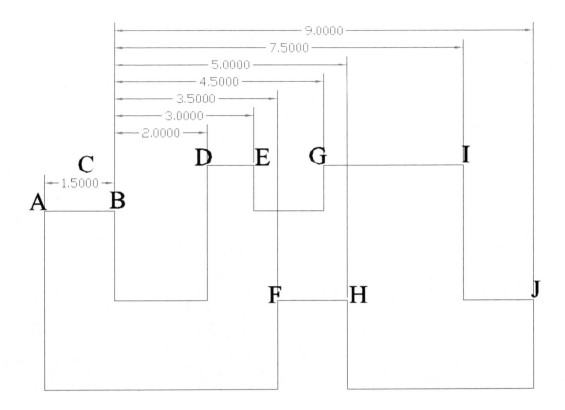

Figure 11.14

DIMDLI:

The **DIMDL** command is used to set the value that controls the spacing in between each Dimension Line. You will notice that the spacing between the dimension lines, are equally spaced using the default setting of **0.38** in Figure 11.14

Setting **DIMDL** to a new value helps to control the spacing of the dimension lines in your drawing. This will create an Offset between dimension lines using the value set at **DIMDL.**

This value can be changed to suit each drawing that you work on. The following is the step taken to change the default value of **0.38** in the **DIMDL**

318

91. Type **DIMDL** at the Command prompt, and press the Enter key. A message pops up requesting you to:

92. **Enter new value for DIMDLI <0.3800>:**

93. Type **0.500** and press the Enter key.

94. Use the Baseline Dimension to add new dimension to the sketch and check the difference.

CONTINUE:

Another Dimension Style that makes reference to the original dimension is the Continue Dimension. Unlike the Baseline dimension, the Continue as its name implies continue to add dimension on the same line as you move along the drawing, end to end of each other.

95. Click on Dimension from the Main Menu and select the Linear Dimension. The pointer turns into a crosshair and A Message pops up requesting you to:

96. **Specify first extension line origin or <select objects>:**

97. Click on the endpoint by the letter 'A' A Message pops up requesting you to

98. **Specify second extension line origin:**

99. Click on the endpoint by the letter 'B'. A Message pops up requesting you to

100. **Specify dimension arc line or [Mtext / Text / Angle]:**

101. Click on the Graphics area closer to the letter 'C' to place the Linear Dimension.

You are now going to add **Continue Dimension** to the Drawing. Refer to Figure 11.15

102. Click on Dimension from the Main Menu and select Baseline. The pointer turns into a Pick Box and A Message pops up requesting you to

103. **Select base dimension:**

104. **Click on the 2.551 Linear dimension just placed on the Graphics area by the letter 'C'.** A Message pops up requesting you to

105. **Specify a second extension line origin or [Undo / Select] <Select>:**

106. Click on the endpoint by the letter **'D'** and continue on to the letter **'G'** and press the Enter key 2Xs when finished to exit the Baseline Dimension. Refer to Figure 11.15

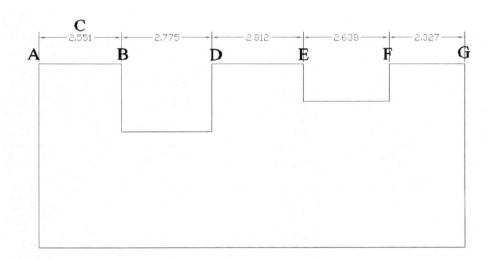

Figure 11.15

Tolerances

Tolerances are used in conjunction with **Dimensions** to obtain the Maximum yield of parts. The higher the Tolerance on a Part the more expensive that Part will cost to manufacture.

In the Pressure Vessel Industry for an example, A Bore of a cylinder is given as **(+/-1/32)** and **(+/-1/16)** when the Dimensional size is **12 inches** and **ABOVE.**

A company for an example can improve its profit by using proper tolerance, thus improving production and reducing waste.

Tolerancing helps to add proper dimensions to a part with regard to its size, position in an assembly and its shape, by showing the Maximum and Minimum values of the dimension for a particular feature. Refer to **(ANSI / ASME Y1.45M-1994)**

In the Pressure Vessel industry for an example, a tolerance of **9.250"+/- (5/32 / 1/32)** added to a Dimension of a Barrel OD, for **900#** class Long Weld Neck Flat Face Nozzle denotes that, the manufactured part may be **9.40625"** for the upper Limit and **9.28125"** for the lower limit or anything in between. The total amount of **Variation** thus tolerated will therefore amount to **0.1875".**

Tolerance is used to control the dimensions of two or more parts in order that such part could be manufactured miles apart and fit without any interference.

For an example if a Part is machined to accommodate a diameter between **7.625"** and **7.623",** the difference of **0.002"** is considered the Tolerance.

There are certain terms and definitions set aside by **(ANSI / ASME Y14.5-1994)** that you must familiarize yourself with since it is the Standard used in the Industry.

Actual Size:

The measured size of the finished part is known as the Actual Size.

Allowance:

This is the minimum clearance space (or minimum interference) that is between the maximum material condition **(MMC)** of mating parts. For an example the difference largest shaft and the smallest hole will be considered as the Allowance, which represents the tightest permissible fit. With a Shaft size of **7.250"** and a hole size of **7.248"** the difference of **0.002"** will be the allowance. The **Clearance Fit** in the difference will be positive and the Interference Fit, negative.

Basic Size:

The process by which Limits of sizes are derived using allowances and tolerances is known as the Basic Size. This is also the theoretical size of the part being measured.

Fits:

It is a general term used to signify the range of tightness, which may result from the application of a specific combination of allowances and tolerances in the design of mating parts

The range of looseness or tightness resulting from the application of a specific combination of allowance and tolerances in between mating parts is known as **Fit.** This is the result of allowances and tolerance that is applied to the specific parts during mating of these parts.

Fit is classified under four general types, namely; **Clearance, Interference, Line** and **Transition Fit**.

Clearance Fit:

The space that occurs while two parts are being-put together in an assembly, the limits in size produced by that space, is known as the clearance fit.

Interference Fit:

In an assembly, the limits in size, which causes interference to occur when parts are being put together, is known as Interference Fit

Line Fit:

In the Line Fit, the limits of size are so specified that a clearance or surface contact may result when mating parts are assembled. You will use practical applications in subsequent drawings regarding Geometric Tolerance.

Refer to **(ANSI / ASME Y14.5M-1994)** for more information on **Manufacturing Tolerancing**

Geometric Tolerance:

When you first click on **Tolerance** on **Dimension** from the Main Menu, the Geometric Tolerance dialogue box pops up. You can then select any Symbol by clicking inside the black box under **Sym** to invoke the Symbol Dialogue box Refer to Figures 11.16 and 11.17

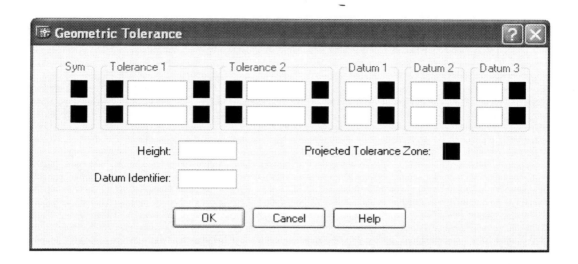

Figure 11.16

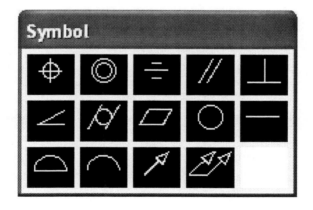

Figure 11.17

Table 11.03

Position	Concentricity	Symmetry	Parallelism	Perpendicularity
Angularity	Cylindricity	Flatness	Circularity	Straightness
Profile of a surface	Profile of a Line	Circular runout	Total runout	

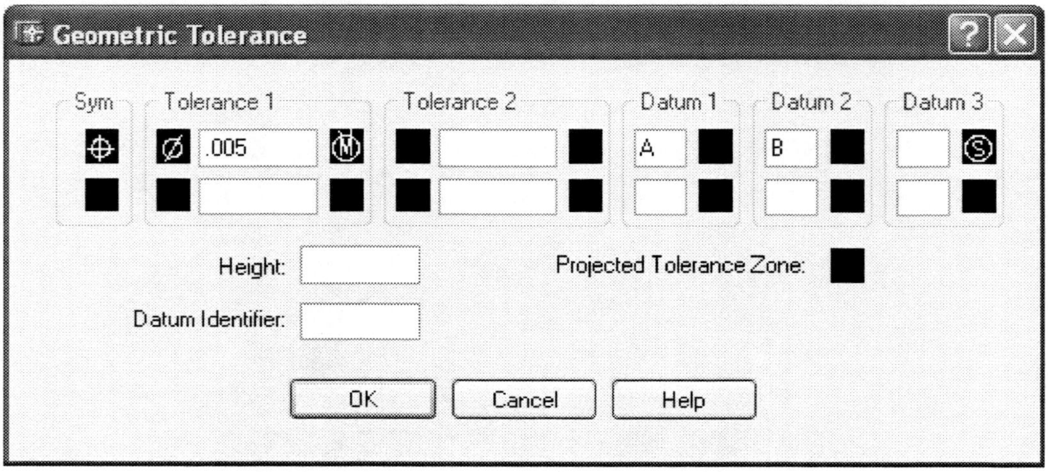

Figure 11.18

⊕ | Ø.005 (M) | A | B | C

Figure 11.19

Radius:

You will use the radius dimension to place dimensions on Arc and Circles. You do so by select the Radius option from the Dimension Menu and clicking on the edge of the circle or Arc.

An arrowhead is also placed to designate the point of reference for the dimension. In certain cases when the **Dimcen** system value is not set to zero, AutoCAD will place a **Center Mark** inside the circle or an arc.

To change this value, type **Dimcen** at the Command prompt and change it to 1 to enable you to place a center mark on the circle or arc.

Note that the larger the number the bigger the center mark will be displayed. A center mark of **0.85** is smaller than **1.00**.

Follow these steps to place dimensions on a Circle:

107.   Open a new file and Save as Radius Dimension.

108.   Type **Dimcen** at the Command prompt and press the enter key. A Message pops up requesting you to:

109.   **Enter new value for Dimcen<0.0000>:**

110.   Change the current value to 1 and press the Enter key.

111.   Click on Draw from the Main Menu highlight **Circle** and select **Center Radius (CR).** A Message pops up requesting you to:

112.   **Specify first center point for circle of [3P / 2P / Ttr (tan tan radius)]:**

113.   Type **0, 0** to place the center of the circle on the Origin and press the Enter key. A Message pops up requesting you to:

114.   **Specify radius of circle or [Diameter]: <0.0000>:**

115.   Type the letter '**R**' short for radius and type press the Enter key.

116.   Type **1.500** and press the enter key to place the circle on the origin.

117.   Click on Dimension from the Main Menu and select Radius. A Message pops up requesting you to:

118.   **Select arc or circle:**

119.   Click on the circle by '**A**' and click on the point by '**B**' to place the dimension.

120.   The center mark is also positioned in the center of the circle.

121.   Change the value of **Dimcen** into **0.00**, and add dimension to the circle and notice what happens to the center mark.

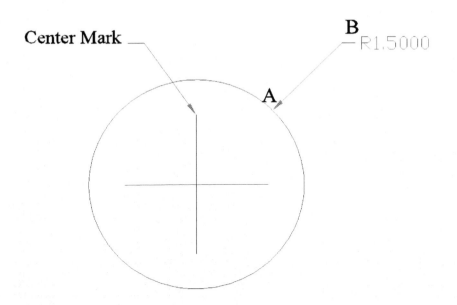

Figure 11.20

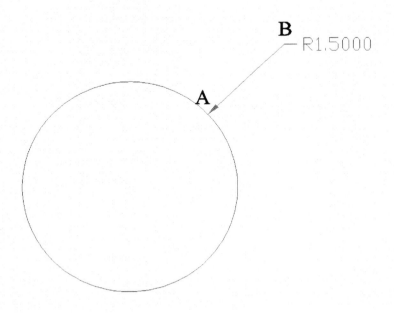

Figure 11.21

Diameter:

122. Open a new file and Save as Diameter Dimension.

123. Type **Dimcen** at the Command prompt and press the enter key. A Message pops up requesting you to:

124. **Enter new value for Dimcen<0.0000>:**

125. Change the current value to **1** and press the Enter key.

126. Click on Draw from the Main Menu highlight **Circle** and select **Center, Radius (CR).** A Message pops up requesting you to:

127. **Specify first center point for circle of [3P / 2P / Ttr (tan tan radius)]:**

128. Type **0, 0** to place the center of the circle on the Origin and press the Enter key. A Message pops up requesting you to:

129. **Specify radius of circle or [Diameter]: <0.0000>:**

130. Type the letter **'D'** short for diameter and press the Enter key.

131. Type **1.500** and press the enter key to place the circle on the origin.

132. Click on **Dimension** from the Main Menu and select **Diameter.** A Message pops up requesting you to:

133. **Select arc or circle:**

134. Click on the circle by **'A'** and click on the point by **'B'** to place the dimension.

135. The center mark is also positioned in the center of the circle.

136. Change the value of **Dimcen** to **0.00** and add dimension to the circle and notice what happens to the center mark.

On using the diametric dimension, you have the option of place the lead arrow of the text on the tangent of the circle, or inside the circle. This option is accessed through the Dimension Style dialogue box. Follow these steps to set the how the Arrow is positioned in your sketches.

137. Click on **Dimension** from the Main Menu and select **Style** from the list of items.

138. Click on Modify and select Fit.

139. Click inside the **Radio Button** by **Both Text and Arrows**

140. Click on Ok, Set Current and close.

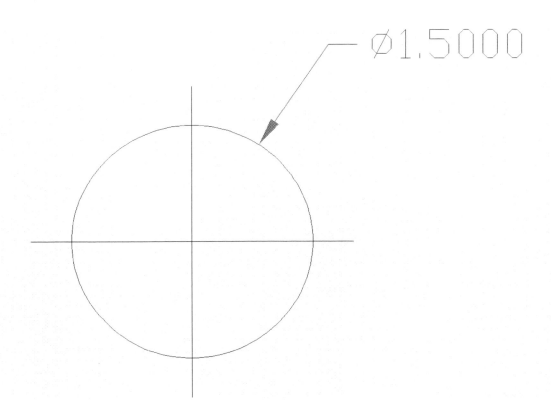

Figure 11.22

141.   Click on Dimension from the Main Menu and select **Diameter**. A Message pops up requesting you to select **arc or circle:**

142.   Click on the circle and click away from it to place the dimension inside the circle. Refer to Figure 11.12

143.   Click on **Dimension** from the Main Menu and select **Style** from the list of items.

144.   Click on Modify and select **Fit.**

145.   Click inside the **Radio Button** by **Either the Text or the Arrow**

146.   Click on Ok, **Set Current** and close.

Figure 11.23

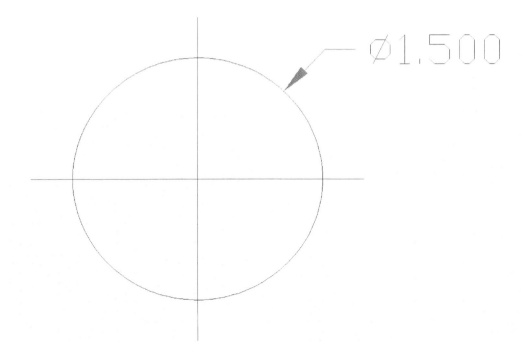

Figure 11.24

Angular Dimension:

Angular dimension is used to measure angles between crossing lines, two or more end points or to measure the angle of circular radii of two points. The process is very simple. When you invoke the Angular dimension option, you will have the option of selecting an arc, circle, line or the vertex. In the case of two lines ending at a common point, you will click on the first line, click on the second line and click in between the two lines to place the angular measurement of the two lines.

With the measurement on an arc, you will also be requested to an arc, circle, line or the vertex. Just click on the arc to place an Angular Dimension of the arc.

There are several ways when it comes to placing an Angular Dimension on a Circle. One of the steps to do that is to first place points as a guide, Format the Point Style to locate the Point and use the Angular Dimension to complete your measurement.

332

You will be shown how to properly use the Angular Dimensions in all the three aspects starting with that of two Line with a common endpoint. Start by opening AutoCAD if it is not already loaded on your system.

147. Type **'LINE'** at the Command prompt and press the Enter key. A Message pops up requesting you to:

148. **Specify the first point:**

149. Type **0, 0** and press the Enter key. A Message pops up requesting you to:

150. **Specify next point or [Undo]:**

151. Type **8, 0** and press the Enter key 2xs, to place the first Line on the Graphics area

152. Press the Enter key again to activate the Line command. A Message pops up requesting you to:

153. Type **0, 0** and press the Enter key. A Message pops up requesting you to:

154. **Specify next point or [Undo]:**

155. Type **@8<27.5** and press the Enter key 2xs to place the next line from the origin.

156. Type Zoom and press the Enter key. A Message pops up requesting you to

100. **[All / Center / Dynamic / Extents / Previous / Scale / Window] <real time>:**

101. Press the Enter key to accept real time and center your sketch on the Graphics area.

You are now going to add Angular Dimension to the two Lines. Refer to Figure below.

102. Click on Dimension from the Main Menu and select the Angular Dimension.

103. The pointer turns into a Pickbox and A Message pops up requesting you to:

104. **Select arc, circle, line, or <specify vertex>:**

105. Click on the Line just below the letter **'A'**. A Message pops up requesting you to

106. **Select second line:**

107. Click on the Line below the letter '**B**'. A Message pops up requesting you to

108. **Specify dimension arc line or [Mtext / Text / Angle]:**

109. Click on the Graphics area closer to the letter '**C**' to place the Angular Dimension.

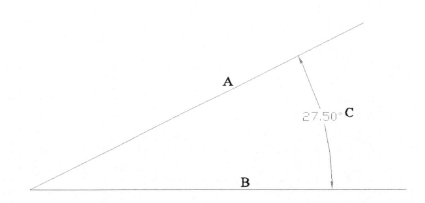

Figure 11.25

The next dimension to cover is the Arc. You will be guided to draw an arc and use the Angular dimension, to place a dimension text on the arc. The first thing to do is to draw an arc. To do so, open a new file or bring in the Template.

110. Click on Draw from the Main Menu and highlight Arc and select 3 Points from the list. A Message pops up requesting you to

111. **Specify start point of arc or [Center]:**

112. Click anywhere on the Graphics area. A Message pops up requesting you to

113. **Specify second point of arc or [Center / End]:**

114. Move the pointer to another location away from the first point and click again. A Message pops up requesting you to

115. **Specify end point of arc:**

116. Click on the graphics area away from the second point to place the arc.

You are now going to add **Angular Dimension** to the Arc. Refer to Figure below.

117. Click on Dimension from the Main Menu and select the Angular Dimension.

118. The pointer turns into a Pick box and A Message pops up requesting you to:

119. **Select arc, circle, line, or <specify vertex>:**

120. Click on the Arc just below the letter '**A**'. A Message pops up requesting you to

121. **Specify dimension arc line location or [Mtext / Text / Angle]:**

122. Click on a point just below the letter '**B**' to place the text for the dimension.

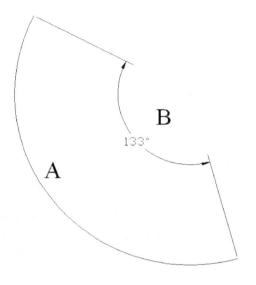

Figure 11.26

The next dimension to cover is the Circle. You will be guided to draw a circle and use the Angular dimension to place a dimension text on the circle by placing point at selected locations. The first thing to do is to draw a circle. To do so, open a new file or bring in the Template.

123. Click on Draw from the Main Menu and highlight Arc and select 3 Points from the list. A Message pops up requesting you to

124. **Specify center point for circle or [3P / 2P / Ttr (tan tan radius)]:**

125. Type **0, 0** and press the Enter key. Click anywhere on the Graphics area. A Message pops up requesting you to

126. **Specify radius of circle or [Diameter]:**

127. Type the letter '**D**' short for diameter and press the Enter key. A Message pops up requesting you to

128. **Specify diameter of circle:**

129. Type **5** and press the Enter key to place the circle on the Graphics area.

130. Type **Zoom** and press the Enter key. A Message pops up requesting you to select

131. **[All / Center / Dynamic / Extents / Previous / Scale / Window]<real time>:**

132. Press the Enter key to accept the option, real time to zoom out the circle.

You will be guided to Format the Point tool. Start by opening a new file and Save it as Circle dims.

133. Click on Format and select **Point Style.** The **Point Style** dialogue box pops up. Refer to Figure 11.27. Select one of the Points and click on OK.

134. Type **PDMODE** at the command prompt. A Message pops up requesting you to select

135. Enter new value for **PDMODE** <0.000>:

136. Type the number **2** at the Command and press the Enter key.

137. Finally click on draw from the Main Menu, highlight Point and click on Multiple Point. A Message pops up requesting you to select

138. **Specify a point:**

139. Click on the section of the Circle below the letter '**B**', move the pointer to the opposite side of the circle, and click on the section of the circle above the letter '**A**' to place the next point

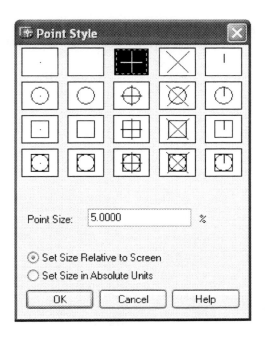

Figure 11.27

You are now going to add **Angular Dimension** to the Circle. Refer to Figure11.29 below.

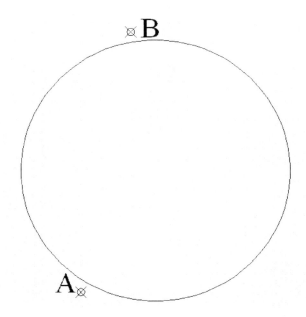

Figure 11.28

140. Click on Dimension and select **Angular**. The pointer should turn into a Pick Box and a Message pops up requesting you to:

141. **Select arc, circle, line or <Specify Vertex>:**

142. Click on section of the Circle below the Point closer to the letter '**A**'. A Message pops up requesting you to select

143. **Specify second angle endpoint:**

144. Click on the point by the letter '**B**'. A Message pops up requesting you to select

145. **Specify dimension arc line location or [Mtext / Text / Angle]:**

146. Click in front of the letter '**C**' to place the Dimension text for the Angular circle.

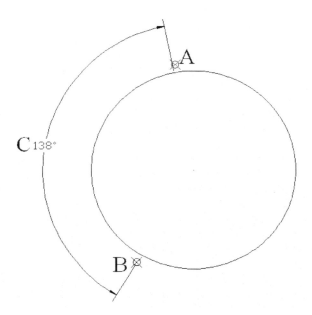

Figure 11.29

147. Click on Dimension from the Main Menu and select the Angular
Dimension. The pointer turns into a Pick box and A Message pops up
requesting you to:

148. **Select arc, circle, line, or <specify vertex>:**

149. Click on the Arc just below the letter '**A**'. A Message pops up requesting
you to

150. **Specify dimension arc line location or [Mtext / Text / Angle]:**

151. Click on a point just below the letter '**B**' to place the text for the dimension.

<u>Summary:</u>

This chapter covered all aspects of Dimensioning. Topics included how to:

- ♣ Use Quick Dimensioning
- ♣ Use Linear Dimensioning
- ♣ Use Aligned dimension
- ♣ Use Ordinate Dimension
- ♣ Create Baseline Dimensioning
- ♣ Be able to know what DIMDLI stands for and its uses
- ♣ Create Dimension with Continue
- ♣ Be able to know of what Actual size means
- ♣ Be able to know what Allowance means in dimensioning
- ♣ Create Basic Size
- ♣ Create Fits
- ♣ Create Clearance, Line and Interference Fit
- ♣ Be able to add Geometric Tolerance to your drawing

Exercise

Using different designs from previous Chapters, add all the various types of Dimensions just covered, from Linear to Ordinate.

The next lesson will cover **3D Modeling.** You will be introduced to Advanced AutoCAD starting with **3D Modeling**.

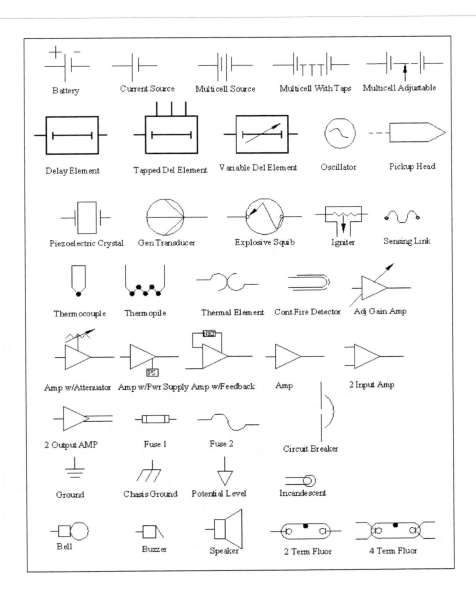

Chapter 12:

Advanced AutoCAD:

After completing this lesson you will be able to:

♣ Design 3D Modeling

♣ Learn about Mtext

♣ Setup Views with UCS

♣ Learn about different views

♣ Use Extrude and Subtract options

♣ Use Path to Extrude objects

♣ Create Title Block

♣ Define and Create Attributes

♣ Create Block setup

♣ Learn about Refedit

3D Modeling:

3D Modeling in AutoCAD involves so many steps and certain principles. You should have covered the introduction as well as the Intermediate AutoCAD before attempting to draw in 3D. Once you understand the basic concepts and know the rudiments to take to accomplish a particular task, everything will fall in place like pieces of a puzzle.

The design intent for generating a drawing in Solid Modeling should be brought into play when approaching a design, since drawings completed with AutoCAD program is cut in stone and cannot be altered. If all the Tools are acquired before starting the drawing the Design intent will be like second nature.

. You will be able to visualize the end product before you even start the sketch.

3D modeling in AutoCAD is like taking a block of clay and hewing away to come up with a sculpture, once the clay is taken off it is hard to stick it back on. You will be instructed step by step as to how to approach your design, develop design intent to visualize the finished product before you even start and all the necessary tools you will need to accomplish your goal.

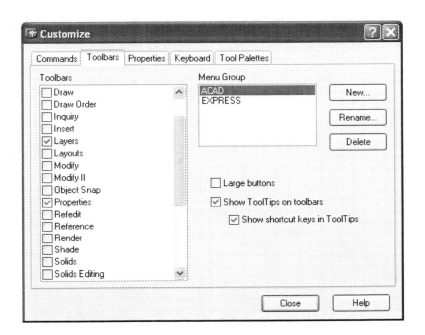

Figure 12.00

Start AutoCAD program and open a new file or your saved Template.

1. Make sure your **View Toolbar** is loaded unto the Graphics area if not follow these steps to load it.
2. Click on **View** from the Main Menu and click on Toolbars. The **Customize** Dialogue box opens up.

3. Click to highlight **ACAD** under <u>**Menu Group**</u> and click on Toolbars from the Titles.

4. Scroll down the list of items and click to place a checkmark in the adjacent box besides **View** and click on Close to exit. Refer to Figure 12.00

For your information, you can click and drag the **View Toolbar** and place it in any location of your preference.

Figure 12.01

<u>Tool Tip:</u>

When you leave the pointer on top of any Tool, a text pops up at its base revealing the name of that particular icon. This is the Tool Tip. For an example place the pointer on top of the icon third from right of the screen and receive the following information.

5. At the base of the icon will be written, **SE Isometric View.**

6. On the bottom left of your screen will be an explanation of what the icon does. In this case it tells you that this:

7. **Sets the View Point to Southeast Isometric: View**

8. Click on the **SE Isometric** icon after reading the Text. The UCS (User Coordinate System) symbol will be oriented with the **X-Axis** and **Y-Axis** lying flat on the Screen with the **Z-Axis** pointing vertically upwards.

9. Type BOX at the Command Prompt and press the Enter key. **A message pops up requesting you to:**

10. **Specify corner of box or [CEnter]: <0, 0, 0>**

11. Press the Enter key to accept the default parameters of '0, 0, and 0'. A message pops up requesting you to:

12. **Specify corner or [Cube / Length]:**

13. Type '**L**' short for the word **Length** and press the Enter key again. A message pops up requesting you to:

14. **Specify length:**

15. Type '**6**' and press the Enter key. A message pops up requesting you to:

16. **Specify width:**

17. Type '**5**' and press the Enter key. A message pops up requesting you to:

18. **Specify height:**

19. Type '**4**' and press the Enter key. You should see a box on top of the graphics area with the UCS placed to the Bottom left corner...

You are going to use this box to learn how to manipulate the UCS together with the various views and with that, you will be able to understand any approach you choose to design state of the art Models.

There are certain hidden commands in the AutoCAD program and unless they are revealed to you, it will be difficult to even conceptualize how to create a simple Model.

For an Example when you type UCS at the Command prompt a list of commands pops up to choose from to create a design with.

You will be requested to:

Enter an option [New / Move / orthographic / Prev / Restore / Save / Del / Apply /? /World <World>: Hidden in this list of actions are other commands like '**X**', '**Y**', '**Z**' and '**3**', '**O**', '**E**', '**A**', '**G**', '**N**', and '**E**'.

Pressing any of the letters listed above will invoke a command for the next action.

For now, we are going to narrow our selection down to **'X'**, **'Y'**, **'Z'** and **'3'**

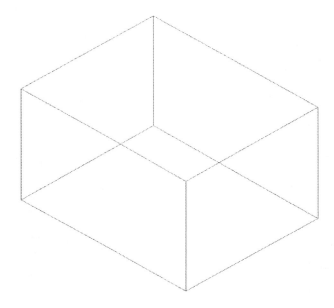

Figure 12.02

20. Type UCS at the Command prompt and press the enter key. A message pops up requesting you to:

21. **Enter an option [New / Move / orthographic / Prev / Restore / Save / Del / Apply /? /World] <World>**

22. Type the number **'3'** and press the Enter key. A message pops up requesting you to:

23. **Specify new origin point <0, 0, 0>:**

24. Move the pointer closer to the Box and click on the corner by the letters **'A'** then **'B'** and **'C'**. **Notice how the UCS changes position.**

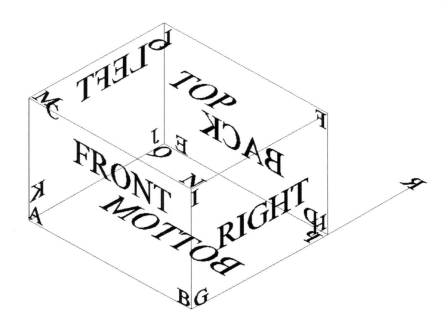

Figure 12.03

Figure 12.04

25. Type **MTEXT** at the Command prompt and press the Enter key. Your pointer should change into a **Crosshair** with the letters **'ABC'** at its base.

26. Click on the **Top Left** corner of the Box, hold down the left mouse button, drag the pointer to the **Bottom Right** corner of the box and click to place an

empty screen on top of the Box. This is the Text Formatting dialogue box. Figure 12.04

27. Click on the Arrow by 'Txt'and select **Times New Roman**.

28. Click on the Arrow by the **Text height** and change it to the figure '**1**'

29. Click on the open tablet and type '**FRONT**' and click on OK at the top right corner of the Text Format.

30. Type **UCS** at the Command prompt and press the Enter key. A message pops up requesting you to:

31. **Enter an option [New / Move / orthographic / Prev / Restore / Save / Del / Apply /? /World] <World>**

32. Type the number '**3**' and press the Enter key. A message pops up requesting you to:

33. **Specify new origin point <0, 0, 0>:**

34. Move the pointer closer to the Box and click on the corner by the letters '**D**' then '**E**' and '**F**'. **Notice how the UCS changes position.**

35. Type **MTEXT** at the Command prompt and press the Enter key. Your pointer should change into a **Crosshair** with the letters '**ABC**' at its base.

36. Click on the **Top Left** corner of the Box, hold down the left mouse button, drag the pointer to the **Bottom Right** corner of the box and click to place an empty screen on top of the Box. This is the Text Formatting dialogue box.

37. Click on the Arrow by 'Txt'and select **Times New Roman**.

38. Click on the Arrow by the **Text height** and change it to the figure '**1**'

39. Click on the open tablet and type '**BACK**' and click on OK at the top right corner of the Text Format.

40. Type **UCS** at the Command prompt and press the enter key. A message pops up requesting you to:

41. **Enter an option [New / Move / orthographic / Prev / Restore / Save / Del / Apply /? /World] <World>**

42. Type the number '**3**' and press the Enter key. A message pops up requesting you to:

43. **Specify new origin point <0, 0, 0>:**

44. Move the pointer closer to the Box and click on the corner by the letters '**G**' then '**H**' and '**I**'. **Notice how the UCS changes position.**

45. Type **MTEXT** at the Command prompt and press the Enter key. Your pointer should change into a **Crosshair** with the letters '**ABC**' at its base.

46. Click on the **Top Left** corner of the Box, hold down the left mouse button, drag the pointer to the **Bottom Right** corner of the box and click to place an empty screen on top of the Box. This is the Text Formatting dialogue box. Refer to Figure 12.04

47. Click on the Arrow by '**Txt**'and select **Times New Roman**.

48. Click on the Arrow by the **Text height** and change it to the figure '**1**'

49. Click on the open tablet and type '**RIGHT**' and click on OK at the top right corner of the Text Format.

50. Follow the above steps to place all the Views at its appropriate positions. The last operation will be that of the Bottom Text.

51. Type **UCS** at the Command prompt and press the enter key. A message pops up requesting you to:

52. **Enter an option [New / Move / orthographic / Prev / Restore / Save / Del / Apply /? /World] <World>**

53. Type the number '**3**' and press the Enter key. A message pops up requesting you to:

54. **Specify new origin point <0, 0, 0>:**

55. Move the pointer closer to the Box and click on the corner by the letters '**P**' then '**Q**' and '**R**'. **Notice how the UCS changes position.**

56. Type **MTEXT** at the Command prompt and press the Enter key. Your pointer should change into a **Crosshair** with the letters '**ABC**' at its base.

57. Click on the **Top Left** corner of the Box, hold down the left mouse button, drag the pointer to the **Bottom Right** corner of the box and click to place an empty screen on top of the Box. This is the Text Formatting dialogue box.

58. Click on the Arrow by **'Txt'**and select **Times New Roman**.

59. Click on the Arrow by the **Text height** and change it to the figure **'1'**

60. Click on the open tablet and type **'RIGHT'** and click on OK at the top right corner of the Text Format.

SEQUENCE OF OPERATION:

Use the values in the Table to complete the **Views** exercise.

Table: 12.00

POINTS	TYPE
ABC	FRONT
DEF	BACK
GHI	RIGHT
JKL	LEFT
MNO	TOP
PQR	BOTTOM

Figure 12.05

You will need to test the Views to find out everything came out right. You do so by using the icons on the Views Toolbar. With the Box still loaded on the Graphics area as in Figure, click on the Top Icon under View as in Figure. This is the second Icon from the left; your Box should turn to reveal the Word **TOP**. Click on the next icon, the box should turn to reveal the word Bottom. Go through all the icons to find out it all came out. Save the Project. You are now going to use the same concept to create 3D Models. Start AutoCAD if it is not already running and open a new File.

Follow the steps below to create your first project.

61. Click on **SE Isometric** View from the **View toolbar**, Refer to Figure

62. Type BOX at the Command Prompt and press the Enter key. **A message pops up requesting you to:**

63. **Specify corner of box or [CEnter]: <0, 0, 0>**

64. Press the **Enter** key to accept the default parameters of '**0, 0, 0**'. A message pops up requesting you to:

65. **Specify corner or [Cube / Length]:**

66. Type '**L**' short for the word **Length** and press the Enter key again. A message pops up requesting you to:

67. **Specify length:**

68. Type '**6**' and press the Enter key. A message pops up requesting you to:

69. **Specify width:**

70. Type '**4**' and press the Enter key. A message pops up requesting you to:

71. **Specify height:**

72. Type '**2**' and press the Enter key. You should see a box on top of the graphics area with the UCS placed to the Bottom left corner…

Extrude:

The next tool that you will learn is very useful and essential. It is advisable to highlight certain portions of the Text in the Book if you have the need to go over again for clarification.

Extrusion is a process whereby 2D sketches which has been converted into one entity using either **PEDIT** or **BOUNDARY** could be generated along a path to form a Solid 3D Model. The part now Extruded can be used in an assembly, merged together with other Parts as in UNION, the Faces copies for other operations and even the Color changed to suit other parts.

Additional Solids can be created anywhere on the original part and used as a TOOL to take away chunks of material from the Base part, thus forming cuts. You will be introduced to different kinds of Extrusion to familiarize yourself with all aspects of 3D modeling in AutoCAD. You will begin these Tutorials with a basic drawing of a **BOX** and add and or subtract other objects from the Box.

Open AutoCAD if it is not already loaded on the Graphics area.

Figure 12.06

73. Click on the **SE Isometric** The UCS (User Coordinate System) symbol will be oriented with the **X-Axis** and **Y-Axis** lying flat on the Screen with the **Z-Axis** pointing vertically upwards.

74. Type BOX at the Command Prompt and press the Enter key. **A message pops up requesting you to:**

75. **Specify corner of box or [CEnter]: <0, 0, 0>**

76. Press the Enter key to accept the default parameters of '0, 0, 0'. A message pops up requesting you to:

77. **Specify corner or [Cube / Length]:**

78. Type '**L**' short for the word **Length** and press the Enter key again. A message pops up requesting you to:

79. **Specify length:**

80. Type '**6**' and press the Enter key. A message pops up requesting you to:

81. **Specify width:**

82. Type '**5**' and press the Enter key. A message pops up requesting you to:

83. **Specify height:**

84. Type '**4**' and press the Enter key. You should see a box on top of the graphics area with the UCS placed to the Bottom left corner...

You are going to use this box to learn how to add other sketches and Extrude the sketch through the initial BOX drawn.

You will then use the SUBTRACT Tool to create a cut in the BOX and save your drawing.

85. Type **UCS** at the Command prompt and press the enter key. A message pops up requesting you to:

86. **Enter an option [New / Move / orthographic / Prev / Restore / Save / Del / Apply /? /World] <World>**

87. Type the number '**3**' and press the Enter key. A message pops up requesting you to:

88. **Specify new origin point <0, 0, 0>:**

89. Move the pointer closer to the Box and click on the corner by the numbers '**1**' then '**2**' and '**3**'. **Notice how the UCS changes position.**

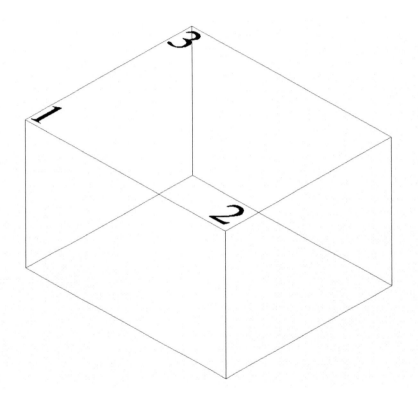

Figure 12.07

90. Click on **Draw** from the Main Menu and select **Rectangle**. A message pops up requesting you to:

91. **Specify first corner point or [Chamfer / Elevation / Fillet / Thickness / width]:**

92. Click on the endpoint of the box by the number '**2**' and release your finger off the Mouse button. A Message pops up requesting you to:

93. **Specify other corner or [Dimension]:**

94. Type **-3, 2** and press the Enter key. You should have a rectangle placed at the corner of the BOX Refer to Figure.12.08

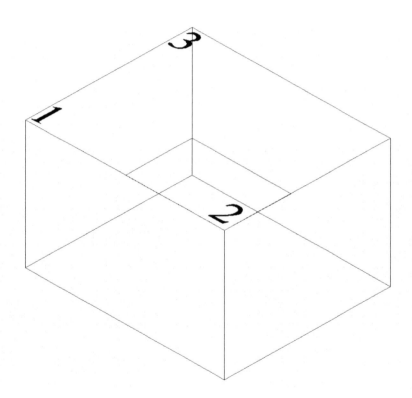

Figure 12.08

The next step is to **Extrude** the **Rectangle** just drawn into the body of the Box. Certain **guidelines MUST** be followed when it comes to Extruding parts in AutoCAD. There are two different ways that, objects get extruded. One is to

356

direct the object being Extruded to follow a set **PATH** and the other is follow the '**Z**' direction. You will use the '**Z**' coordinate to Extrude the Rectangle and learn how to use the PATH command at a later lesson.

On using the 'Z' coordinate care should be taken as to what direction to follow whether the positive or the negative direction.

When you look at the **UCS,** you will notice that, all the three coordinates; 'X' 'Y' 'Z' are pointing in the **POSITIVE** direction.

For an example, the rectangle you have just drawn will have to be extruded in the **NEGATIVE** direction in order for it to go through the BOX. Also you should always make the length of the Extruded part a little over the length of the Base part, in order not to leave traces of uncut parts. Follow these steps to Extrude the Rectangle through the BOX.

95.   Type **Extrude** at the Command prompt. A message pops up requesting you to:

96.   **Select Objects:**

97.   Click on one of the lines bounding the rectangle just drawn and press the Enter key. A Message pops up requesting you to:

98.   **Specify height of extrusion or [Path]:**

99.   Type **-6**(Negative six) since the height of the Box is **4inches**. A Message pops up requesting you to:

100.   **Specify angle of taper for extrusion<0>:**

110. Press the Enter key to accept the Default value of 0 to add the Extrusion to the BOX. Refer to Figure12.09

To create a **CUT** you have to use the **SUBTRACT** tool to remove the PART encased within the boundaries of the Solid Box. Follow these steps to subtract the part from the BOX.

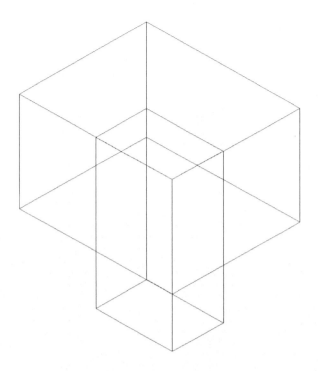

Figure 12.09

101. Click on **Modify,** highlight **Solid Editing** and select **Subtract**. The pointer turns into a Pickbox and a Message pops up requesting you to:

102. **Select object:**

103. Click on the part you will like to keep first, which is the BOX and press the Enter key. A Message pops up requesting you to again:

104. **Select objects:**

105. Click on the Extruded Rectangle next and press the Enter key to remove the Extruded part from the Base Part the BOX. Refer to Figure 12.09

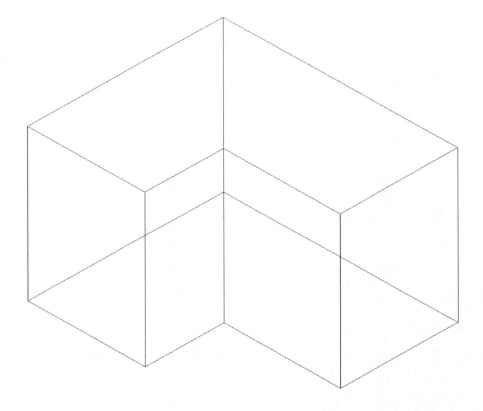

Figure 12.10

PATH:

Another very useful Feature in AutoCAD is the **PATH**, without which certain Geometries would have been very difficult to generate. The PATH tool forces an object to follow a guided line whiles executing the Extrude command. The next Tutorials will cover **PATH** and its functions. We will use an angular cut on an object together with PATH to extrude the sketch.

106. Click on the **SE Isometric** The UCS (User Coordinate System) symbol will be oriented with the **X-Axis** and **Y-Axis** lying flat on the Screen with the **Z-Axis** pointing vertically upwards.

107. Type BOX at the Command Prompt and press the Enter key. **A message pops up requesting you to:**

108. **Specify corner of box or [CEnter]: <0, 0, 0>**

109. Press the Enter key to accept the default parameters of '**0, 0,** and **0**'. A message pops up requesting you to:

110. **Specify corner or [Cube / Length]:**

111. Type '**L**' short for the word **Length** and press the Enter key again. A message pops up requesting you to:

112. **Specify length:**

113. Type '**6**' and press the Enter key. A message pops up requesting you to:

114. **Specify width:**

115. Type '**4**' and press the Enter key. A message pops up requesting you to:

116. **Specify height:**

117. Type '**4**' and press the Enter key. You should see a box on top of the graphics area with the UCS placed to the Bottom left corner...

The next step is to place your geometric sketch on the BOX to be used for the Extrusion.

118. Click on Draw from the Main Menu and select **Line**. Follow the steps for drawing Lines and place a triangular shape on the BOX with points at '**A**' '**B**' and '**C**'. Refer to Figure 12.12

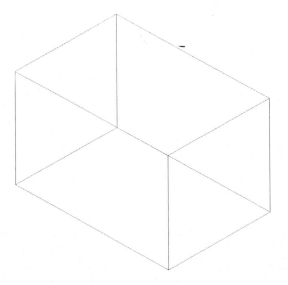

Figure 12.11

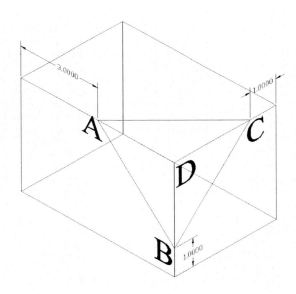

Figure 12.12

119. Type **UCS** at the Command prompt and press the enter key. A message pops up requesting you to:

120. **Enter an option [New / Move / orthographic / Prev / Restore / Save / Del / Apply /? /World] <World>**

121. Type the number '**3**' and press the Enter key. A message pops up requesting you to:

122. **Specify new origin point <0, 0, 0>:**

123. Move the pointer closer to the Box and click on the corner by the letters '**1**' then '**2**' and '**3**'. **Notice how the UCS changes position.**

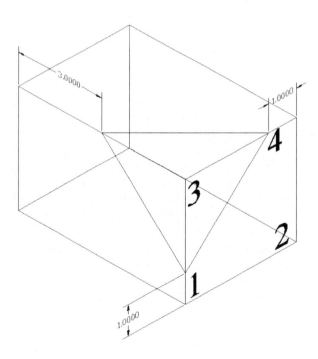

Figure 12.13

The next step is for you to create a Polyline of the Triangle to be used in the Extrusion. Follow these steps to convert the Lines on the triangle into a Polyline. Note that you can only use Polyline in extruding a part thus the conversion.

124. Click on **Draw** from the Main Menu and select **Polyline** from the list of tools. A Message pops up requesting you to:

125. **Specify start point:**

126. Click on the endpoint by the number **'1'** A message pops up requesting you to:

127. **Specify next point or [Arc / HalfWidth Length / Undo / Width]:**

128. Click on the endpoint by the number **'3'**. A Message pops up requesting you to:

129. **Specify next point or [Arc / HalfWidth Length / Undo / Width]:**

130. Click on the endpoint by the number **'4'**. A Message pops up requesting you to:

131. **Specify next point or [Arc / HalfWidth Length / Undo / Width]:**

132. Click on the endpoint by the number **'1'** and hit the Enter key to complete the Polyline

You are now going to use PATH for the Extrusion of the Triangle.

133. Type **Extrude** at the Command prompt and press the Enter key. A Message pops up Requesting you to:

134. **Select objects:**

135. Click on one of the Line of the Triangle and press the Enter key. A Message pops up Requesting you to:

136. **Specify height of extrusion or [Path]:**

137. Type '**P**' for the **PATH** and press the Enter key, the pointer turns into a Pickbox, with a Message requesting you to:

138. **Select extrusion path or [Taper angle]:**

139. Click on the endpoints of the Line with numbers '**5**' and '**4**', the Triangle gets Extruded along that Line. Refer to Figure 12.15

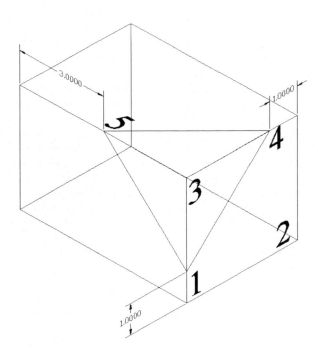

Figure 12.14

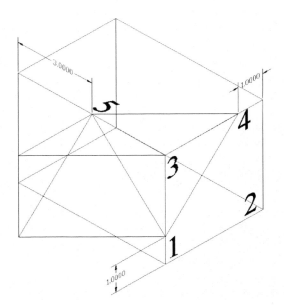

Figure 12.15

You are now going to use Subtraction to take out the unwanted parts.

140. Type Subtraction at the Command prompt and press the Enter key. A
    Message pops up requesting you to:

141. **Select objects:**

142. Click first on the Part you would like to retain, which is the BOX and press
    the Enter key.

143. Next click on the parts to be taken out, which is the Extruded Triangle and
    press the Enter key again. Refer to Figure 12.16 for the final Model of the Part.

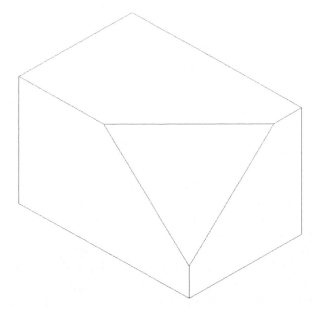

Figure 12.16

Summary:

In this Tutorial, you covered topics that included:

♣ Designing 3D Modeling

♣ Learning about Mtext

♣ Setting up Views with UCS

♣ Learning about different views

♣ Using Extrude and Subtract options

♣ Using Path to Extrude objects

♣ Creating Title Block

♣ Defining and Create Attributes

♣ Creating Block setup

♣ Learning about Refedit

Exercise:

Create a Title Block for an up coming project and add all the necessary text to the Title Block.

Make a Block out of this Project and save it.

The next Chapter will cover **Title Block** and **Attributes**

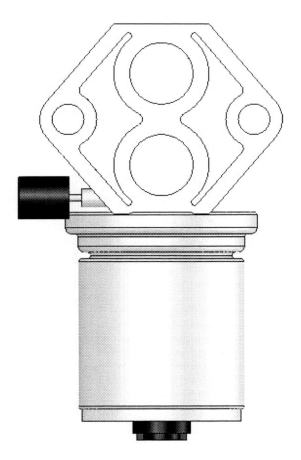

Chapter 13

After completing this Chapter you will be able to:
- Create Title Blocks
- Learn about Test
- Create Data table
- Use Offset command
- Learn to create Attributes
- Know the difference between Tag and prompt
- Create company LOGO
- Setup Wblock
- Test the Attribute Definition
- Work with Refedit

TITLE BLOCK:

Title Blocks also known as Sheet Layout, comes in different sizes. The European Standard is referred to as International Standard and that of North America is known as American National Standard. The International Standard's units are set in metric and that of American National Standard is in Feet and Inches. The American Standard is designated with the letters **A-E** and that of the International Standard, **A4-A0.**

In these Tutorials, you will be guided in drawing one American National Standard Title Block as well as one for the International Standard.

Refer to the Table below for the list of items to be used in designing an **"8.50 X 11.00"** Title Block.

TABLE 13.00

Company LOGO	Number REQD.	Sales Order	Work Order	Part Description
Material	Drawn By	Date	Checked By	Date Chkd
Scale	Revision	Notes	Cust Name	Part Num

Start AutoCAD if it is not already running on you system, and open a new file.

1. Click on Draw from the Main Menu and select Rectangle. A Message pops up requesting you to:

2. **Specify first corner point or [Chamfer / Elevation / Fillet / Thickness / Width]:**

3. Type '**0, 0**' and press the Enter key. A Message pops up requesting you to:

4. **Specify other corner point or [Dimensions]:**

5. Type '**8.50, 11.00**' and press the Enter key a Rectangle should be place at the Origin of the UCS.

6. Type **Zoom** and press the Enter key. A Message pops up requesting you to: A Message pops up requesting you to select an option from the list below:

7. **[All / Center / Dynamic / Extents / Previous / Scale / Window] <real time>:**

8. Type '**E**' short for Extents and press the Enter key, the Rectangle will be scaled out to cover the screen.

The next step is to use the Offset from the Modify Toolbar to add a copy of the Rectangle for the Border.

9. Click on Modify and select Offset from the list of options. A Message pops up requesting you to:

10. **Specify offset distance or [Through] <Through>:**

11. Type **0.25** and press the Enter key. The pointer turns into a Pickbox and a Message pops up requesting you to:

12. **Select object to offset or <exit>:**

13. Click on one of the **four** lines bounding the Rectangle and click inside the Rectangle to place a copy.

Figure 13.00

You are now going to add Lines and use the Offset tool to create a Table-like Title Strip in which you will make all the Entries as per the Table.

Type Line at the Command prompt

TABLE 13.01

Company LOGO	Number REQD.	Sales Order	Work Order	Part Description
Material	Drawn By	Date	Checked By	Date Chkd
Scale	Revision	Notes	Cust Name	Part Num

Start AutoCAD if it is not already running on you system, and open a new file.

14. Click on Draw from the Main Menu and select Rectangle. A Message pops up requesting you to:

15. **Specify first corner point or [Chamfer / Elevation / Fillet / Thickness / Width]:**

16. Type '**0, 0**' and press the Enter key. A Message pops up requesting you to:

17. **Specify other corner point or [Dimensions]:**

18. Type '**8.50, 11.00**' and press the Enter key a Rectangle should be place at the Origin of the UCS.

19. Type **Zoom** and press the Enter key. A Message pops up requesting you to: A Message pops up requesting you to select an option from the list below:

20. **[All / Center / Dynamic / Extents / Previous / Scale / Window] <real time>:**

21. Type '**E**' short for Extents and press the Enter key, the Rectangle will be scaled out to cover the screen.

The next step is to use the Offset from the Modify Toolbar to add a copy of the Rectangle for the Border.

22. Click on Modify and select Offset from the list of options. A Message pops up requesting you to:

23. **Specify offset distance or [Through] <Through>:**

24. Type **0.25** and press the Enter key. The pointer turns into a Pickbox and a Message pops up requesting you to:

25. **Select object to offset or <exit>:**

26. Click on one of the four lines bounding the Rectangle and click inside the Rectangle to place a copy.

Figure 13.02

You are now going to add Lines and use the Offset tool to create a Table-like Title Strip in which you will make all the Entries as per the Table.

Type Line at the Command prompt and press the Enter key, you will be requested to:

373

27. **Specify first point:**

28. Use the Line Tool to draw the boxes as depicted in Figure 13.19 adding all
the necessary Dimensions.

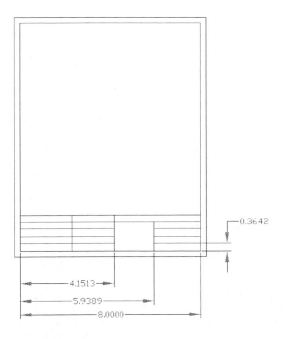

Figure 13.03

You will be using Text from the Draw option on the Main Toolbar insert text in the
allotted spaces.

29. Click on Draw from the Main Menu, highlight Text and select Multiline
Text. A Message pops up requesting you to:

30. **Specify first corner:**

31. Click on the number '1' release your finger from the left mouse button, move the pointer down and click on the number '2'. The Text Formatting box pops up. Refer to Figure 13.05

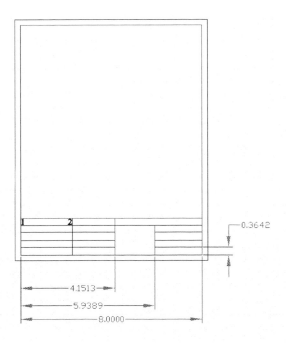

Figure 13.04

32. Click on the arrow by **Text** and select **Times New Roman** from the list of items.

33. Click on **Text Height**, which is the arrow to the right of Text box type **0.25**, and press the Enter key.

34. Type '**No. Reqd.**' in the allotted box and click on the OK button.

35. Repeat this action for the next box and use Figure 13.06 to fill the rest of the values in the boxes.

375

Figure 13.05

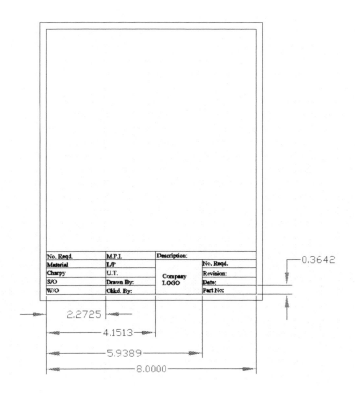

Figure 13.06

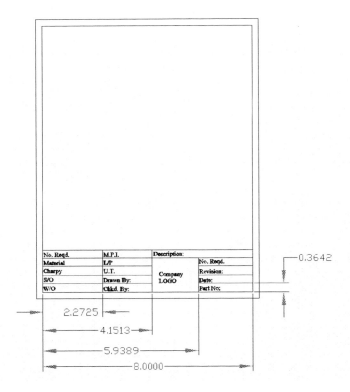

Figure 13.07

Creating Attributes:

Planning the type of Values to be used in setting up an Attribute must be the first step to take in creating Attributes.

You set the Values by exploring the nature of the particular Drawing or Part, to enable you define the Attribute to suit your needs.

Although changes could be made after setting up an Attribute, it is advisable to do it right for the very first time.

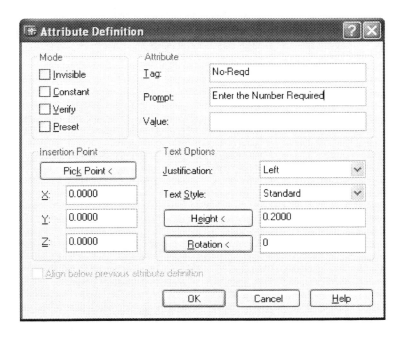

Figure 13.08

You are now going to create an Attribute Definition to be used in the Title
Block.

Start AutoCAD if it is not already running on your system and open a new File
or your Template. There are certain Rules you should be aware of when making
your entries.

- Never leave a blank space in between text when making entries in the box
  for the **TAG**.

- Underscore and hyphen will be accepted but not commas, backslash or
  other such characters.

- The PROMPT can take any characters as well as Spaces as long as it does
  not exceed 256 characters.

378

The boxes that you created on the Title Block will be used as a guide to place the Attribute Tag in the right place.

Some of the elements to be defined in the Attribute include the **TAG;** used to identify the Attribute in the Title Block.

The user interacts with the **PROMPT** in order to enter certain set values. The **VALUE;** which will be the information relating to the Prompt text.

The **PICK POINT;** allows you to specify a particular location to insert the Attribute Definition.

The **TEXT HEIGHT;** controls how large the text will appear in the Block.

The **JUSTIFICATION;** aligns the text to the **Left; Right; Center;** and other orientations you so choose to place the text.

These are the main parameters you will need to create an Attribute for the Title Block.

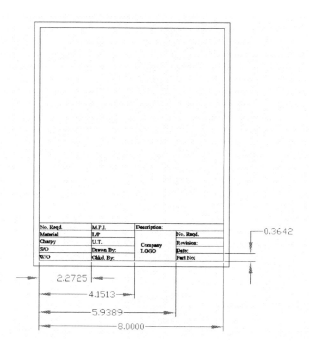

Figure 13.09

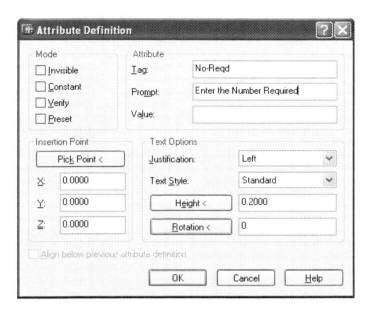

Figure 13.10

You are now going to create an **Attribute Definition** to be used in the Title Block.

Start AutoCAD if it is not already running on your system and open a new File or your Template. There are certain Rules you should be aware of when making your entries.

- **NEVER** leave a blank space in between text when making entries in the box for the **TAG**. Underscore and hyphen will be accepted but not commas or other such characters.

- The **PROMPT** can take any character as well as Spaces as long as it does not exceed 256 characters.

36. Click on **Draw** from the Main Menu, highlight **Block** and select **Define Attribute**, the **Attribute Definition** dialogue box pops up with the cursor blinking inside the box adjacent to the '**Tag:**'

37. Type in **No.-Reqd:** and press the **Tab** key on the keyboard.

38. In the Prompt box type, **'Enter the Number required'** click in the box by **Height** under the **Text Options** and change the value to **0.125.**

39. Move to the left side of the dialogue box and click on **Pic<u>k</u> Point<** under **Insertion Point** the pointer changes into a crosshair on the Graphics area.

40. Click inside the box by **'No.Reqd'**. You will be brought back to the dialogue box

41. Click on OK to **insert** the first Attribute definition in the Title Block.

Use the Table below to add the rest of the Attribute Definitions to the Title Block.

Table 13.02

Tag: No-Reqd **Prompt:** Enter Num Required	**Tag:** M.P.I. **Prompt:** Enter MPI value	**Tag:** Description: **Prompt:** Enter Description
Tag: Material **Prompt**: Enter type of Material	**Tag:** L.P. **Prompt:** Enter Value	**Tag:** Sheet-Number **Prompt:** Enter Sheet Number
Tag: Charpy **Prompt:** Enter Charpy value	**Tag:** U.T. **Prompt:** Enter percent U.T.	**Tag:** Revision **Prompt:** Enter Revision type
Tag: S/O **Prompt:** Enter Sales Order Number	**Tag:** W/O **Prompt:** Enter Work Order	**Tag:** Drawn **Prompt:** Enter Name
Tag: Chkd-By **Prompt:** Enter name of Checker	**Tag:** Date **Prompt:** Enter Today's Date	**Tag:** Part-Num **Prompt:** Enter the Part Num.

Company LOGO:

The Company Logo normally depicts the company's operation but many have chosen unrelated insignia.

You first have to create a particular design suitable for the Company LOGO and use it as an insert into the Title Block. You will use one of the drawings already completed as the company's logo.

42. Type **Insert** at the Command prompt and press the Enter. The Insert dialogue box opens up

43. Click on Browse, search for the Folder your Drawings are saved in and Pick a design for the Company LOGO.

44. Click on Open to place a copy on the Graphics area and scale it to fit the given space on the Title Block. Refer to Figure 13.13

The next step is to write a Block for the Title Block together with the Attribute Definition and combine the two as one. You will be able to program the values and insert it into any drawing with the Title Block and add Text in the form of an Attribute as listed on the Title Block. Make sure the Title Block is centered on the Graphics area with about 0.5in on the Top and bottom of the block.

WBLOCK Setup:

45. Type **WBLOCK** at the Command prompt and press the Enter key, the **Write Block** dialogue box pops up for certain entries to be performed. Refer to Figure 13.13

Figure 13.11

46. Click on the icon with three dots on it also known as Browse, which is located at the end of the box by **File name and path:**

47. Search for the Folder you would like to save your Title Block in and enter a name by the **Filename.**

48. Click on Save to come back to the Write Block dialogue box.

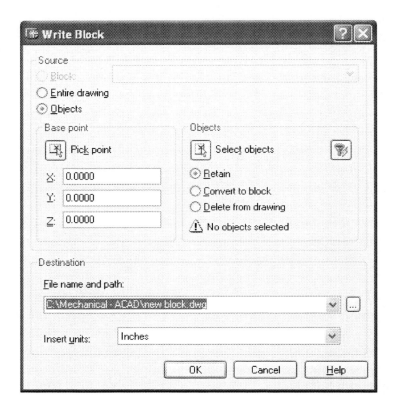

Figure 13.12

This stage is very **essential** and **important** in that, the way you pick the Attributes will determine in what order it will appear on your drawing when it is invoked. You can choose to select the Definitions in ascending order, descending order, diagonal order or any preferred order to set it up.

49. Move the pointer to the Objects and click on **Select objects:** the Graphics area opens up again allowing you to select all necessary objects.

Follow the Vertical order for this Tutorials starting with **NO-REQD: IN ORDER WORDS GO FROM LEFT TO THE RIGHT WHILES PICKING THE ATTRIBUTES.** Refer to Figure 13.12

You will click on NO-REQD, MATERIAL, and CHARPY in that order. When finished click on the outside Top left corner of the Title Block, release your Finger, move the pointer to the Bottom right corner of the Title Block and click on the graphics area again to highlight the entire Title Block.

Hit the Enter key once to go back to the **Write Block** dialogue box.

50. Move to the **Base point** and click on **Pick point.** A Message pops up requesting you to

51. **Specify Insertion Base point:**

How the Base Point is selected, determines how the Title Block is inserted in a drawing. You can click any corner of your preference, but normally I have used the Top Right corner as a preference.

52. Click on the **Top right** corner of the **Title Block**, which brings you back to the **Write Block** dialogue box.

This final **STEP** will determine if the Attribute Definition was setup right and the program worked.

Move your head and gaze at the **Top Left** corner of your screen whiles you place the mouse pointer over the **OK** button.

When you click on the **OK** button, a **PICTURE** of the **Title Block** will **FLASH** in a second denoting that everything went well. If you do not see the Flash then you might have done something wrong.

Click on the OK button to complete this Tutorial.

Testing the Attribute Definition:

Testing the Attributes Definition is so easy; all you do is Invoke the Attributes from the Folder where it is saved and makes the entries at the Prompt.

53. Open up a **new** drawing, type **Insert** at the Command Prompt, the Insert dialogue box opens up.

54. Browse to the location of the block just created and click to select it. When you click on OK a Message comes up requesting you to:

55. **Specify insertion point or [Scale / X / Y / Z / Rotate / PScale / PX / PY / PZ / PRotate]:**

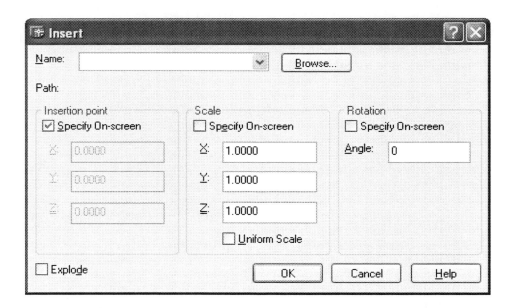

Figure 13.13

56. Click on the Graphics area to insert the Block. The Insert dialogue box, Refer to Figure 13.13 pops up.

57. Click on OK and at the bottom of your screen; you will be prompted to make certain entries by answering the questions being asked and pressing the Enter key for the next Attribute. Refer to Figure 13.13

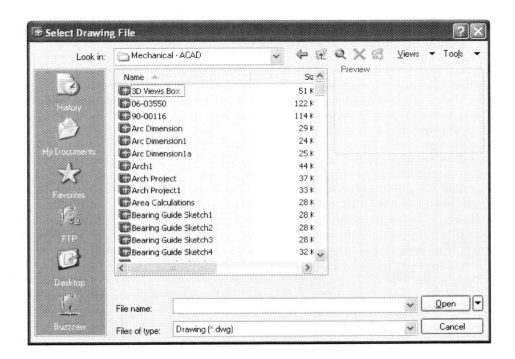

Figure 13.14

388

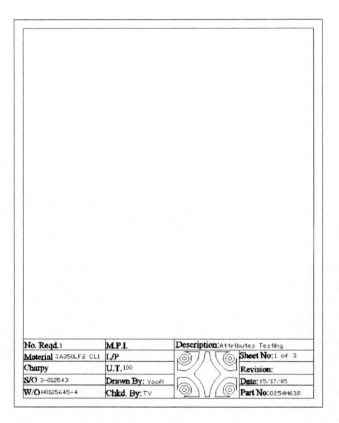

Figure 13.15

REFEDIT:

Block Editing

Refedit allows you to edit your block and make corrections to mistakes you made whiles designing the Block. You will be able to Scale the Block and or change the color if you choose to. Follow these steps to edit a Block.

The next Tutorials will introduce you to Lighting: After going through these lessons you will be able to setup lighting, Render and create Scenes.

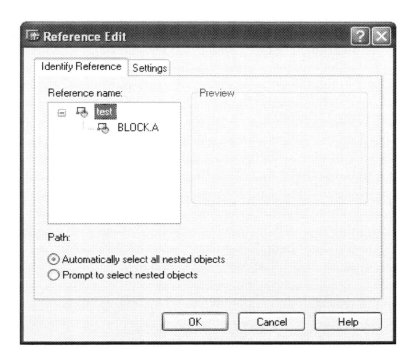

Figure 13.16

Figure 13.17

58. Double-click on the Block to be edited; the **Reference Edit** dialogue box opens up.

59. Select **Identity Reference** and click inside the radio button **Prompt to select nested objects**, under **Path**: Refer to Figure 13.16 Click OK

60. The **Refedit** dialogue box opens up.

61. Click on Edit block or Xref, which is the first icon on the dialogue box. The pointer turns into a Pickbox.

62. Drag an invincible window around the block to highlight everything and change the color from the ByLayer or Scale the Block.

63. Click on **save back changes to reference** to complete the Edit.

Summary:

:

This Chapter introduced you to different aspects of using design tools in

- Creating Title Blocks
- Learning about Test
- Creating Data table
- Using Offset command
- Learning to create Attributes
- Know the difference between Tag and prompt
- Creating company LOGO
- Setting up Wblock
- Testing the Attribute Definition
- Working with Refedit

Exercise

- Set up an Attributes definition using the Furniture around your workplace, create Blocks and edit the Blocks using Refedit.
- Using Spline, draw the Dinosaur below and Extrude with the Path option. Figure 13.18
- Draw a Circle and use the Extrude command to create a cylindrical pipe with a branch on its side. Figure 13.19

The next Lesson will cover **Lights** and its many uses

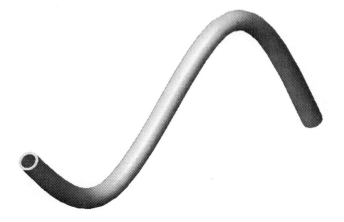

Figure 13.18

Figure 13.19

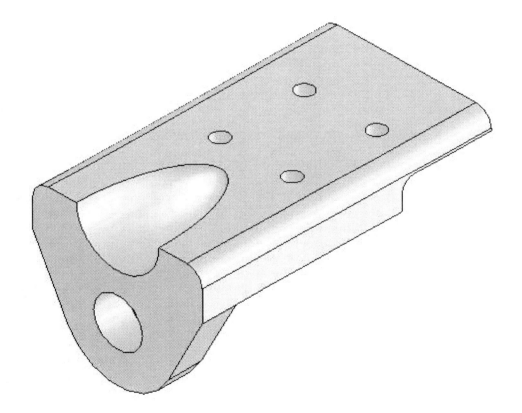

Chapter 14:

Lights:

In this chapter you will be introduced to Lighting and everything that has to do with Lights and Shadows. Explore many other functions to make your designing quicker and easier. You will be introduced to short cuts and basic designing tools in the exercises that would be covered.

After going through this Chapter, you will be able to:

      i.   Create Light and Insert it in your Drawing

      j.   Learn to create Shadow on your Objects.

      k.   Learn about different types of Lightning

      l.   Learn of Ambient Light

      m. Learn about Distance, Point and Spot Light

      n.   Add Lights to objects

      o.   Create Render and cover Tolerances

Light and its applications in AutoCAD are endless and with the aid of the Rendering Tool, objects appear real to the naked eye and Parts that you design, come alive on the Screen.

Light can be added to an entire assembly of Parts or just a Part. It can also be placed in a darkened place to illuminate the area being specified. Whatever you do with lights in real life for an example in your house could also be applied to your Drawings in AutoCAD.

There is no such thing as too many Lights in a drawing, since the Lights that you add can also are deleted or altered.

You can always turn the lights off by setting its Intensity to **ZERO** or make it brighter by turning the **Intensity** higher value.

Lights can be placed in a Molded Cavity to enhance its appearance and reveal all the cuts and crevices.

Lights cannot be swapped but deleted. In sense you cannot decide to swap an Ambient Light for a Spot Light in your drawing. What you can do is first delete the unwanted Ambient Light and inserts a Spot Light.

Shadow:

Designers intending to use Shadows in their drawing will have to do so with the aid of the Rendering Tool together with **Photo Real** or **Photo Raytrace** since the four types of lights in AutoCAD software do not cast any shadow.

There are several types when considering Lights in your drawing which include:

- Ambient Light
- Distant Light
- Point Light
- Spot Light

These together with certain geometrical objects and colors, provide all the light that is needed in a Drawing environment. Refer to the AutoCAD Help document for further explanation to Lights. For now you will be given the definitions of the Four Types of lights as listed above and a practical example of each one of them.

Ambient Light:

Ambient light provides **Constant Illumination** to every surface in a Part Drawing. It is like a surrounding body of bright light with no particular source or direction, embodying the Model. Ambient should be used together with other options to produce realistic images, since it engulfs the object thus making it look like a washed-off part. The Designer has the flexibility of turning the Intensity of the Ambient light off or lowered to adjust its brightness as needed.

Distance Light:

Think about the **Sun** when you use the Distance Light. Although the intensity of the sun do minimize as it reaches the surface of the Earth because of radiation that of the Distant Light does not diminish with distance and it is bright at every step of the way.

In Distance Light, parallel light rays are emitted uniformly in one direction only.

To properly apply Distant Light to your Drawing, you will need to explore the right direction of the Distant Light since this will determine how the objects get well lighted. Architectural firms normally use the Distance Light together with rendering to simulate the position of the Sun by the day

Point Light:

The further away a Point Light is located the lesser its intensity in lighting up an object. Unlike the Distance Light, the Point Light will light an object from all directions.

Consider the light bulb in the house, one can simulate a light bulb with a Point Light and other general lighting needs for your drawing. You can also fill in a location with a Point Light to bring out hidden parts that will normally not show on the drawing.

Spot Light:

A Spot Light uses a **directional cone** to emit light from a source to an object. The user to achieve proper lighting can control the size and direction of the cone. The Intensity of Point Lights also diminishes with distance because of what is known as hotspots and falloff angles, which together determines the intensity or the strength of the light. Refer to the Help Files for more on Hotspots and Falloff cone angles.

Adding Light:

To add light to a Model you first have to plan and determine what type of light you are going to use, how many lights to use and the intensity what spots needed for the lighting.

You then place the Model or Parts on the Graphics area, to add light to and type **Light** at the Command prompt. Alternatively, click on **View** from the Main menu; highlight **Render** and select Light, the **Lights Dialogue** box pops up.

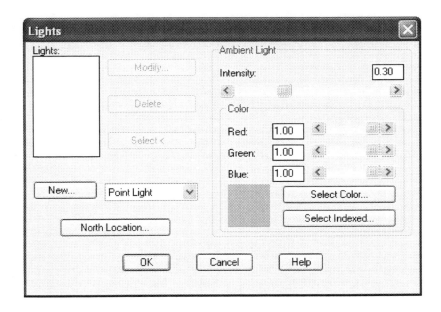

Figure 14.00

In the Light dialogue box, you will notice a list of buttons to enable you start a particular action needed for the environment. All the values are set as default and the dial can be adjusted as and when necessary.

1. Click on New to bring up the next dialogue box, which is the New Point Light. Notice that the cursor is blinking in the empty box by Light Name.

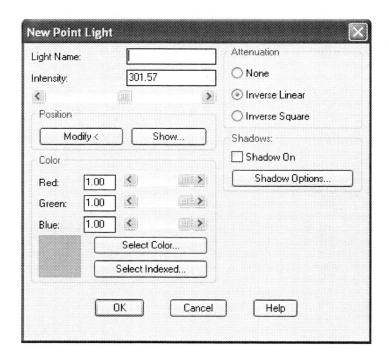

Figure 14.01

2. Type in the Part number and the type of light but not exceeding 8 characters and no spaces in between text. Your entries can be alphanumeric (combination of alphabets and numbers) or alphabets only or numbers only.

3. Backslash and forward slash is not allowed as the name.

Spot Light:

A Spot Light uses a directional cone to emit light from a source to an object. The user to achieve proper lighting can control the size and direction of the cone. The Intensity of Point Lights also diminishes with distance because of what is known as hotspots and falloff angles, which together determines the intensity or the strength of the light. Refer to the Help Files for more on Hotspots and Falloff cone angles. Before we continue our Light project, let us draw a Box with holes in it to use for placing lights at the darkened places.

Start AutoCAD and open up a new file.

Figure 14.02

4. Click on View in the Main Menu and select 3D Views and click on SE Isometric. Alternatively, click on the SE Isometric from the View Toolbar above.

5. Type Box at the Command prompt. A message pops up requesting you to:

6. **Specify corner of box or [Center] <0, 0, 0, >**

7. Press the Enter key to accept the Default values of **0, 0,** and **0.** A message pops up requesting you to:

8. **Specify corner or [Cube / Length]**

9. Type '**L**' short for the word Length and press the Enter key. A message pops up requesting you to:

10. **Specify Length:**

11. Type **8** and press the Enter key. A message pops up requesting you to:

12. **Specify width:**

13. Type **7** and press the Enter key. A message pops up requesting you to:

14. **Specify height:**

15. Type **6** and press the Enter key to complete the drawing for the box

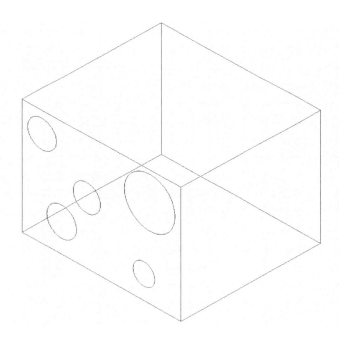

Figure 14.03

16. Place the UCS in the Front view of the box; refer to Chapter on UCS Setup.

17. Add about five Circles on the Front of the Box.

18. Extrude the circles **2 ½"** inside the box and use the **Subtract** option to remove the cylinders from the Box in order to create the holes. Refer Figure 14.05

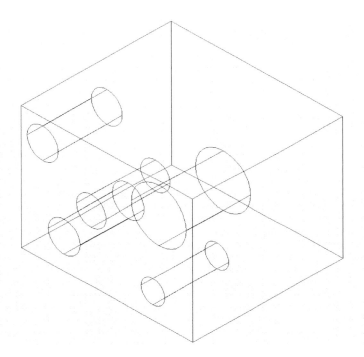

Figure 14.04

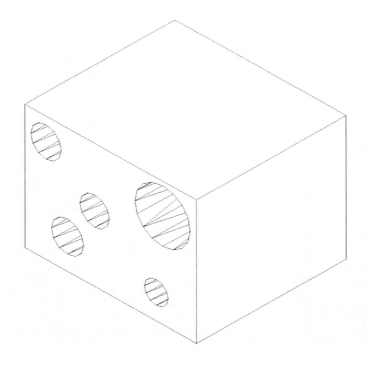

Figure 14.05

Adding Light:

To add light to a Model you first have to plan and determine what type of light you are going to use, how many lights to use and the intensity, what spots needed for the lighting.

You then place the Model or Parts on the Graphics area, to add light to and type **Light** at the Command prompt. Alternatively, click on **View** from the Main menu; highlight **Render** and select Light, the **Lights Dialogue** box pops up.

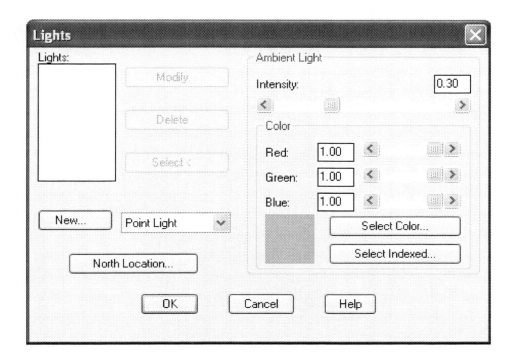

Figure 14.06

In the Light dialogue box, you will notice a list of buttons to enable you start a particular action needed for the environment. All the values are set as default and the dial can be adjusted as and when necessary.

19. Click on **New** to bring up the next dialogue box, which is the New Point Light. Notice that the cursor is blinking in the empty box by **Light Name.**

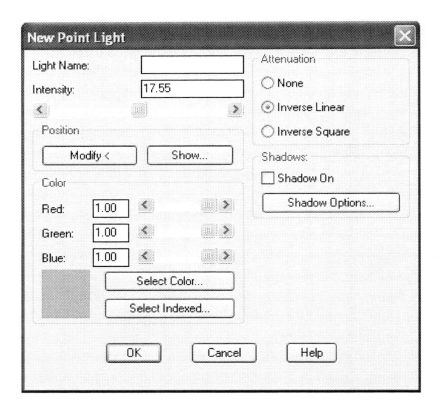

Figure 14.07

20. Type in the Part number and the type of light but not exceeding 8 characters and no spaces in between text. Your entries can be alphanumeric (combination of alphabets and numbers) or alphabets only or numbers only.

21. Backslash and forward slash are not allowed in the **Light Name box.**

22. Do not make any other adjustments after typing in the Part number in the Light Name box, just click on **OK** The name you Entered will be displayed under **Lights** box

23. Click on **OK** again to exit the Light command.

Adding Light:

Note that you will have to use the **Light** together with **Render** to see results of the projection of the Light intensity.

To add light to a Model you first have to plan and determine what type of light you are going to use, how many lights to use and the intensity, what spots needed for the lighting.

You then place the Model or Parts on the Graphics area, to add light to and type **Light** at the Command prompt. Alternatively, click on **View** from the Main menu; highlight **Render** and select Light, the **Lights Dialogue** box pops up.

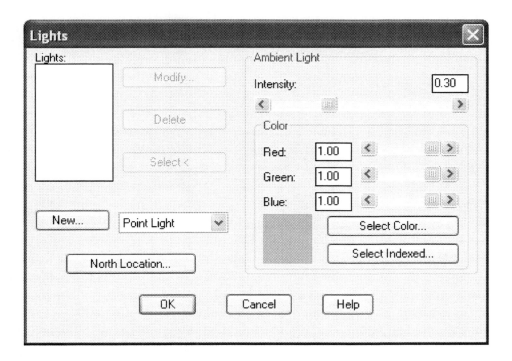

Figure 14.08

In the Light dialogue box, you will notice a list of buttons to enable you start a particular action needed for the environment. All the values are set as default and the dial can be adjusted as and when necessary.

24. Click on **New** to bring up the next dialogue box, which is the New Point Light. Notice that the cursor is blinking in the empty box by **Light Name.**

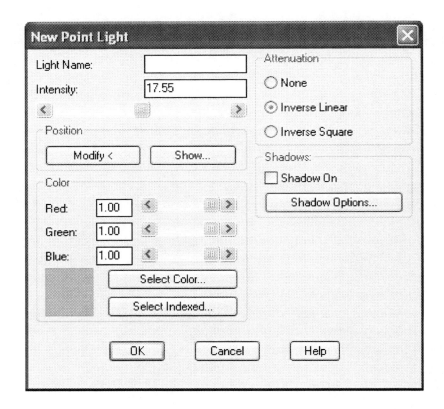

Figure 14.09

25. Type in the Part number and the type of light but not exceeding **8** characters and no spaces in between text.

26. Your entries can be alphanumeric (combination of alphabets and numbers) or alphabets only or numbers only.

27. Backslash and forward slash are not allowed in the **Light Name box.**

28. Do not make any other adjustments after typing in the Part number in the Light Name box, just click on OK The name you Entered will be displayed under **Lights** box

29. Click on OK again to exit the Light command.

Rendering:

Render uses different colors and materials to enhance the appearance of a Model After inserting the Light into your Model, a circular shape with the given light name appears on the Model.

You have the option of using the Move command to place it anywhere on your Model.

Once the Render process is completed, moving the Light to another spot will be very difficult to accomplish.

30. Click on **View** from the **Main Menu**, highlight **Render** and click to select the render from the list of items.

31. The Render dialogue box opens up with different options.

32. Click on the arrow by Rendering Type and select **Photo Raytrace**

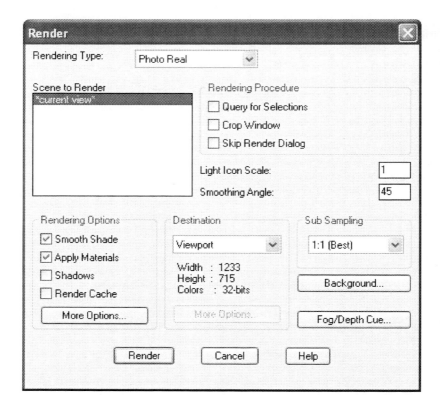

Figure 14.10

33. Move to Destination, click to expand the arrow and select **Render Window.**

34. Leave the rest of the options intact and click on **Render** to see the change in your Model.

Using the **Render Window** option is very essential, in that Rendered Models can be saved as Bitmap, Printed, Opened as well as Tiled to reveal all the rest of the Render. You can also use the Edit command to copy the Rendered Model to other Files.

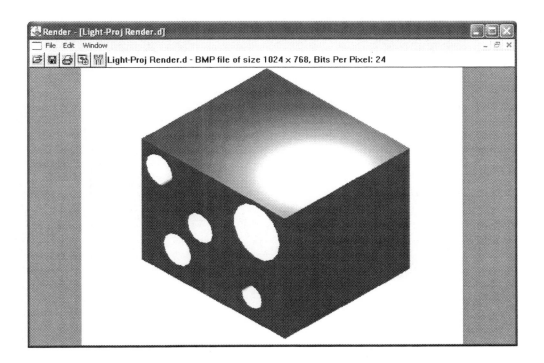

Figure14.11

Distant Light:

The next Light to explore is the **Distant Light**.

35. Open a new File and type **Light** at the Command prompt and press the Enter key or

36. Click on **View** from the **Main Menu**, highlight **Render** and select **Light**.

37. Expand the arrow by **New** and select **Distant Light**.

38. Click on **New,** enter a new Part Name in the allotted box and click on OK.

You can see from the New Distant Light dialogue box in Figure 14.12 of other options like **Azimuth** and Altitude together with color selection and Sun-Angle Calculator. For further tutorials refer to the AutoCAD Help files.

Click on OK to go back to the Distant Light dialogue box.

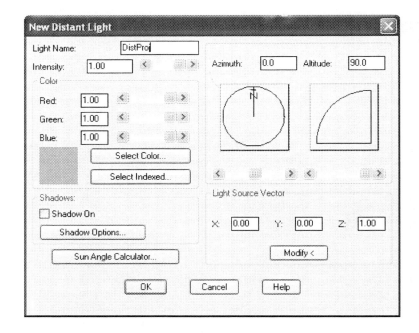

Figure 14.12

When you click on **OK** in the Lights dialogue box, the Model will be Rendered in a window. You will now be able to manipulate the light by moving it to different location and Rendering again to see the other views.

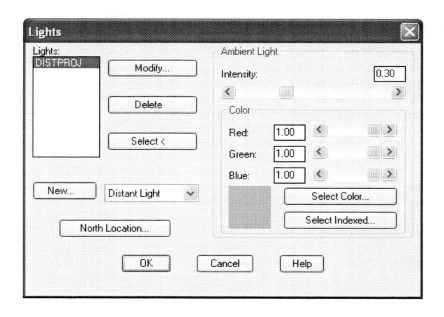

Figure 14.13

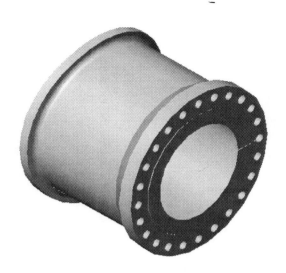

Figure 14.14

Spot Light:

The next Light to explore is the **Spot Light**.

39. Open a new File and type **Light** at the Command prompt and press the Enter key or;

40. Click on **View** from the **Main Menu**, highlight **Render** and select **Light.**

41. Expand the arrow by **New** and select **Spot Light**.

42. Click on **New,** enter a new Part Name in the allotted box and click on OK. Refer to Figure

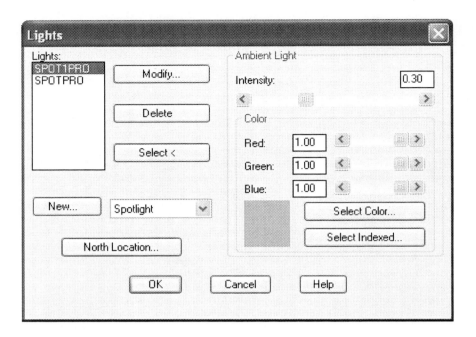

Figure 14.15

The **Spot Light** you have placed on the Desktop can now be moved to a different location, copied to any side of the Part or deleted from the Part. For now let us go on and add more copies of the Spotlight to our Model.

43. Click on Modify from the Main Menu and select copy. A Message pops up requesting you to:

44. **Select objects:**

45. Click on the Spot light symbol on the graphics area and press the Enter key. A Message pops up requesting you to:

46. **Specify base point or displacement, or [Multiple]:**

47. Type **'M'** short for Multiple and press the Enter key. A Message pops up requesting you to specify base point.

48. Click any where on the graphics area. A Message pops up requesting you to:

49. **Specify second point of displacement or <use first point as displacement>:**

50. Click on different locations to place as many Spotlights as so desire and press the **'esc'** key when finished. However do not over do it.

51. Click on **View** from the Main Menu again, highlight **Render** and select Light.

52. You will notice the additional light in the List box under Lights

53. Click on **OK** and add Render to your Model by selecting **Photo Raytrace** and **Render Window**

414

Summary:

You were introduced to Lights that included:

p. Creating a Light feature and Insert it in your Drawing

q. Learning to create Shadow on your Objects.

r. Learning about different types of Lightning

s. Learning of Ambient Light

t. Learning about Distance, Point and Spot Light

u. Adding Lights to objects

v. Creating Render and cover Tolerances

Exercise

Create a Model with several cavities and insert different kinds of Lights in it, to bring out all kinds of shadows and scene. Start with the shape in Figure 13.16

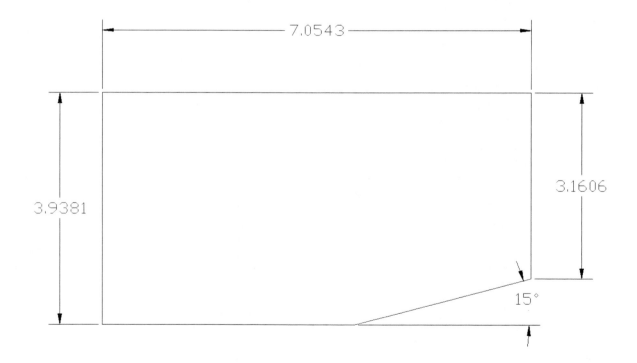

Figure 14.16

Extrude the shape 3 Units and orient it in SE Isometric View.

Figure 14.17

Place the UCS on top of the part and add a circular extrusion and a hole to the object. Refer to Figure 14.18

Add Lights to the object by following the Tutorials in Chapter 14

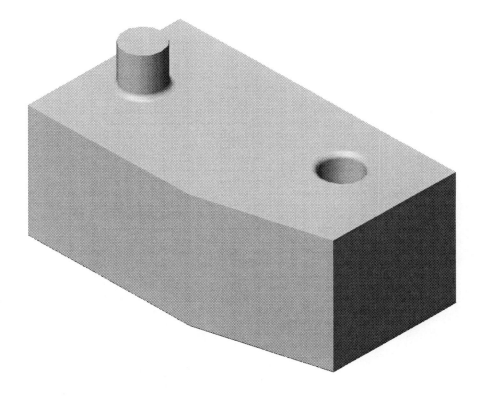

Figure 14.18

The next Lesson will cover **AutoLisp, Script File, Slideshow** and program writing

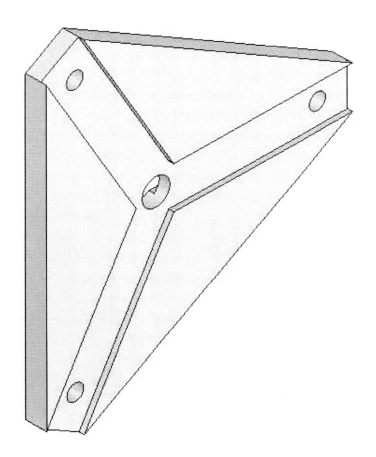

Chapter 15:

Programming is in very essential when it comes to design of repetitive part design. This helps the designer not to redraw parts all over again, which slows down production of goods.

AutoLisp and Script files are two such programming software, which, can be utilized in achieving such goal.

You will be guided in this Chapter to write an AutoLisp and Script, and then use a Slide show to view the Script.

After completing this Chapter, you will be able to:

   w. Know what Script files do

   x. Learn of what Delay is in Script writing

   y. Understand terminologies such as GRAPHSCR, RESUME, RSCRIPT, and TXTSCR and what it is used for.

   z. Use Script to design Polygon and Ellipse.

   aa. Know of the Text Editor and Code writing

   bb. Write a program for a Slide and learn about Vslide and Mslide

   cc. Create a Slideshow.

   dd. Learn how to program with AutoLisp

   ee. Know of defun, setq, getpoint and many more words in code writing.

SCRIPT:

AutoCAD is loaded with many other programs that could be used in generating drawings and automatically displayed on the Graphics area for ease of reference, for presentations as well as trade shows and conferences.

These include AutoLisp, Visual Basic Editor, Visual Lisp, Script, Slide, Diesel and many more.

A script is a text file with one command on each line.

In this chapter, you will be introduced to AutoLisp, Script and Slide programming. All the three programs can be written with a Text editor such as Microsoft® Windows Notepad, a word processor such as Microsoft® Word or the built in Text editor from AutoCAD, which can be assessed through the Command prompt.

An extension of '.SCR' should be added to the saved files to be recognized as script file, also make a note of the folder to which files are saved to be able to load them.

Script can either be run within AutoCAD or invoked from the Startup whichever is preferable will work.

Although writing Script files is that easy, care must be taken in writing the commands on each line since spaces and blanks are considered as pressing the Enter key.

To properly write a Script file, you first use the commands from AutoCAD and write down its responses to be used in the same sequence in the Script file.

Make sure of the names you assign to the script file since certain abbreviations will be easily forgotten with time. For an example do write **Chair** and not **Chr** to represent a piece of furniture. If you have to have two names to represent a single object, place a hyphen or an underscore to link the names.

For an example, **Brown Chair** should be written as **Brown_Chair** or **Brown-Chair**

You can always revise a Script file by invoking it and adding or deleting lines of code to reflect any future changes.

Note that with the exception of dialog boxes, a script file can and will execute any command at the AutoCAD command prompt. This is the only item covered by AutoCAD through the command line.

To add a comment to your script, just place a semicolon **(;)** at the beginning of the line.

There are other very useful commands in writing scripts that include DELAY, RSCRIPT, ESC, RESUME, TEXTSCR and GRAPHSCR

DELAY

Delay is used as a timer within a script to momentarily pause the script in milliseconds. Adding a 1000 for an example will represent a second and 15,000 will represent approximately 15-second pause in between displays.

GRAPHSCR

Like pressing the F2 function key, typing GRAPHSCR at the Command prompt, toggles between the text window and the drawing or graphics area.

RESUME

Shows that are interrupted through break or escape (Esc) restarts with the RESUME command.

RSCRIPT

This line of code is placed at the end of the script program when repetitions are required in the script file.

TEXTSCR

You can switch to the text window by simply typing TEXTSCR at the command prompt.

Follow these steps to write a Script program that displays different drawings on the Graphics area. You will generate drawings for a Rectangle, a Circle, a Donut and an Ellipse. To begin our script writing, we will have to type the commands at the Command Prompt and note down the responses to the sketches.

Start AutoCAD and open a new file. Type rectangle at the Command Prompt and press the Enter key

1. Command: **Rectangle** (Press the Enter key after typing rectangle) A Message pops up requesting you to:

2. **Specify first corner point or [Chamfer / Elevation / Fillet / Thickness / Width]:**

3. Type **0, 0** and press the Enter key A Message pops up requesting you to:

4. **Specify other corner point or [Dimensions]:**

5. Type **8, 12** and press the Enter key.

6. Type Zoom at the Command prompt and press the Enter key. A Message pops up requesting you to select:

7. **[All / Center / Dynamic / Extents / Previous / Scale / Window]<real time>:**

8. Type **'A'** short letter for **All** and press the Enter key.

Now that we have finished drawing the Rectangle, it is time to collect all the necessary information to write the Script file with. First we typed Rectangle and

422

pressed the Enter key.

Script Translation:

Rectangle 0,0 8,12

Zoom A

After pressing the Enter key, you were requested to Specify first corner, therefore the Script line reflects that above. Notice the space in between the 0,0 and 8,12 that represents the Enter key. There is also a space between **Zoom** and **A** meaning that you are requesting the Script command to use the Enter key at this point. The next drawing will be a CIRCLE.

9. Command: Circle and press the Enter key. A Message pops up requesting you to

10. **Specify center point for circle or [3p / 2p / Ttr (tan tan radius)]:**

11. Type **4, 6** and press the Enter key. A Message pops up requesting you to:

12. **Specify radius of circle or [Diameter] <0.000>:**

13. Type **2** for the Diameter and press the Enter key

Script Translation:

Circle4, 6 2

After pressing the Enter key, you were requested to Specify center point for circle; therefore the Script line reflects the line of code, above. Notice the space in between the 4,6 and 2 that represents the Enter key. The 4,6 is the X and Y coordinates of centerpoint of the circle and the 2 represents the Diameter of the circle. The next drawing will be a DONUT

14. Command: Polygon (Type Polygon at the Command Prompt and press the Enter key) A Message pops up requesting you to:

15. **Enter number of sides<4>:**

16. Type **6** and press the Enter key. A Message pops up requesting you to:

17. **Specify center of polygon or [Edge]:**

18. Type **3,4** and press the Enter key A Message pops up requesting you to:

19. **Enter an option [Inscribed in circle / Circumscribed about circle]<I>:**

20. Type **'C'** short for Circumscribed and press the Enter key. A Message pops up requesting you to:

21. **Specify radius of circle:**

22. Type **1** and press the Enter key.

Script Translation:

Polygon 6 3,4 C 1

After pressing the Enter key, you were requested to enter number of sides therefore the Script line reflects the line of code, above. Notice the space in between the **6 3,4 C** and 1 that represents the Enter key. **6** is the number of sides of the polygon **3,4** represent the center of the polygon, **C** tells the program to use **Circumference** instead of **Inscribed**. The number **1** defines the radius of the polygon. The next drawing will be an ELLIPSE

Type Ellipse at the Command prompt and press the Enter key.

23. Command: Ellipse A Message pops up requesting you to:

24. **Specify axis or [Arc / Center]:**

25. Type '**C**' and press the Enter key. A Message pops up requesting you to:

26. **Specify center of ellipse:**

27. Type **3,4** and press the Enter key. A Message pops up requesting you to:

28. **Specify distance to other axis or [Rotation]:**

29. Type **@0,3** and press the Enter key A Message pops up requesting you to:

30. **Specify distance to other axis or [Rotation]:**

31. Type **4,0** and press the Enter key.

Script Translation:

Ellipse C 3,4 @0,3 4,0

After pressing the Enter key, you were requested to specify axis therefore the Script line reflects the line of code, above. Notice the space in between **C 3,4 0,3 4,0** that represents the Enter key. **C** is the center of the Ellipse. **3,4** denote the X and Y coordinate of the Ellipse. **@0,3** and **4,0** represent the distances from the center of the Ellipse to the end of the axis.

The next step in this lesson is to actually write the code that will direct AutoCAD to do all these drawings automatically.

SCRIPT:

You will be directed to use the Text Editor that comes with AutoCAD to write the lines of code, you can also use any text editor of your choice so long as you add SCR as an extension when saving your file. Make sure you know the Folder name and the location you would like to save your script file in or it will not work.

Follow these steps to write the codes for the Script. At the Command prompt enter EDIT and press the Enter key

32. Command: Edit when you press the Enter key, a message pops up requesting you to write the name of:

33. **File to edit:** (For an example this Script will be saved in **C:\Yoofi\Shapes.Scr**

34. Type **Shapes.Scr** and press the Enter key.

When you do press the Enter key, a Text Editor opens up with a blank Dark-Blue screen. Make the following entries and save it

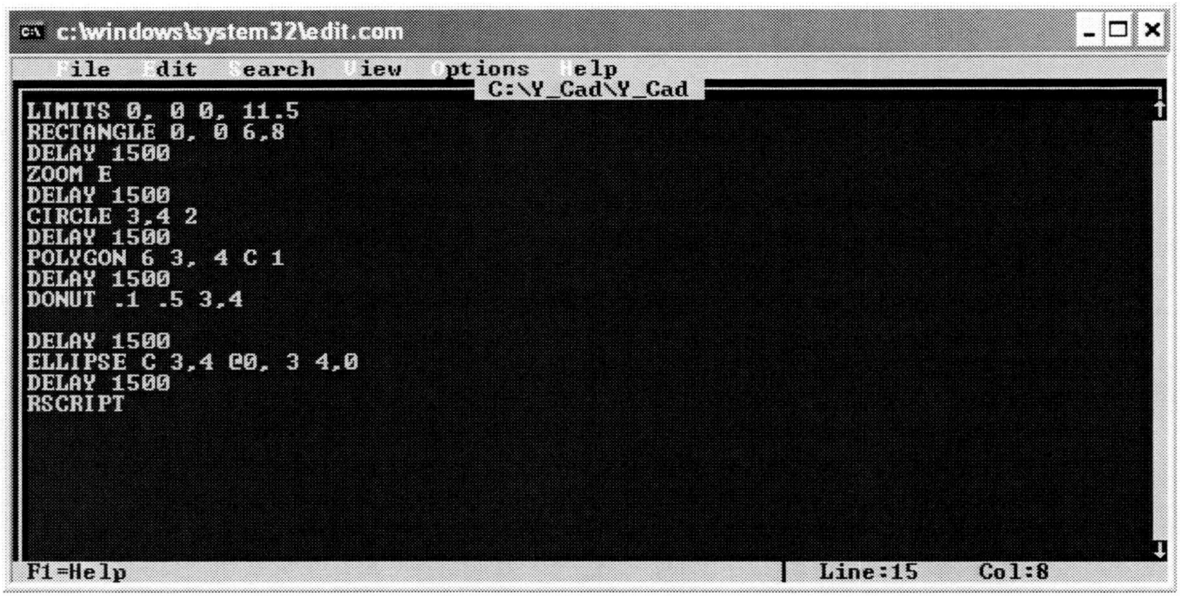

```
c:\windows\system32\edit.com                                    _ □ ×
   File   Edit   Search   View   Options   Help
                              C:\Y_Cad\Y_Cad
LIMITS 0, 0 0, 11.5                                               ↑
RECTANGLE 0, 0 6,8
DELAY 1500
ZOOM E
DELAY 1500
CIRCLE 3,4 2
DELAY 1500
POLYGON 6 3, 4 C 1
DELAY 1500
DONUT .1 .5 3,4

DELAY 1500
ELLIPSE C 3,4 @0, 3 4,0
DELAY 1500
RSCRIPT



                                                                 ↓
F1=Help                                        Line:15    Col:8
```

Figure 15.00

Interpretation of CODE:

- LIMITS **0,0 8,11.5** instructs the computer to create a drawing space of **8" X 11.5"** for the drawings.

- The next line Rectangle, directs AutoCAD program to produce a rectangular drawing starting at the zero origin, with a distance of 6 in the X-direction and 8 in the Y-direction.

- Delay informs the system pause for 15 seconds before the next command.

- Zoom E instructs AutoCAD to extend the drawing to its full size.

- Delay informs the system pause for 15 seconds before the next command.

- Circle requests the system to generate a circle at the center of **3" X 4"** with Diameter of **2**

- Delay informs the system pause for 15 seconds before the next command.
- Polygon gives the sides as **6** the center as **3" x 4"** with circumscribed and a radius of **1inch**
- Delay informs the system pause for 15 seconds before the next command.
- Donut has an inside hole of **0.1**, outer diameter of **0.5** and a center of **3"x 4"**
- Delay informs the system pause for 15 seconds before the next command.
- The Ellipse is at a center of **3" x 4"** and with a distance of 0,3 of one axis and **4,0** for the other. The '@' sign instruct the program to begin the drawing at that particular point.
- Finally RSCRIPT tells the program to do it all over again until stopped. Pressing the **"Esc"** (escape key) will temporary pause a script and RESUME will start it again.
- Click on File and select Save.
- Next click on File and select Exit to end the program.

You now know how to write a Script using AutoCAD text Editor. The next exercise will cover **SLIDE**

SLIDE:

To create a Slide, you first have to make the drawings or the parts to be used in the slide then write a program for the slide show. We are going to draw a Part in this lesson and use it in our Slide.

35. Start AutoCAD and use the Line tool to generate the drawing in Figure 15.01

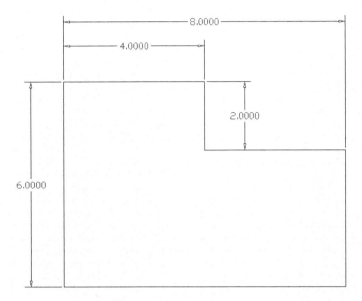

Figure 15.01

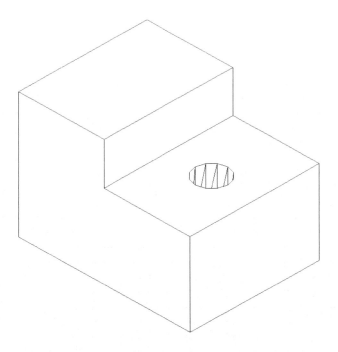

Figure 15.02

36. Extrude the sketch and add '**Ø1.5**' as shown in Figure 14.02. (Refer to chapter on Extrusion and Subtraction of objects)

Figure 15.03

37. Using the View toolbar as in Figure 14.03, orient the drawing to the **Top view**. Type **MSLIDE** at the Command prompt and press the Enter key

38. Command: **Mslide,** the **Create Slide File** opens up for you to save your drawing. The filename in this case will be given as **TOP_SLIDE.** When you

click on Save, AutoCAD will automatically add '**.sld**' as an extension classifying it as a Slide.

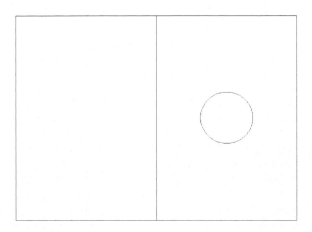

Figure 15.04

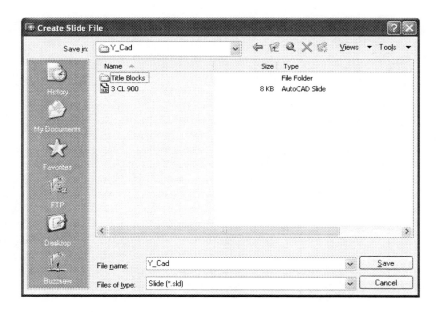

Figure 15.05

39. Click on the **Front View** from the View toolbar and make a slide of that view.

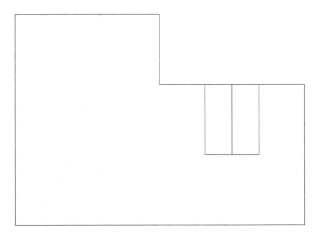

Figure 15.06

40. Command: **Mslide**

41. Save the slide as **FRONT_SLIDE** and change the view to Right side view.

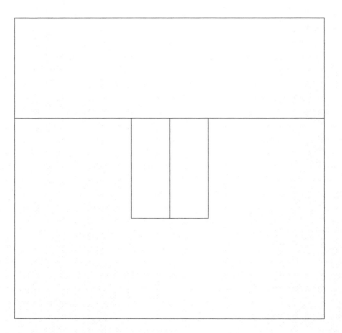

Figure 15.07

42. Command: **Mslide** (Type Mslide at the Command prompt and press the Enter key)

43. In the Create Slide File, save it as **RIGHT_SLIDE** and change into the Isometric view.

44. Command: **Mslide** (Type Mslide at the Command prompt and press the Enter key)

45. In the Create Slide File, save it as **SE_SLIDE** and change into the Isometric view.

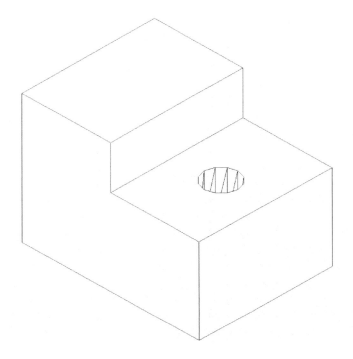

Figure 15.08

Now that we have created all the views required for the Slide, it is time to write the program for the Slide. Type Edit at the Command prompt and press the Enter key. In the File to Edit, type **SlideShow1.Scr**

46. Command: **Edit**

47. **File to edit: SlideShow1.Scr**

Enter the code as in Figure 15.10 and save your drawing

434

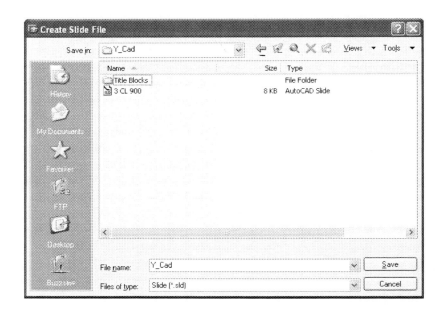

Figure 15.09

```
c:\windows\system32\edit.com                                    _ □ ×
  File  Edit  Search  View  Options  Help
─────────────────────────── C:\Y_Cad\Slideshow ────────────────────
    VSLIDE TOP_SLIDE
    DELAY 1500
    VSLIDE FRONT_SLIDE
    DELAY 1500
    VSLIDE RIGHT_SLIDE
    DELAY 1500
    VSLIDE SE_SLIDE
    RSCRIPT




 F1=Help                                    │     Line:8      Col:7
```

Figure 15.10

SLIDESHOW:

To run the Slide show, type **SCRIPT** at the Command Prompt and press the Enter key. From the list of files in the Select Script File dialogue box, highlight SlidShow1.Scr and click on open.

Sit back and watch the views change in seconds.

Press the '**Esc**' key to exit the Slideshow. This concludes the tutorials on Script and Slide programming. The next lesson will cover **AutoLisp**

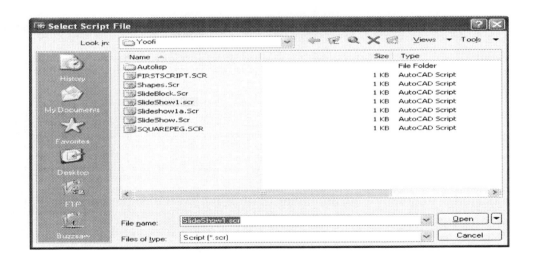

Figure 15.11

AutoLisp:

This section will introduce you to basic AutoLisp programming. AutoLisp enhances your drawing and design by creating drawings you make very often so as it will be generated, by entering values at the keyboard. There is an endless use of AutoLisp once you get the hang of it. Short for List Processor, the program was developed by Autodesk, Inc.

You learned how to write Script and create Slides, in earlier lessons, this will cap off programming in AutoCAD in this book. Do research and explore all the capabilities of these three programs and see how far you will go with it. For more on AutoLisp, refer to the AutoLisp Programmers Manual from Autodesk.

The sketch you are about to create will involve a Rectangle. You can use a Text editor like the Notepad or a Word processor to type in the Codes, but make sure it is saved with an 'lsp' extension In essence RECT will be saved as **Rect.lsp** in a known Folder.

You can also use the Command Prompt of AutoCAD to type in the code, but be careful of closing parenthesis. When you use the Command prompt to enter the Code, AutoLisp automatically uses the current layer to make the sketch.

To add comments to your Code, add a semicolon **(;)** in front of the sentence and AutoLisp will overlook it as a Code.

You will first have to learn certain terminologies and functions to be able to piece everything together. This will be explained in the order of operation for a typical coding.

Defun:

Defun like the abbreviated word goes, is used to define a function in the AutoLisp program, **Lline** being the name of the function.

You therefore start your coding by specifying what to be used in a particular exercise. For an example if you will like to program AutoLisp to draw a Line, you start by defining the line and add other codes to it. A typical line of code will look like:

Defun C: Lline ()

This will allow the function **'Lline'** to run at the Command prompt. The letter 'C' indicates entries at the Command prompt.

Setq:

You will need to assign a value to variables that you create and you do so by using **'setq'** to write the code. In our example **setq P1** will request the user to enter a value for the first point of the rectangular sketch. This works in conjunction with getpoint.

Setq P1

Getpoint:

Points that make up the x and y coordinates of a sketch are entered through the keyboard. In order for the user to enter the assigned coordinates for each point, the getpoint function pause the program to enable the process to be carried out. Thus a 2inch Line drawn from the origin on the positive x-axis, will be entered as **2, 0.** For an example:

(Setq P1 (getpoint "\n Specify the First point:"))

"\n

The backslash and n short for new line is used as a carriage return and the statement specify the First point of the Rectangle, will be printed on the next line.

"\n Specify the First point of the Rectangle:"

Printed below, is a complete set of codes that will generate a rectangle on the graphics' area. Type in the code at the Command Prompt and run the program by typing '**Rect**' at the Command prompt with the following entries.

(Command "Line" P1 P2 P3 P4 "C"))

At the Command Prompt, this function will be used to draw a line from point P1 to P2 to P3 to P4 forming a rectangle.

Now enter the code exactly as it appears below and run it to generate a rectangle.

```
; This program will prompt the user to enter four points from the keyboard
; and generate a rectangle sketch with the set points, P1 P2 P3 and P4.

(defun C: Rect()
(Setq P1 (getpoint "\n Specify the First point of the Rectangle :"))
(Setq P2 (getpoint "\n Specify the Second point of the Rectangle :"))
(Setq P3 (getpoint "\n Specify the Third point of the Rectangle :"))
(Setq P4 (getpoint "\n Specify the Fourth point of the Rectangle:"))
(Command "Line" P1 P2 P3 P4 "C"))
```

)

Do the following to load and run the program.

After writing all the code as indicated above in the Notepad text, click on File and Save as Rect.lsp in a known location.

With AutoCAD opened, click on Tools from the Main Menu, highlight Autolisp and click on Load. The Load/Unload Application dialogue box pops up.

Click on Rect.lsp once and click on Load. Rect.lsp successfully loaded appears in the box below as in Figure 15.12. Click on close to exit the command.

Back at the Command prompt, type Rect and press the Enter key.

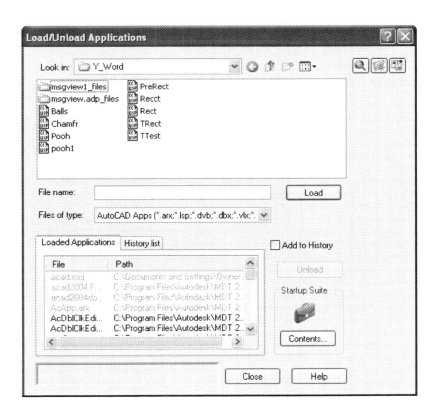

Figure 15.12

Command: **Rect** (type Rect and press the enter key): A Message pops requesting you to:

48. **Specify the First point of the Rectangle:**

49. Enter **0, 0** and press the enter key A Message pops requesting you to

50. **Specify the Second point of the Rectangle**

51. Enter **4, 0** and press the enter key A Message pops requesting you to

52. **Specify the Third point of the Rectangle:**

53. Enter **4, 4** and press the enter key A Message pops requesting you to

54. **Specify the Fourth point of the Rectangle**

55. Enter **0, 4** and press the enter key A Message pops requesting you to

A rectangle with dimensions of **4" x 4"** is drawn on the graphics area.

Special Characters:

Code	Results
%%P	Yields +/- tolerance symbol
%%C	Yields Diameter (Ø)
%%D	Yields Degree (°)
Alt +248	Yields Degree (°)
%%U	Yields Underscore
%%O	Yields Overscore
\P	Yields the end of a Paragraph
%%O%%U	Yields Overscore and Underscore

Start AutoCAD and open a new file.

56. Click on Dimension from the Tool bar, highlight **Linear** and press the Enter key. A Message on the Command line requests you to:

57. **Specify first extension line origin or <Select object>:**

58. Click anywhere on the graphics area. A Message on the Command line requests you to:

59. **Specify second extension line origin:**

60. First press the **F8** function key to turn the **Ortho** on.

61. Move the mouse pointer horizontally away from the first point, type **2** and hit the Enter key on the keyboard. A Message on the Command line requests you to add:

62. **[Mtext / Text / Angle / Horizontal / Vertical / Rotated]:**

63. Click to exit the dimension tool.

Summary:

This Chapter introduced you to a little bit of Code and programming and you got to have the feel of drawing with programs as against conventional sketches. Some of the topics covered include:

ff. Familiarizing yourself with what Script does

gg. Learning of what Delay is in Script writing

hh. Understanding different terminologies that included GRAPHSCR, RESUME, RSCRIPT, and TXTSCR and what it is used for.

ii. Using Script to design Polygon and Ellipse.

jj. Knowing of the Text Editor and Code writing

kk. Writing a program for a Slide and learn about Vslide and Mslide

ll. Creating a Slideshow.

mm. Learning how to program with AutoLisp

nn. Knowing of **defun**, **setq**, **getpoint** and many more words in code writing.

Exercise

a. Using the steps covered above; write an **AutoLisp** program to create a Triangle. Load the triangle from the Tools option and run it.

b. Create a slide with a 3D model and write a Script for the show. Good Luck!

The next Chapter will introduce you to **Customizing Toolbars** to suit the environment you are working in.

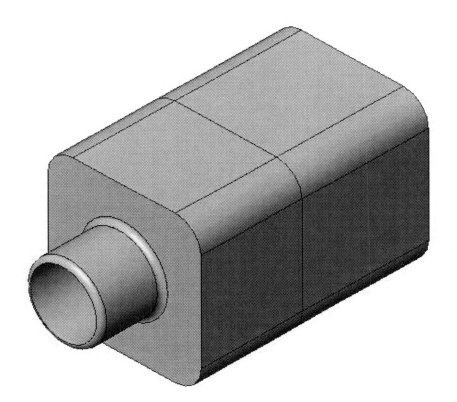

Chapter 16:

In this chapter you will create Custom toolbars and learn of the differences between **2D Mirror** and that of **3D** options.

        oo. Learn to Setup Custom Toolbar

        pp. Introduced to the New Toolbar

        qq. Learn how to create an empty toolbar and populate it with selected Tools.

        rr. Learn to use short cuts

        ss. How to use 3 Point arc

        tt. Learn to use the Isometric view to draw

        uu. Use the Normal and Sketch icons

        vv. Learn to use Relations

        ww. Learn to use the Boss and Extrude cut commands

Custom Toolbar:

1. Type Toolbar at the Command Prompt; a Toolbar Button should be active under a **Customize** dialog box.

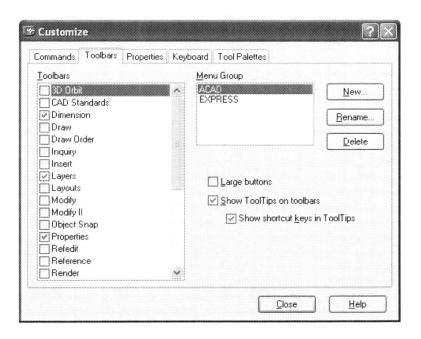

Figure 16.00

2. Click on New, the New Toolbar dialog box opens up

3. In the box under Toolbar Name, enter a related name and click on OK. For an example Tooling Project if were working in a project of designing tools.

Figure 16.01

446

4. Click on OK after selecting ACAD under the Save Toolbar and notice a new empty toolbar inserted on the graphics area.

Figure 16.02

5. Click on **Commands** under Customize then drag and drop all the tools needed on the project.

Follow these steps to add different tools to the new Toolbar

6. Click on Commands and under Categories; highlight an option for an example File.

7. Move to the Commands box, click on **New** hold down the left mouse button, drag and drop it onto the space allotted under the Tooling Project Toolbar. Refer to Figure 16.03 below.

8. Select the OPEN icon, drag and drop it by the NEW icon under the Tooling Project toolbar.

Figure 16.03

9. Click to highlight **Edit** next and hold down the left mouse button on **UNDO**, drag and drop it by the **OPEN** icon

10. Go through the list of tools and follow the steps above to place them on the Toolbar.

Follow these steps to remove a Tool from the Tolling Toolbar.

11. Open up the tool under Commands, hold down on the Tool to delete, drag and drop on the same area you first copied it from.

12. Click on close to exit the command when finished and all the tools will be loaded on your new Toolbar ready to be used.

13. You can now move the new toolbar and dock it on top of the Main Menu and remove the duplicate toolbars from the Menu.

Mirror Objects

2D Mirror

You will only need two-reference point of a line about which to mirror a sketch when working with 2D. Follow these steps to create a mirror for a sketch.
Start AutoCAD if it not already running on your computer and open a new file.
Draw the sketch below using the Rectangle tool.

14. Click on Draw from the Main Menu and select **Rectangle**. A Message pops

448

up requesting you to:

15. **Specify first corner point or [Chamfer / Elevation /Fillet / Thickness / Width]:**

16. Type **0, 0** and press the Enter key. A Message pops up requesting you to:

17. **Specify other corner point or [Dimensions]:**

18. Type **6, 4** and press the Enter key

Figure 16.04

To create a mirror image of the rectangle, click on Modify from the Main Menu and select Mirror from the list of tools. A Message pops up requesting you to:

19. **Select objects:**

20. Click on one of the four lines that bound the rectangle and press the Enter key. A Message pops up requesting you to:

21. **Specify first point of mirror line:**

22. Click on the endpoint by the letter **'A'**. A Message pops up requesting you to:

23. **Specify second point of mirror line:**

24. Click on the endpoint by the letter **'B'**. A Message pops up requesting you to:

25. **Delete source objects? [Yes/No] <No>:**

26. Press the Enter key to accept No. A mirror image should be placed side by side of the original rectangle.

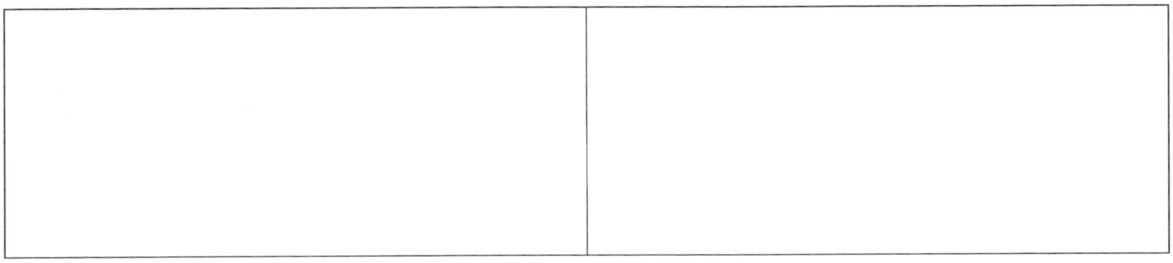

Figure 16.05

The other option is to plane a line parallel to a side of the object at any specified distant and pick the endpoints to place the mirror image of the original object. To accomplish this, draw a line parallel to the rectangle and add a dimension of **0.25"** between the reference line and one side of the rectangle.

450

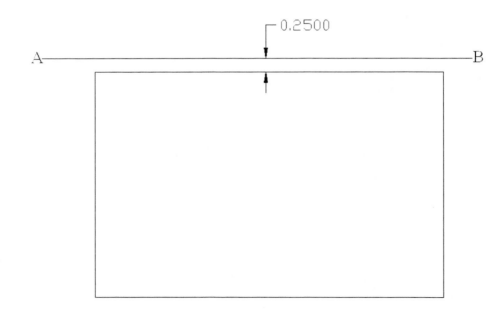

Figure 16.06

27. Click on Modify from the Main Menu and select Mirror from the list of tools. A Message pops up requesting you to:

28. **Select objects:**

29. Click on one of the four lines that bound the rectangle and press the Enter key. A Message pops up requesting you to:

30. **Specify first point of mirror line:**

31. Click on the endpoint by the letter 'A'. A Message pops up requesting you to:

32. **Specify second point of mirror line:**

33. Click on the endpoint by the letter **'B'**. A Message pops up requesting you to:

34. **Delete source objects? [Yes/No] <No>:**

Press the Enter key to accept **No.** A mirror image should be placed side by side of the original rectangle.

451

Figure 16.07

Mirror different Objects:

Objects with different shapes; like lines and circles, are approached by selecting individual shapes before using the Mirror tool or by dragging a selection window around the group before the mirror. Follow these steps to create a group of objects and add mirror to the group.

Start AutoCAD if it is not already running on your computer and open a new file. Use different tools to draw the objects in Figure 16.08 and save your drawing.

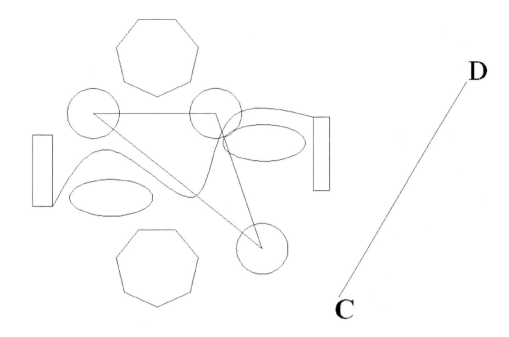

Figure 16.08

35. Click on Modify from the Main Menu and select Mirror from the list of tools. A Message pops up requesting you to:

36. **Select objects:**

37. Type **ALL** at Command prompt and press the Enter key 2x's (Two times). A Message pops up requesting you to:

38. **Specify first point of mirror line:**

39. Click on the endpoint by the letter '**C**'. A Message pops up requesting you to:

40. **Specify second point of mirror line:**

41. Click on the endpoint by the letter '**D**'. A Message pops up requesting you to:

42. **Delete source objects? [Yes/No] <No>:**

Press the Enter key to accept **No.** A mirror image should be placed side by side of the original rectangle.

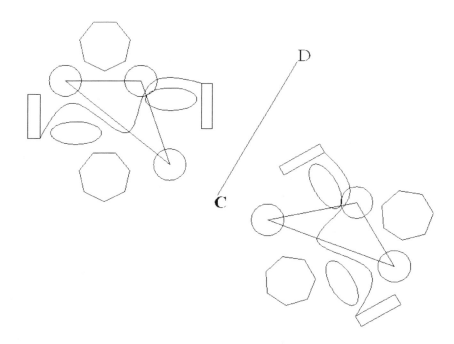

Figure 16.09

<u>3D Mirror</u>

Certain objects like Circle, Ellipse and Polygons are extruded without converting individual lines into a Polyline or making an enclosed part a Boundary before turning it into a 3D model. 3D Mirror is used with Solids

Other objects that do not fall under this category get converted into Polyline or Boundaries before extrusion or revolving the sketch. You will be introduced to both options for these Tutorials but first let us draw a sketch for this exercise.

Start AutoCAD if it is not already running on your Computer and open a new File.

43. Type '**LINE**' at the Command prompt and press the Enter key. A Message pops up requesting you to:

44. **Specify first point:**

45. Draw the sketch as in Figure 16.10

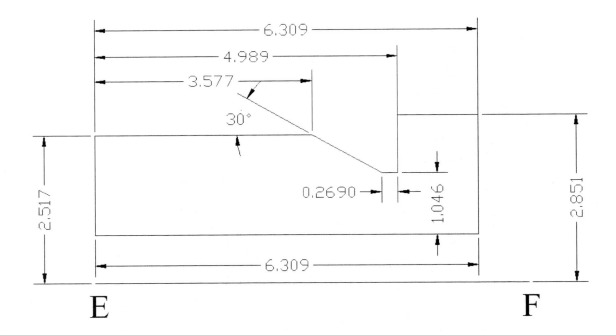

Figure 16.10

To turn the Sketch in Figure 16.10 into a 3D Model, you first have to convert all the connecting lines into a Polyline turning it into a one entity. To do those follow these steps.

46. Type **PEdit** at the Command Prompt and press the Enter key. A Message pops up requesting you to:

47. **Select Polyline or [Multiple]:**

48. Click on one of the lines in the sketch. A Message pops up asking:

49. **Do you want to turn it into one? <Y>?**

50. Press the Enter key to accept the Yes option. A Message pops up requesting you to:

51. **Enter an option: [Close / Join / Width / Edit vertex / Fit / Spline / Decurve / Ltype gen / Undo]:**

52. Type '**J**' short for Join and press the Enter key. A Message pops up requesting you:

53. **Select objects:**

54. Type **'All'** and press the Enter key **three** times to exit the command. All the lines should now turn into one entity. Click on one of the line and grips should appear t all the endpoints.

55. Type **Revolve** at the Command prompt and press the Enter key. A Message pops up requesting you to:

56. Click on one of the Lines and press the Enter key again. A Message pops up requesting you to:

57. **Define axis by [Object / x (axis) Y (axis)]:**

58. Click on the endpoint by **'E'**, a message pops up requesting you to:

59. **Specify endpoint of axis:**

60. Click on the endpoint by **'F'** A Message pops up requesting you to:

Figure 16.11

61. **Specify angle of revolution <360>:**

62. Press the Enter key to accept the 360-revolution option. The sketch should turn into a 3D Model

63. Click on View from the Main Menu, highlight 3D Views and select SE Isometric.

Now click on View again highlight Shade and select Gouraud Shaded to view the 3D Model

64. Click on Modify from the Main Menu, highlight 3D Operation and select Rotate 3D

Do the following to create 3D Mirror of Parts. With the Model in Figure 16.11 still on the Graphics area, click on Modify highlight 3D Operations and select **Mirror 3D.** A Message pops up requesting you to:

65. **Select objects:**

66. Click on the object to highlight it and press the Enter key. A Message pops up requesting you to:

67. **Choose [Object / Last / Zaxis / View / XY / TZ / 3Points] <3Points>:**

68. Press the Enter key to accept the default option of **<3 Points>:** A Message pops up requesting you to:

69. **Specify first point on mirror plane:**

70. Type **'CEN'** short for center and press the Enter key.

71. Move the Pointer closer to the center of the part and when you see the image of a circle, click on it A Message pops up requesting you to:

72. **Specify second point on mirror plane:**

73. Type **'QUAD'** short for Quadrant and press the Enter key.

74. Move the Pointer closer to edge of the part and when you see the image of a diamond-shape object, click on it. A Message pops up requesting you to:

75. Specify the third point on mirror plane:

76. Type **'QUAD'** short for Quadrant and press the Enter key.

77. Move the Pointer closer to edge of the part and when you see the image of a diamond-shape object, click on it. A Message pops up requesting you to:

78. **Delete source objects [Yes / No] <No>:**

79. Press the Enter key to accept No, A Mirror of the Part should be placed on the face of the original part. Refer to Figure 16.12

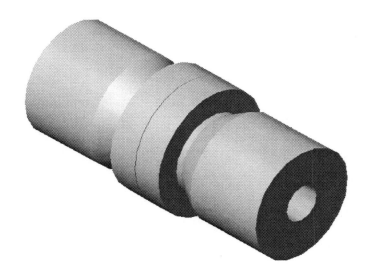

Figure 16.12

Summary:

In this Chapter you learned how to create 2D Mirror of sketches and also 3D Mirror of Solid Models. You were introduced to Topics that included:

      xx. Learning to Setup Custom Toolbar

      yy. Being Introduced to the New Toolbar

      zz. Learning how to create an empty toolbar and populate it with selected Tools.

      aaa.   Learning to use short cuts

      bbb.   Knowing how to use 3 Point arc

      ccc.   Learning to use the Isometric view to draw

      ddd.   Using the Normal and Sketch icons

      eee.   Learning to use Relations

      fff.   Learning to use the Boss and Extrude cut commands

Exercise

Follow the same concept and with the aid of already saved models, create Mirror images of sketches and 3D Models of Four different Drawings.

The next Lesson will cover **Built-in Solids**

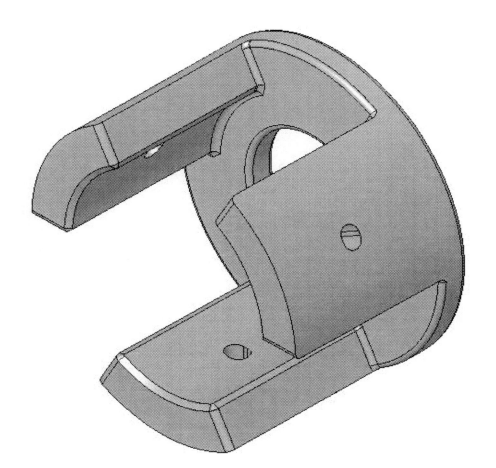

Chapter 17:

In this chapter you will cover other forms of **Solids** loaded with AutoCAD program. After completing this section, you will be able to create solids that will include:

- Creating Sphere
- Creating Cylinder
- Creating a Cone
- Creating a Wedge
- Creating Torus

SURFACES

AutoCAD is loaded with several tools that include Surfaces. We have already covered Solid Modeling under solids using the Box tool and now you will be introduced to ready made Solid Tools as well as Mesh and Wireframe.

SPHERE

1. Start AutoCAD if it is not already running on your computer and open a Template or a new File.
2. Click on Draw, highlight Solids and click on **Sphere**. A Message pops up requesting you to:
3. **Specify center of Sphere <0, 0, 0>**
4. Type **0, 0** and press the Enter key
5. **Specify radius of Sphere or [Diameter]:**
6. Type 1 and press the Enter key to insert a Sphere at the Origin.

Figure 17.00

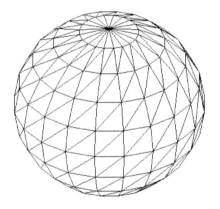

Figure 17.01

To view the **Sphere,** click on one of the views from the **View** toolbar for an example SE Isometric view as in Figure 17.00.

7. Click on **View** from the **Toolbar**, highlight **Shade** and click on **Gouraud Shaded.**

8. Click on the body of the Sphere, click on the arrow from **ByLayer** to expand the list of colors click to select a different color and hit the **'Esc'** key on the keyboard.

CYLINDER

9. Click on Draw, highlight Solids and click on **Cylinder.** A Message pops up requesting you to:

10. **Specify center point for base of Cylinder or [Elliptical]: <0, 0, 0>**

11. Type **0, 0** and press the Enter key

12. **Specify radius for base of cylinder or [Diameter]:**

13. Type **1** and press the Enter key A Message pops up requesting you to:

14. **Specify height of cylinder or [Center of the other end]:**

15. Type **2** and press the Enter key to place a cylinder on the Graphics area.

16. Click on **View** from the **Toolbar**, highlight **Shade** and click on **Gouraud Shaded.**

17. Click on the body of the Cylinder, click on the arrow from **ByLayer** to expand the list of colors click to select a different color and hit the **'Esc'** key on the keyboard.

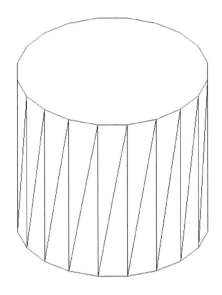

Figure 17.02

CONE

18. Click on Draw, highlight Solids and click on **Cone.** A Message pops up requesting you to:

19. **Specify center point for base of Cone or [Elliptical]: <0, 0, 0>**

20. Type **0, 0** and press the Enter key

21. **Specify radius for base of cone or [Diameter]:**

22. Type **1** and press the Enter key A Message pops up requesting you to:

23. **Specify height of cone or [Apex]:**

24. Type **3** and press the Enter key to place a cone on the Graphics area.

25. Click on **View** from the **Toolbar**, highlight **Shade** and click on **Gouraud Shaded.**

26. Click on the body of the Cone, click on the arrow from **ByLayer** to expand

the list of colors click to select a different color and hit the **'Esc'** key on the keyboard.

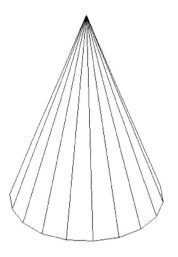

Figure 17.03

WEDGE

27. Click on Draw, highlight Solids and click on **Wedge.** A Message pops up requesting you to:

28. **Specify first corner of wedge or [CEnter]: <0, 0, 0>**

29. Type **0, 0** and press the Enter key

30. **Specify corner or [Cube / Length]:**

31. Type **'L'** and press the Enter key A Message pops up requesting you to:

32. **Specify length:**

33. Type **1** and press the Enter. A Message pops up requesting you:

34. **Specify width:**

35. Type '**2**' and press the Enter key. A Message pops up requesting you to:

36. **Specify height:**

37. Type '**2**' and press the Enter key to place a Wedge on the Graphics area.

38. Click on **View** from the **Toolbar**, highlight **Shade** and click on **Gouraud Shaded.**

39. Click on the body of the Wedge, click on the arrow from **ByLayer** to expand the list of colors click to select a different color and hit the '**Esc**' key on the keyboard.

Figure 17.04

TORUS

40. Click on **Draw**, highlight Solids and click on **Torus**. A Message pops up requesting you to:

41. **Specify center of Torus <0, 0, 0>**

42. Type **0, 0** and press the Enter key

43. **Specify radius of Torus or [Diameter]:**

44. Type **1** and press the Enter key. A Message pops up requesting you to:

45. **Specify radius of tube or [Diameter]**

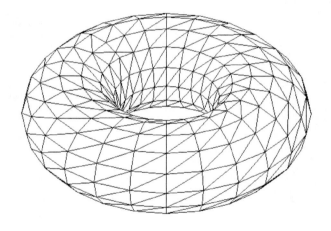

Figure 17.05

46. Type **0.5** and press the Enter key.

47. Click on **View** from the **Toolbar**, highlight **Shade** and click on **Gouraud Shaded.**

48. Click on the body of the Torus, click on the arrow from **ByLayer** to expand

the list of colors click to select a different color and hit the **'Esc'** key on the keyboard.

<u>Summary:</u>

You were introduced to Topics that included:

- Creating Sphere

- Creating Cylinder

- Creating a Cone

- Creating a Wedge

- Creating Torus

Exercise

Experiment with the Solid option as detailed in this Chapter. Change different values to see how it comes out.

The next Lesson will cover **Section and Slides**

Chapter 18:

Follow these steps to create a **Section** and then **Slice.**

Start AutoCAD, if it is not already running on your computer and open the part.

After completing this section, you will be able to:

ggg.   Learn of the steps taken to draw a Bearing Guide

hhh.   Create a Boundary

iii.   Use the Extrude option to add depth to your sketch

jjj.   Add a Groove inside a part

kkk.   Use Subtract to remove excess parts

lll.   Create Section and a Slice.

Section and Slice

Now that you know how the Solids work you will move on to **Section** and **Slide.**

Clients would occasionally request for sections of parts in order to ascertain the correctness of the internal structures. Sections are created to reveal the making of such internal parts with an outline view of the whole internal design.

A section in AutoCAD is generated with 3D models by picking three different points on the Model. The base part is then relocated with the move optional tool to show the sectioned part. You will need to open a 3D drawing or draw one to be used in this tutorial.

Follow these steps to create a section of a Solid part.

Open AutoCAD if it is not already running on your Computer and draw a sketch.

1. Type Circle at the Command prompt and press the Enter key. A Message pops up requesting you to:

2. **Specify center point for circle or [3P / 2P / Ttr (Tan tan radius)]**

3. Type **0, 0** and press the Enter key. A Message pops up requesting you to:

4. **Specify radius of circle or [Diameter] <0.0000>**

5. Type **'D'** short for diameter and press the Enter key. A Message pops up requesting you to:

6. **Specify diameter of circle <0.000>**

7. Type **3.5** and press the Enter key, a circle should be placed on the Origin.

Follow similar steps and add the rest of the circles to the sketch and make sure you enter **'R'** short for radius, when the system requests you to enter the radius. Refer to Figure 18.00 below.

You are now going to add **Tangential Lines** to the circles and convert it into one entity.

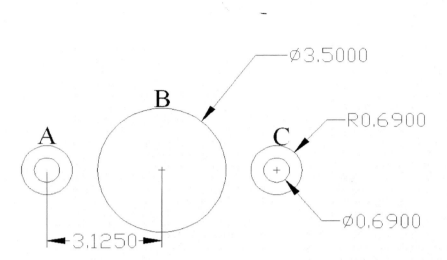

Figure 18.00

8. Using the Line tool draw lines tangent to the circles. Refer to Figure 18.01 Follow these steps for placing Tangential Lines on a circle.

9. Type **Line** at the Command prompt and press the Enter key. A Message pops up requesting you to:

10. **Specify first point:**

11. Type **'tan'** and press the enter key. A Message asks **' to'**

12. Move the pointer on the outline of the circle closer to letter **'A'** and it should change to a tangent symbol.

13. Click on the circle the moment you see the symbol.

14. Type **'tan'** again and move to the other circle closer to the letter **'B'**, click to place a tangential line on the two circles.

15. Repeat these steps for the rest of the circles and save your model.

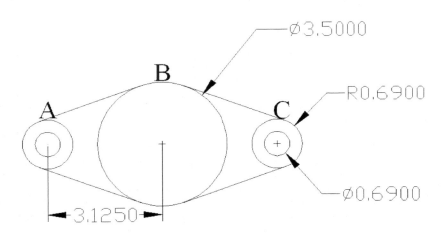

Figure 18.01

You are now going to use the **Trim** tool to remove excess Lines for your model

16. Click on Modify from the Main menu and select Trim. A Message pops up requesting you to:

17. **Select objects:** Press the Enter key once and a Message will pop up requesting you to:

18. **Select object to trim or shift-select to extend or [Project / Edge / undo]**

19. Click on the arc of the larger circle first, then that of the smaller circles. Refer to Figure 18.01

20. Click on the 'Esc' key on the keyboard when finished to exit the trim command tool.

You will now use the **Boundary** tool to combine all the broken arcs into one entity to enable the Extrude option to work properly.

21. Click on **Draw** from the Main Menu and select **Boundary,** the Boundary Creation dialogue box pops up as in Figure

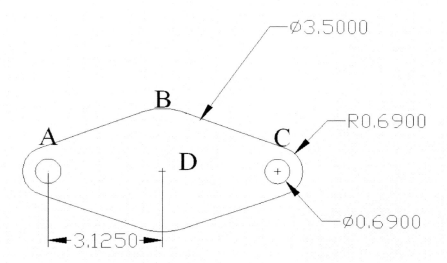

Figure 18.02

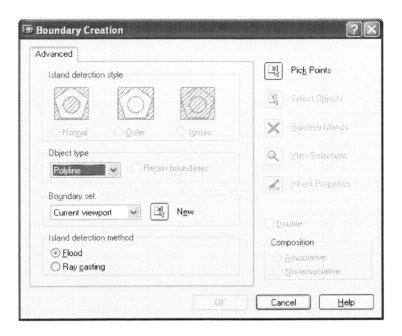

Figure 18.03

22. Click on Pick Points. A Message pops up requesting you to:

23. **Select internal point**

24. Click on '**D**' located inside the sketch in Figure 18.02 and press the Enter key.

You will now use the **Extrude** option to add depth to the sketch. To better see the change in the sketch you would need to change it to the 3D view.

Click to select **SE Isometric** from the **View** toolbar to change the orientation of the sketch. Refer to Figure 18.04

25. Click on **Draw** from the **Main Menu**, highlight **Solids**, and select **Extrude**. A Message pops up requesting you to:

26. **Select objects:**

476

Figure 18.04

27. Click on the outline of the sketch and click on the two remaining circles. A Message pops up requesting you to:

28. **Specify height of extrusion or [Path]**

29. Type **0.63** and press the Enter key. A Message pops up requesting you to:

30. **Specify angle of taper for extrusion <0>:**

31. Press the Enter key to accept the default option of zero to complete the Extrusion. Refer to Figure 18.05

You will continue the tutorial, by placing a circle on top of the Model and adding another extrusion to do this, you will need to rotate the UCS in order for the X and Y coordinates to be parallel with the surface or lie flat on the top of the Model

32. Type **UCS** and press the Enter key. A Message pops up requesting you to:

33. Enter an option **[New / Move / orthoGraphic / Prev / Restore / Save / Del / Apply /? /World] <World>**

34. Type **'X'** and press the Enter key [Notice that **'X'** is not one of the choices above because it is a hidden command and not included in the list of items.] A Message pops up requesting you to:

35. **Specify rotation angle about x axis <90>:**

36. Press the Enter key to accept the default of 90. The UCS changes its orientation and lies flat on the surface.

The next step is to move the UCS to the Top face of the model. To do this:

37. Type **UCS** again and press the Enter key. A Message pops up requesting you to:

38. Enter an option **[New / Move / orthoGraphic / Prev / Restore / Save / Del / Apply /? /World] <World>**

39. Type **'M"** short for move and press the Enter key. A Message pops up requesting you to:

40. **Specify new origin point or [Zdepth] <0,0,0, >:**

41. Type **'cen'** short for center and press the Enter key. A Message asks **of**

42. Move the pointer to the curved part of your model in the middle, the center symbol is inserted at the center of the part

43. Click to Move the UCS to the center of the Model, the moment you see the circle symbol.

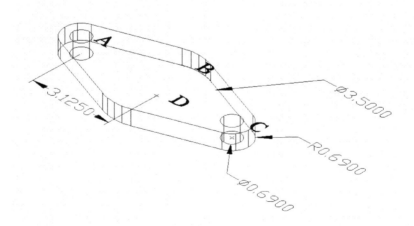

Figure 18.05

You are now going to use the **Subtract** editing tool to remove the cylindrical pieces from the main model to create a hole.

44. Click on Modify from the Main Menu, highlight Solids Editing and select **Subtract.** The pointer turns into a Pickbox and a Message pops up requesting you to:

45. **Select objects: [Here** you click to select the objects you would like to keep first, in this case click on the body of the model]

46. **Select object:**

47. Click on the two circles and press the Enter key to bore the holes.

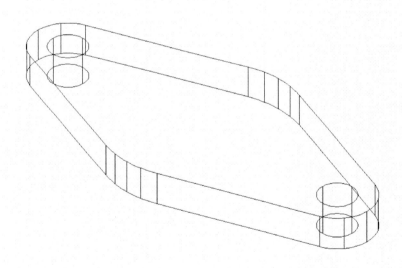

Figure 18.06

You are now going to place a **CIRCLE** sketch on top of the Model.

48. Type **Circle** at the Command prompt and press the Enter key. A Message pops up requesting you to:

49. **Specify center point for circle or [3P / 2P / Ttr (tan tan radius)]**

50. Type **0, 0** and press the Enter key. A Message pops up requesting you to:

51. **Specify radius of circle or [Diameter] <0.000>:** [Notice that if no prior entries have been made, the program will register <0.000> as above.]

52. Type **'D'** short for diameter and press the Enter key. A Message pops up requesting you to:

53. **Specify Diameter of circle <0.000>:**

54. Type **3.50** and press the Enter key to place a circle on top of the model.

You are now going to **Extrude** the circle on top of the model.

55. Click on **Draw** from the **Main Menu**, highlight **Solids**, and select **Extrude**. A Message pops up requesting you to:

56. **Select objects:**

Figure 18.07

57. Click on the Circle on top of the Model. A Message pops up requesting you to:

58. **Specify height of extrusion or [Path]**

59. Type **0.50** and press the Enter key. A Message pops up requesting you to:

60. **Specify angle of taper for extrusion <0>:**

61. Press the Enter key to accept the default option of zero to complete the

   Extrusion. [Note that whichever direction the **Z-axis** point is positive.

If Z is pointing downwards and your extrusion needs to go upwards, you will

have to make the value a negative number]

   Since the two parts are now separate, we will have to make it into one entity

before proceeding to the next lesson. You will therefore use the Union option to join

the two entities.

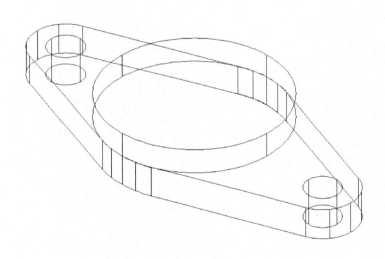

Figure 18.08

62. Click on **Modify** from the main Menu, highlight **Solids Editing** and select

   Union from the list of tools. A Message pops up requesting you to:

63. **Select objects:**

64. Type **'ALL'** and press the Enter key **2** times, the two parts are now one entity.

You are now going to bore a hole in the center of the Model and use the Subtract editing tool to remove the **Cylindrical-Shaped** objects leaving holes behind.

65. Move the UCS on top of model and place a circle with diameter **Ø2.38** from the center. Refer to **#22** on moving the UCS.

The next step is to extrude the circle beyond the body of the Model.

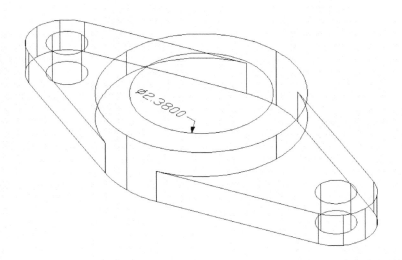

Figure 18.09

66. Click on **Draw** from the **Main Menu**, highlight **Solids**, and select **Extrude**. A Message pops up requesting you to:

67. **Select objects:**

68. Click on the Circle on top of the Model. A Message pops up requesting you to:

69. **Specify height of extrusion or [Path]**

70. Type **4.50** and press the Enter key. A Message pops up requesting you to:

71. **Specify angle of taper for extrusion <0>:**

72. Press the Enter key to accept the default option of zero to complete the Extrusion. [Note that whichever direction the **Z-axis** point is positive.

If **Z** is pointing downwards and your extrusion needs to go upwards, you will have to make the value a negative number.

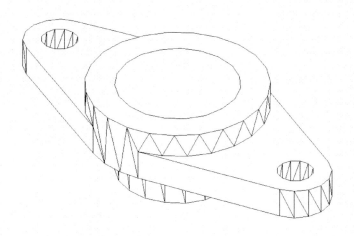

Figure 18.10

483

You are now going to use the **Subtract** editing tool to remove the cylindrical piece from the center of the model to create a hole.

73. Click on Modify from the Main Menu, highlight **Solids Editing** and select **Subtract.** The pointer turns into a **Pickbox** and a Message pops up requesting you to:

74. **Select objects:** [Here you click to select the objects you would like to keep first, in this case click on the body of the model]

75. **Select object:**

76. Click on the circle in the center of the model and press the Enter key to bore the hole.

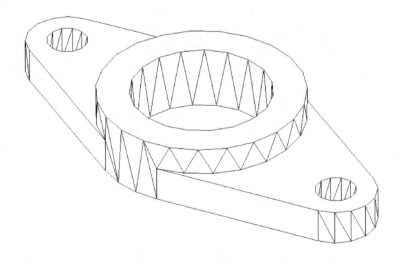

Figure 18.11

Next in this tutorial is to add a **GROOVE** inside on the circular shape. Follow these steps to add the groove to the Model. You will do so by first moving the UCS **0.44** down from the top and place a circle.

77. Type **UCS** and press the Enter key. A Message pops up requesting you to:

78. Enter an option **[New / Move / orthoGraphic / Prev / Restore / Save / Del / Apply /? /World] <World>**

79. Type '**M**" short for move and press the Enter key. A Message pops up requesting you to:

80. **Specify new origin point or [Zdepth] <0,0,0, >:**

81. Type **0, 0, -0.44** and press the Enter key.

82. The UCS icon moves down **0.44** units from the top of the Model.

You are now going to place a circle on the origin of the UCS.

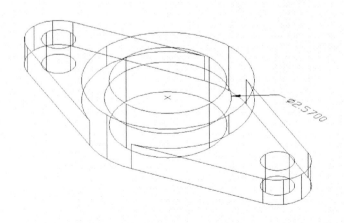

Figure 18.12

83. Type **Circle** at the Command prompt and press the Enter key. A Message pops up requesting you to:

84. **Specify center point for circle or [3P / 2P / Ttr (tan tan radius)]**

85. Type **0, 0** and press the Enter key. A Message pops up requesting you to:

86. **Specify radius of circle or [Diameter] <0.000>:** [Notice that if no prior entries have been made, the program will register **<0.000>** as above.]

87. Type **'D'** short for diameter and press the Enter key. A Message pops up requesting you to:

88. **Specify Diameter of circle <0.000>:**

89. Type **2.57** and press the Enter key to place a circle on the Origin of the UCS icon.

The next step is to extrude the circle to be used for the groove cut.

90. Click on **Draw** from the **Main Menu**, highlight **Solids**, and select **Extrude**. A Message pops up requesting you to:

91. **Select objects:**

Figure 18.13

92. Click on the Circle on the UCS icon. A Message pops up requesting you to:

93. **Specify height of extrusion or [Path]**

94. Type **0.19** and press the Enter key. A Message pops up requesting you to:

95. **Specify angle of taper for extrusion <0>:**

96. Press the Enter key to accept the default option of zero to complete the Extrusion. [Note that whichever direction the Z-axis points is the positive. If Z is pointing downwards and your extrusion needs to go upwards, you will have to make the value a negative number

You are now on the final steps to use the **Subtract** editing tool to create the groove inside of the Model.

97. Click on **Modify** from the Main Menu, highlight **Solids Editing** and select **Subtract.** The pointer turns into a **Pickbox** and a Message pops up requesting you to:
98. **Select objects:** [Here you click to select the objects you would like to keep first, in this case click on the body of the model]
99. **Select object:**
100. Click on the circle in the on top of the UCS icon and press the Enter key to bore the central hole.

Figure 18.14

SECTION:

You will proceed to create a **Section** of the part now that we have a Model with an inside Groove and holes.

Follow these steps to create a Section of the Model

100. Type **Section** at the Command prompt and press the Enter key. A Message pops up requesting you to:

101. **Select objects:**

102. Click on the edge of the model and everything gets highlighted.

103. Press the Enter key and a Message pops up requesting you to:

104. **Specify first point on the Section plane by [Object / Zaxis / View / XY / YZ / ZX / 3points] <3 points>:**

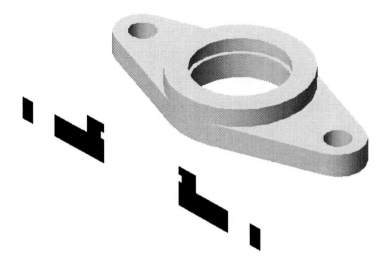

Figure 18.15

105.   Press the Enter key to accept the 3points. A message pops up requesting you to:

106.   **Specify first point on plane:**

107.   Type **'CEN'** short for center and press the enter key, move the pointer to one of the smaller holes of the model and click on it, when the pointer turns into a circle image. Notice that this will anchor the pointer with a line trailing at its end. A Message pops up requesting you to:

108.   **Specify second point on plane.**

109.   Type **'CEN'** short for center and press the enter key, move the pointer to the center and when you see an image of a circle, click to place the second point for the section. A message pops up requesting you to:

110.   **Specify third point on plane:**

111. Type **'CEN'** short for center and press the enter key, move the pointer to the other end of the model and click inside the smaller hole, when the pointer turns into a circular-shaped image.

112. Type **Move** at the command prompt and you will be requested to Select objects:

100. Click on the model and drag it to one side to see the Sectioned part. [Notice that Section leaves the base part intact with an outline of the selected profile.]

The next Tutorial will cover Slice where the Model is cut in half.

SLICE

Slice unlike **Sections**, splits the model in two halves revealing the internal Structure of the part.

Figure 18.16

490

Follow these steps to create a Slice of the part just drawn. Open AutoCAD if it is not already running on your computer.

Click on **Draw** from the Main Menu, highlight **Solids** and select **Slice.** A Message pops up requesting you to:

100.   **Select objects:**

101.   Click on the edge of the part to highlight the model and press the Enter key. A Message pops up requesting you to:

102.   **Specify first point on Slicing plane by [Object / Zaxis / View / XY / YZ / ZX / 3points] <3points>:**

103.   Type 'CEN' short for center and press the Enter key, move the pointer to the first smaller hole, when you see an image of a circle inside the hole, click on the left mouse button to place the first anchor point. A Message pops up requesting you to:

104.   **Specify second point on plane:**

105.   Type 'CEN' short for center and press the Enter key, move the pointer to the larger middle hole, when you see an image of a circle inside the hole, click on the left mouse button to place the second anchor point. A Message pops up requesting you to:

106.   **Specify third point on plane:**

107.   Type 'CEN' short for center and press the Enter key, move the pointer to the last smaller hole, when you see an image of a circle inside the hole, click on the left mouse button to place the third anchor point. A Message pops up requesting you to:

108.   **Specify a point on the desired side of the plane or [keep Both sides]**

109.   Type 'B' short for both and press the Enter key, the part should be split in two halves.

Follow these steps to view the results of the Slice.

110.   Type **MOVE** at the Command prompt and press the Enter key. A Message
        pops up requesting you to:

111.   **Select objects**

112.   Click on the edge of one of the halves. A Message pops up requesting you to:

113.   **Specify base point or displacement:**

114.   Click anywhere on the Graphics area away from the Model. A Message pops
        up requesting you to:

115.   **Specify second point of displacement or < use first point as
        displacement>:**

116.   Drag the mouse to another location and click to place one-half of the part on
        the graphics area.

This concludes the Tutorials on creating **Sections** and **Slice** of Solid Models.

<u>Summary:</u>

Tutorials in this Chapter covered topics that included:

mmm. Creating Section and Slice

nnn.　Creating Boundary

ooo.　Using the Extrude option to add depth to your sketch

ppp.　Adding a Groove inside the part

qqq.　Using Subtract to remove excess parts

rrr.　Creating Section and a Slice.

Exercise:

Design a bearing and go through the steps in adding Sections and Slice as explained in this Chapter

The next Lesson will cover **Dimensioning, Tolerance** and **Fits**

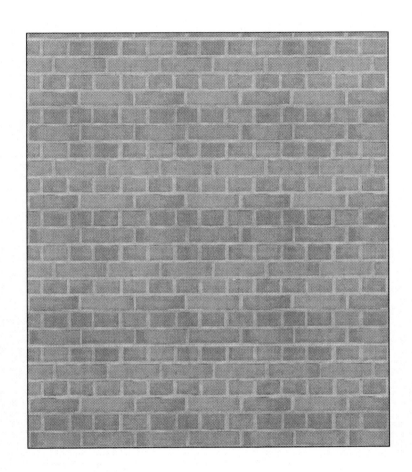

Chapter 19:

After completing this section, you will be able to:

- Add proper Dimensioning and Tolerance to the Part that you design

- Know how to draw Solid Lines

- Lineweight

- Polyline width

- Solid-Fill

- Different usage with polygons

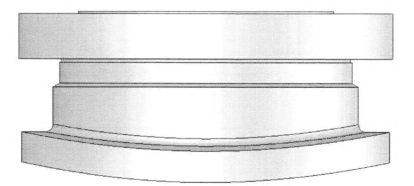

Figure 19.00

In this Tutorial, you will be guided step by step in designing a LWN RFD Long Weld Flange in 300 series class of **2.00" x 9.000"** with a Raised Face.

Start AutoCAD if it is not already running on your Computer and open a new file.

1. Type Line at the Command Prompt and use the sketch in Figure 19.01 below to complete the drawing. To add Dimensions and Tolerance to the sketch, do the following:

2. Click on Dimension from the Main Menu and select Linear. Add dimension as in Figure 19.02

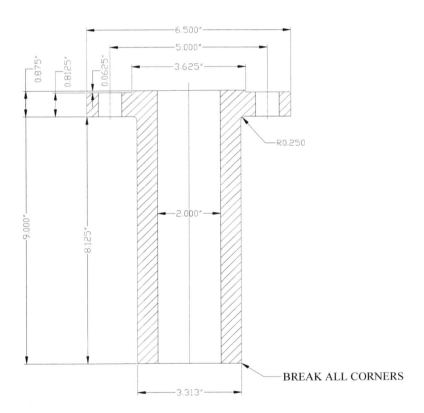

Figure 19.01

Figure 19.02

You are now going to add **Tolerance** and other **Text** to your drawing for manufacturing.

3. Double-click on **the 6.500"** dimension, the Properties dialogue box open up. Click on top of the grey strip by Text and it turns **blue** in color with an image of a **hand**.

4. Click and hold down on the Left mouse button and drag it up until you see **Text override**.

5. Click inside the empty box by the Text override a when you see the cursor blinking, type the following and press the Enter key when Finished.

6.500" %%P1/16 O.D. FLANGE

6. Double-Click on **5.000"** and following the same steps as above, type the following and press the Enter key.

8 EACH 0.750" Holes on A 5.000" %%P1/16 B.C.

7. Double-Click on **3.625"** and following the same steps as above, type the

following and press the Enter key.

$$-$$

3.625"%%P 0.03 Raised Face O.D.

8. Double-Click on **9.000"** and following the same steps as above, type the following and press the Enter key.

9.000" + 1/8\P-0

9. Double-Click on **8.125"** and following the same steps as above, type the following and press the Enter key.

8.125" Reference

10. Double-Click on **0.0625"** and following the same steps as above, type the following and press the Enter key.
0.0625" %%P1/64

11. Double-Click on **0.875"** and following the same steps as above, type the following and press the Enter key.
0.875" 1/8\P-0

12. Double-Click on **0.8125"** and following the same steps as above, type the following and press the Enter key.
0.8125"+1/8\P-0

13. Double-Click on **2.000"** and following the same steps as above, type the following and press the Enter key.
2.000"+3/32\P-1/32

14. Double-Click on **3.313"** and following the same steps as above, type the following and press the Enter key.

3.313"+3/32|P-1/32

15. Use Text to add **STD 125-250 AARH** and place it on the top face of the Flange. Place a **Surface Finish** sign as indicated in front of the STD…

16. Add also a text denoting **BREAK ALL CORNERS** at the bottom right hand corner of the barrel of the nozzle.

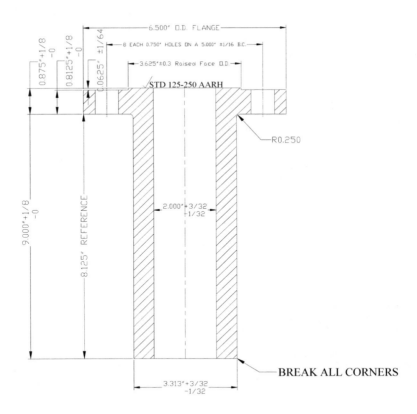

Figure 19.03

Solid-Fill:

At certain times in the design of parts, you would like to show a thick or very darkened line to emphasize a particular point.

There are three ways to accomplish this and any one you choose will work in your drawing.

    a. There is the first option where the Line weight is changed during the Layer setup

    b. Change the Width in the Polyline option to reflect the thickness of the Line

    c. Use the Solid-Filled option to add thickness to your sketch.

Lineweight:

During the setup of the Layers, you have the option to change the Lineweight from the default setting. When you click on the Lineweight under the Layer Properties Manager, the Lineweight dialogue box pops up. Refer to Figure 19.04

Change the weight by selecting a size and click on OK to exit the command.

You will not notice an immediate change in the thickness of the line; it only takes effect when your drawing is plotted.

To edit the Lineweight, double-click on the line and change the Lineweight from the Properties manger.

Polyline:

The second option is to change the width option under the Polyline command to correspond to the thickness of the Line you would like to use. To accomplish that you first type 'pl' short for Polyline and press the Enter key.

    17. Command: Pl (press the Enter key) A Message pops up requesting you to:

    18. Specify start point:

    19. Click anywhere on the graphics area. A Message pops up requesting you to:

500

20. Specify next point or [Arc/Halfwidth/Length/Undo/Width]:

21. Type **'W'** short for width and press the Enter key. A Message pops up requesting you to:

22. **Specify starting width <0.000>:**

23. Type 0.125 and press the Enter key. A Message pops up requesting you to:

24. Specify ending width <0.1250>:

25. Press the Enter key to accept the 0.1250 and press the F8 function key to start drawing the thick lines. Figure 19.05

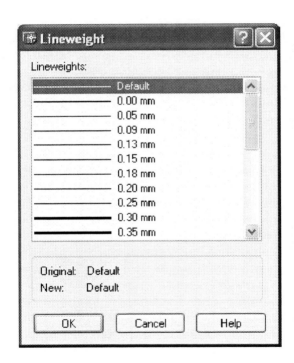

Figure 19.04

501

Figure 19.05

<u>Solid-Fill</u>

The last option is using the Solid-Fill option. To properly use the Solid-Fill you should have a sketch or an outline to be used for the Solid-Fill.

Care must be taken as regards the order in which the outline is selected to properly add the solid-fill. You will be introduced to several shapes to understand the making of Solid-fill. Let us first draw a rectangle to be used as an outline for a Solid-Filled arrowhead.

26. Command: **So** short for Solid and (press the Enter key) A Message pops up requesting you to:

27. **Specify first point:**

28. Type Mid short for midpoint and press the Enter key.

Figure 19.06

29. Move closer to the Line by the letter 'A' you should see a yellow triangular shaped object, click on it to place the first point on the rectangle. A Message pops up requesting you to:

30. Specify second point:

31. Click on the letter 'B' a Message pops up requesting you to:

32. Specify third point:

33. Click on the endpoint by the letter 'C' and press the Enter key to complete the Solid-Fill.

34. Click on one of the lines of the rectangle and press the Delete key on the keyboard. Refer to Figure 19.07

Figure 19.07

You will now use the rectangle as the sketch to add Solid-Fill to. Depending on the order you pick the points the solid-fill create a different pattern with your selection. You will first pick in the order of **'ABCD'**. Next you will pick in the order of **'ADBC'** to see the difference.

35. Command: Enter **'So'** and press the Enter key. A Message pops up requesting you to:

36. Specify first point

37. Click on the endpoint by the letter **'A'**. A Message pops up requesting you to:

38. Specify second point:

39. Click on the endpoint by the letter **'B'**. A Message pops up requesting you to:

40. **Specify third point:**

41. Click on the endpoint by the letter 'C' and. A Message pops up requesting you to:

42. **Specify third point or <exit>:**

43. Click on the endpoint by the letter 'D' to form a solid-filled shape. Hit the 'Esc' key to exit command. Refer to Figure 19.09

Figure 19.08

44. Command: Enter 'So' and press the Enter key. A Message pops up requesting you to:

45. **Specify first point**

Click on the endpoint by the letter 'A'. A Message pops up requesting you to:

Figure 19.09

46. Specify second point:

Click on the endpoint by the letter **'D'**. A Message pops up requesting you

47. Specify third point:

48. Click on the endpoint by the letter **'B'** and. A Message pops up requesting you to:

49. Specify third point or <exit>:

Click on the endpoint by the letter **'C'** to form a solid-filled shape. Hit the **'Esc'** key to exit command. Refer to Figure 19.10

Figure 19.10

You will now use a 5-Sided polygon also known as Pentagon for the Solid-Fill exercise.

50. Command: Pol short for Polygon and press the Enter key. A Message pops up requesting you to:

51. **Enter number of sides<4>:**

52. Type 5 and press the Enter key. A Message pops up requesting you to:

53. **Specify center of polygon or [Edge]:**

54. Type 0,0 and press the Enter key. A Message pops up requesting you to:

55. **Enter an option [Inscribed in circle/Circumscribed about circle <C>:**

56. Type C short for Circumscribed and press the Enter key. A Message pops up requesting you to:

57. Specify radius of circle:

58. Type 5 and press the Enter key to complete the polygon.

59. Type 'So' at the Command prompt and press the Enter key.

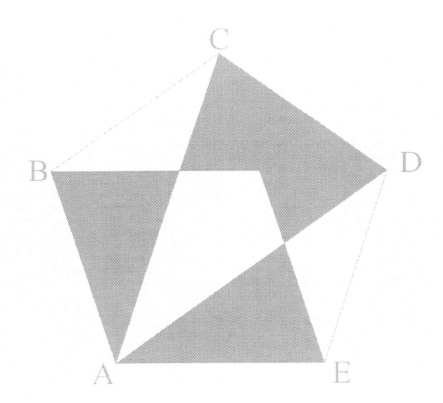

Figure 19.11

60. Command: Enter **'So'** and press the Enter key. A Message pops up requesting you to:

61. **Specify first point**

62. Click on the endpoint by the letter **'A'**. A Message pops up requesting you to:

63. **Specify third point:**

64. Click on the endpoint by the letter **'B'** and. A Message pops up requesting you to:

65. **Specify third point or \<exit\>:**

66. Click on the endpoint by the letter **'C'**. **A Message pops up requesting you to:**

67. **Specify fourth point or \<exit\>:**

68. Click on the end point by the letter **'D'** A Message pops up requesting you to:

69. Specify third point:

70. Click on the endpoint by the letter **'E'**, A Message pops up requesting you to:

71. Specify fourth point or \<exit\>:

72. Click on the endpoint by the letter **'A'** to complete the pattern as in Figure 19.12

Type **'So'** at the Command prompt and press the Enter key. Using the steps just covered above click on the endpoints in this order to find out the different pattern. **'AEBDCD'**

509

Figure 19.12

Summary:

In this chapter, you covered topics that included:

- Adding proper Dimensioning and Tolerance to the Part that you design
- Knowing how to draw Solid Lines
- Lineweight
- Polyline width
- Solid-Fill
- Different usage with polygons

Exercise:

- Use as many polygons as you can think of, starting from a **Hexagon** and add Solid-Fill to each one of them.
- Draw the Nozzle in Figure 19.01 and using the steps just covered add Dimensioning and Tolerance to the Sketch.

The next Chapter will cover **Nozzles** used in **Pressure Vessel** industry.

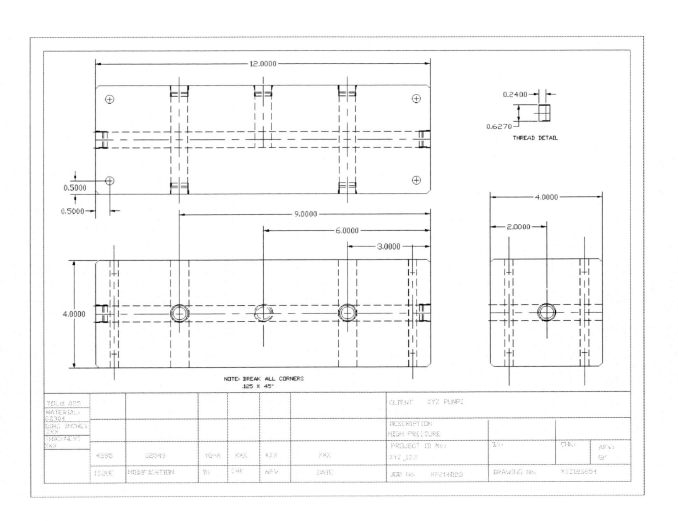

THREAD DETAIL

NOTE: BREAK ALL CORNERS
.125 X 45°

Chapter 20:

After completing this lesson you will be able to:

- ♣ Design a Nozzle and find its weight.

- ♣ Learn of the steps taken to manufacture a Nozzle

- ♣ Nozzles used in the Pressure Vessel Industry

- ♣ Manual calculations of weights of a Nozzle.

- ♣ Know the uses of Mass Properties option.

- ♣ Calculate the Volume of a vessel

- ♣ Learn to use 3D Intersection

Pressure Vessel:

Nozzles used in the Pressure Industry come in all shapes and sizes. There are Stubs, Studding Outlets, and Long Weld Necks, to name a few. A nozzle well engineered is forged machined and bottom contoured as required. The weight on the flat-bottomed straight barrel nozzle is easy to generate, out by finding the Volume of the Cylinder and calculating the weights thereof.

A nozzle with Spherical and Cylindrical contour, which will be welded unto a Head or Shell from the center of the cylinder or the Hillside, will take a lot of calculations to obtain the right results.

With AutoCAD, such complex shapes can be drawn and the Volume and its weight mathematically calculated accurately, with the aid of the **Mass Property** Tool. You will be guided step by step as to how to do all the weight and volume calculation for any Vessel in the Pressure Vessel industry.

For an example the Weight of a hollow cylinder be calculated by first finding the volume of the cylinder using the Formula $V=\Pi*r^2*h$. You will then calculate the weight using the results from the Volume. $V=\Pi*r^2*h$

Given (OD) Diameter = 12.50

Height = 4.00in

ID (Inner Diameter) = 6.00in

Calculate the Weight of the outer Cylinder.

$V=\Pi*r^2*h$ $V = (\Pi*6^2*4)$ $V = 490.873in^3$ .... (1)

$V=\Pi*r^2*h$ $V = (\Pi*3^2*4)$ $V = 113.10\ in^3$ .... (2)

Volume (1) – Volume (2)

$490.873in^2$ - $113.10\ in^2$ = 377.773

There are 0.2833lbs / in^3

Therefore 377.773 * $0.2833in^3$ = 107lbs

The weight of the said Cylinder is therefore equal to: 107.02 lbs.

Now how will you calculate a Complex shape like the one in Figure 16.02?

Pressure Vessel Nozzles:

Nozzles used in the Pressure Vessel Industry come in all shapes and sizes. There are **Stubs, Studding Outlets**, and **Long Weld Necks**, to name a few. A nozzle well engineered is forged machined and bottom contoured as required. The flat-bottomed straight barrel nozzle is easy to figure out by finding the Volume of the Cylinder and calculating the weights thereof.

A nozzle with **Spherical** and **Cylindrical** contour, which will be welded unto a **Head** or **Shell** from the center of the cylinder or the **Hillside**, will take a lot of calculations to obtain the right results.

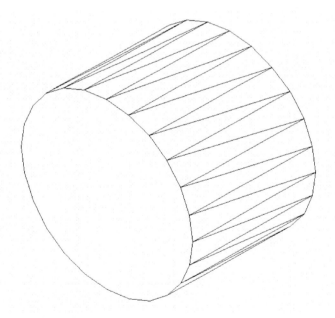

Figure 20.00

Billet

This is a Block of Steel of material **SA182-F11** to be used in producing a **24.00 X 600# X 25.375 V RFD Q-Type W/NS.**

This will go through different processes from **UT** testing to **Turning** and finally **Milling** to achieve the Bottom Contour as indicated in Figure 16.02.

<u>Mass Properties</u>

Mass: 26464.7765

Volume: 26464.7765

Bounding box: X: 0.0000 -- 36.0000

        Y: 0.0000 -- 26.0000

        Z: -18.0000 -- 18.0000

Centroid: X: 18.0000

        Y: 13.0000

        Z: 0.0000

Moments of inertia: X: 8107043.2054

        Y: 12861881.3857

        Z: 16681630.7959

Products of inertia: XY: 6192757.7042

        YZ: 0.0000

        ZX: 0.0000

Radii of gyration: X: 17.5024

        Y: 22.0454

        Z: 25.1064

Principal moments and X-Y-Z directions about centroid:

        I: 3634495.9746 along [1.0000 0.0000 0.0000]

        J: 4287293.7952 along [0.0000 1.0000 0.0000]

K: 3634495.9746 along [0.0000 0.0000 1.0000]

26464.7765lb / in^3 X 0.2833 in^3 = 7497.47lb

Front View

Figure 20.01

Right Side View

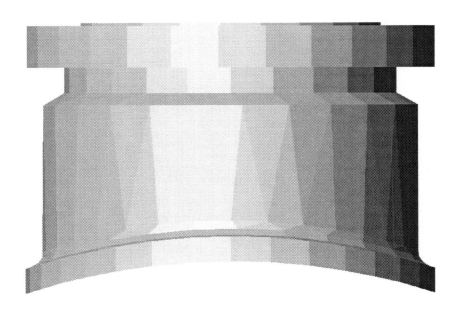

Figure 20.02

Isometric View

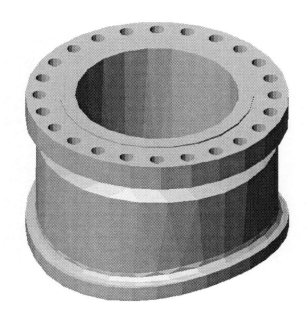

Figure 20.03

Mass: 11543.1651
Volume: 11543.1651
Bounding box: X: -18.5352 -- 18.5353
Y: -25.3130 -- 0.0000
Z: -15.0502 -- 21.9553
Centroid: X: -0.0002
Y: -12.0956
Z: 3.4549
Moments of inertia: X: 3665221.8559
Y: 2637819.2289
Z: 3478159.5320
Products of inertia: XY: 30.4413
YZ: -482377.8088
ZX: -2.4610
Radii of gyration: X: 17.8192

$11543.1651 \text{lb} / \text{in}^3 \times 0.2833 \text{ in}^3 = 3270.18 \text{lb}$

3D Intersection

Summary:

This chapter covered topics that included the user learning about

- Nozzles as used in Pressure Industry

- Designing a Nozzle and finding its weight.

- Learning of the steps taken to manufacture a Nozzle

- Learning of type of Nozzles are used in the Pressure Vessel Industry

- Manual calculations of weights of a Nozzle.

- Knowing the uses of Mass Properties option.

- Calculating the Volume of a vessel

Exercise

- Use the Sketch in Figure 3.10 Extrude the Sketch **10 inches** and use Mass properties to calculate the weight of the Model

- The second object is a 3D studding Outlet model

- The last model is an RH Tool Post, create a drawing and calculate the weight.

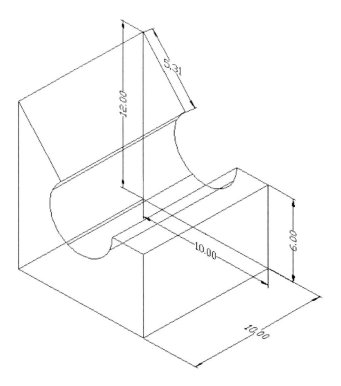

Figure 20.04

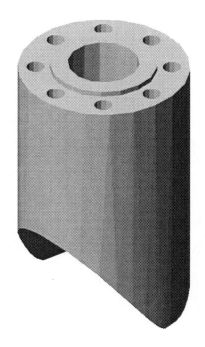

Figure 20.05

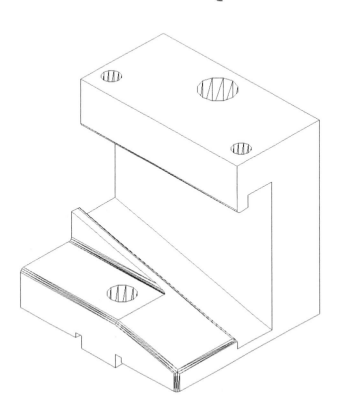

Figure 20.06

The next Chapter will cover **Material Mapping**, **Projection** and **Rendering**

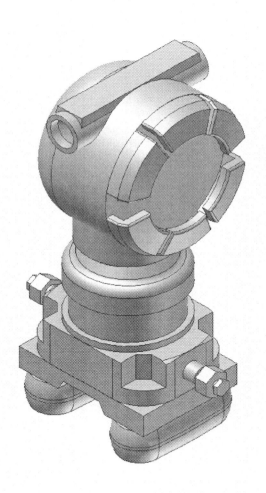

Chapter 21:

After completing this Chapter, you will be able to:

- Use Mapping on Solid Objects
- Draw simple 3D objects and add materials to it
- Use Projection unto Solid Objects
- Know of Planar, Cylindrical, Spherical and Solid Projections
- Know the uses of the Materials dialogue Box
- Know how to Insert Images
- Use the Rendering Tool
- Know of the New Standard Material Dialogue box
- Learn of Bitmap File Dialogue box
- Know the uses of the Attach option

Mapping

Mapping is a process whereby materials are attached to 3D objects to form a Pattern on the surface of the object.

There are two types of Mapping, the Fixed Scale Mapping and the Fit to Object mapping.

In the Fixed scale mapping, the material is not stretched unto the object but tiled to the boundaries.

Fixed Scale mapping is utilized in areas where there appear multiple patterns.

Unlike the Fixed Scale, the Fit to object mapping is stretched or shrunk to Fit the object.

Fit to Objects can be used on Landscape as well as Floor tiling

You will be introduced to steps taken in designing each of the two options.

Projection

Projection as the word implies is used to project an image unto the Surface of a Solid object.

There is **Planar** projection, **Cylindrical**, **Spherical** as well as **Solid** projection

Planar Projection:

Planar projection scales the image to fit the surface and does not distort the texture of the image.

Imagine projecting a film or slide unto a surface this is the form Planar Projection depicts when it is used.

Cylindrical Projection:

Cylindrical objects are used in mapping images unto its surface, leaving the top and bottom surface free of any projected images.

Spherical Projection:

Both the Vertical and Horizontal edges are used to cover the texture unto the surface.

Solid Projection:

Coordinates that the user specifies are used to map the texture unto the Solid object. Solid objects appear in 3D thus it uses three-dimensional coordinates of U,V, W to project the images.

The 'U' corresponds to the X coordinate as related to the UCS, 'V' the Y coordinate and 'W' the Z coordinate.

You will first be introduced to Fixed Scale mapping and to do that start AutoCAD if it is not already running on your machine and open a new file.

1. Type Circle at the Command prompt and press the Enter key. A Message pops up requesting you to:
2. **Specify first point for circle or [3P / 2P/ Ttr (tan tan radius)]:**
3. Type **0, 0** and press the Enter key. A Message pops up requesting you to:

528

4. **Specify radius of circle or [Diameter]:**

5. Type **5** and press the enter key, a Circle is drawn at the Origin of the UCS

You are now going to add depth to the circle to turn it into a 3D model.

6. Type Extrude at the Command Prompt and press the Enter key. A Message pops up requesting you to:

7. **Select the objects:**

8. Click on the circle and press the Enter key. A Message pops up requesting you to:

9. **Specify height of extrusion or [Path]:**

10. Type '**10**' and press the Enter key. A Message pops up requesting you to:

11. **Specify angle of taper for extrusion<0>:**

12. Press the Enter key again to complete the extrusion.

To see the 3D object just created, click on the SE Isometric view from the View Toolbar in Figure 21.00

Figure 21.00

The next objective is to create a new mapping texture and project it unto the surface of the cylinder. AutoCAD is loaded with **.tga** images which could be accessed and loaded from a File and attached to you're the 3D model.
Follow these steps to import and project an image unto the cylinder surface.

13. Click on View; highlight Render and select materials from the list of tools,

the **Materials** dialogue box opens up. Refer to Figure 21.02

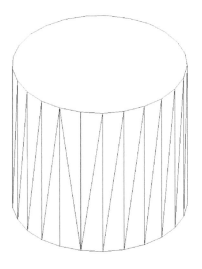

Figure 21.01

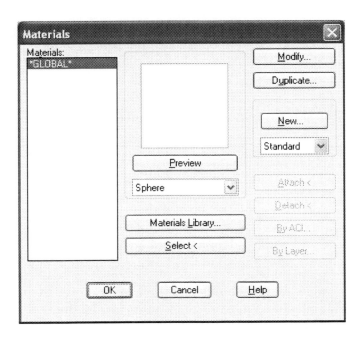

21.02

14. Click on <u>N</u>ew o open the **New Standard Material** dialogue box. Refer to Figure 21.03

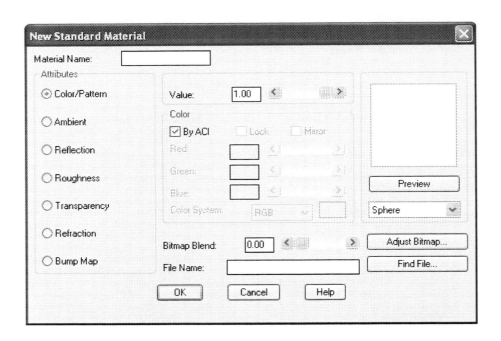

Figure 21.03

15. Inside the empty box by Material Name, enter a related name of the pattern to be projected unto the surface of the cylinder. For our purpose let us enter Pattern1 and click on **Find File**. The Bitmap File opens up with a list of .tga files

16. Highlight a File and click Open. Back in the New Standard Material dialogue box, click on Preview to see the image first hand.

17. Click on Ok to go back to the **Materials** dialogue box.

18. Click on Attach from the Materials dialogue box to go to the Graphics area and you will be requested to:

19. **Select objects to attach 'Pattern1" to:**

20. Click on the Solid Cylinder and press the Enter key

21. Back in the Materials dialogue box, click on OK to complete the attachment.

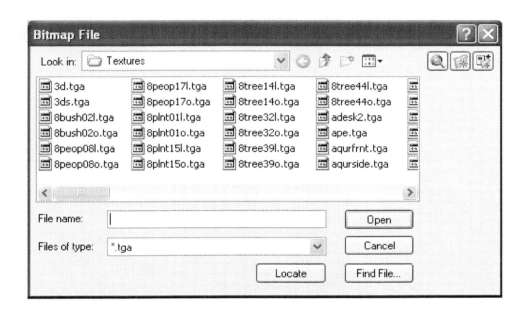

Figure 21.04

Render:

Render is used in creating a photo realistic shaded image of a Solid Model.

You are now going to Render the Model to Project the image unto it.

22. Click on **View** from the Main Menu, highlight **Render** and click on Render, the Render dialogue box opens up. Refer to Figure 21.05

23. Expand the arrow by the **Rendering Type** and select **Photo Raytrace**

24. Click on the arrow under Destination and select **Render Window**

25. Finally click on **Render** at the bottom left of the dialogue box to add the image to the cylinder. Refer to Figure 21.06

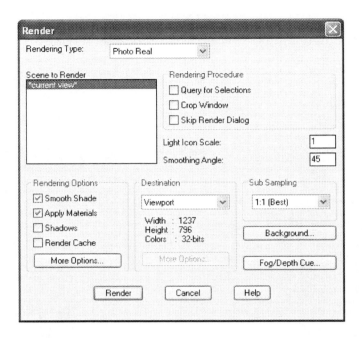

Figure 21.05

Figure 21.06

The next Tutorials will cover Fit to Objects and we will utilize Floor Tiling.

26. Click on Draw from the Main Menu and select Rectangle. A Message pops up requesting you to:

27. **Specify first corner point or [Chamfer / Elevation / Fillet / Thickness / Width]:**

28. Type **0, 0** at the Command prompt and press the Enter key. A Message pops up requesting you to:

29. **Specify other corner point or [Dimension]:**

30. Type **8,8** and press the Enter key

Figure 21.07

31. Click on the SE Isometric from the View Toolbar. Refer to Figure 21.07

You are now going to add depth to the Rectangle to turn it into a 3D Model

32. Click on **Draw** from the Main Menu, highlight **Solids** and select **Extrude**. A Message pops up requesting you to:

33. **Select objects:**

34. Type **'All'** and press the Enter key twice. Note! You are going to type ALL without the colon. A Message pops up requesting you to:

35. **Specify height of extrusion or [Path]:**

36. Type **0.25** and press the Enter key. A Message pops up requesting you to:

37. **Specify angle of taper for extrusion <0>:**

38. Press the Enter key to add the extrusion. Refer to Figure 21.08

Figure 21.08

39. Click on View; highlight Render and select materials from the list of tools, the Materials dialogue box opens up. Refer to Figure 21.09

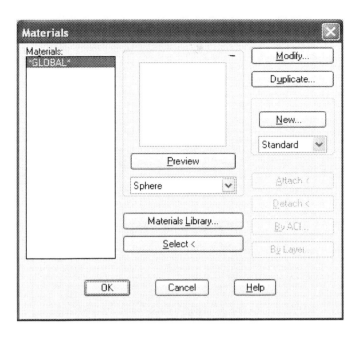

Figure 21.09

40. Click on <u>N</u>ew o open the **New Standard Material** dialogue box. Refer to Figure 21.10

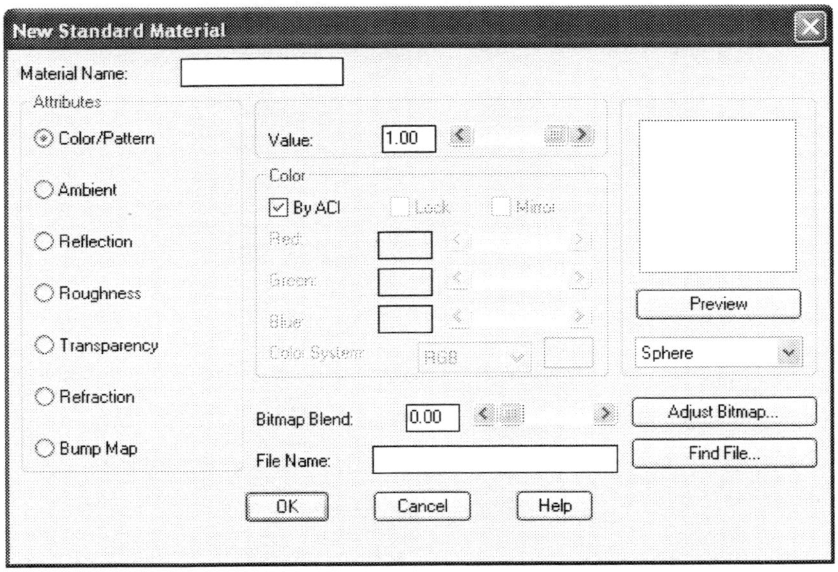

Figure 21.10

41. Inside the empty box by **Material Name**, enter a related name of the pattern to be projected unto the surface of the cylinder. For our purpose let us enter **Tile1** and click on **Find File**. The Bitmap File opens up with a list of .tga files

42. Highlight a File and click Open. Back in the New Standard Material dialogue box, click on Preview to see the image first hand. Refer to Figure 21.12

43. Click on Ok to go back to the **Materials** dialogue box.

44. Click on Attach from the Materials dialogue box to go to the Graphics area and you will be requested to:

45. Select objects to attach 'Tile1" to:

46. Click on the Rectangular solid and press the Enter key

47. Back in the Materials dialogue box, click on OK to complete the attachment.

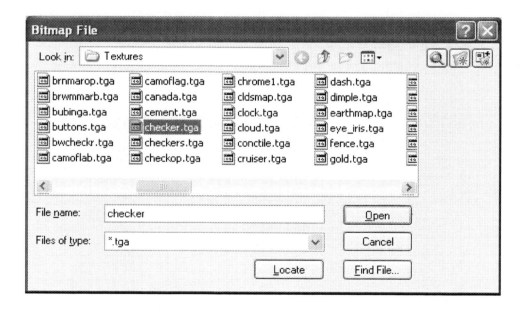

Figure 21.11

48. Click on Ok from the **New Standard Material** to go back to the **Materials** dialogue box. Refer to figure 21.13

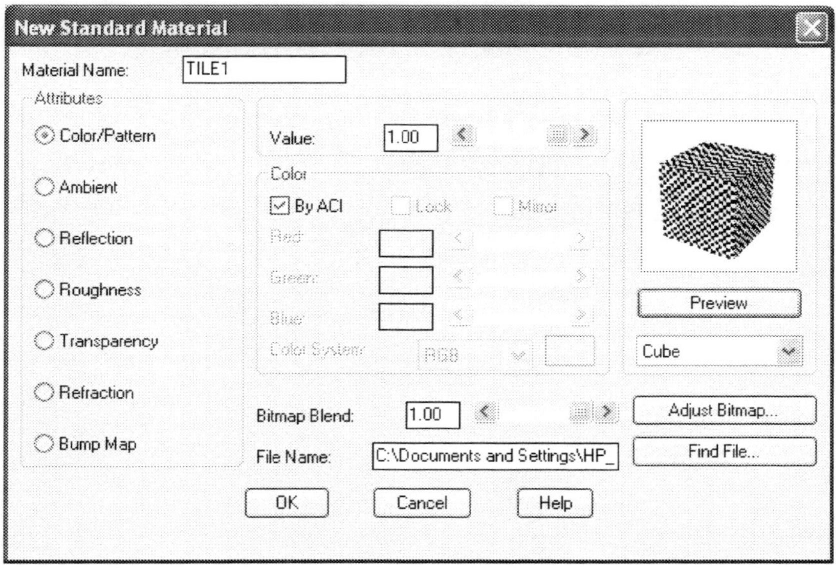

Figure 21.12

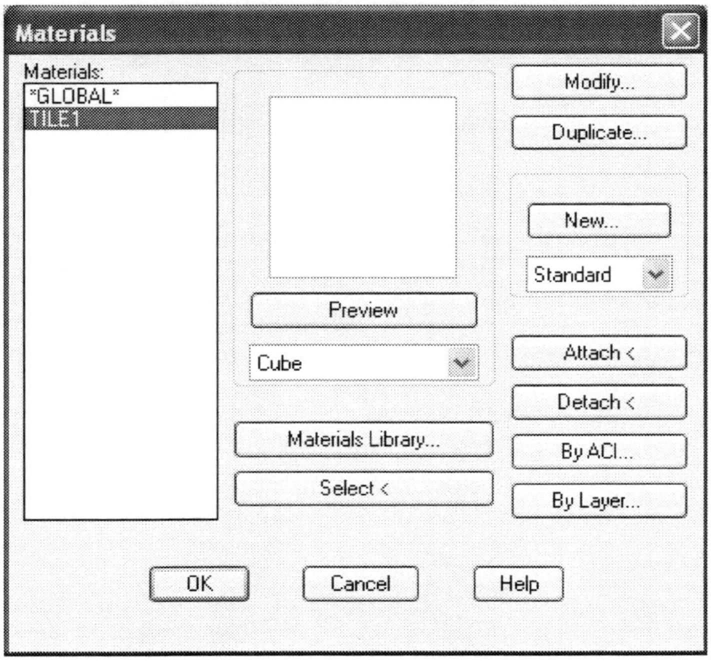

Figure 21.13

49. Click on **Attach** from the Materials dialogue box and click on the Rectangular Solid. A Message pops up requesting you to:

50. Select objects to attach "TILE1" to:

51. Click on the Rectangular Solid and press the Enter key.

52. Back in the Materials dialogue box, click on OK to complete adding the image to the solid.

Render:

Render is used in creating a photo realistic shaded image of a Solid Model.

You are now going to Render the Model to Project the image unto it.

53. Click on **View** from the Main Menu, highlight **Render** and click on Render, the Render dialogue box opens up. Refer to Figure 21.14

54. Expand the arrow by the **Rendering Type** and select **Photo Raytrace**

55. Click on the arrow under Destination and select **Render Window**

56. Finally click on **Render** at the bottom left of the dialogue box to add the image to the rectangular solid. Refer to Figure 21.15

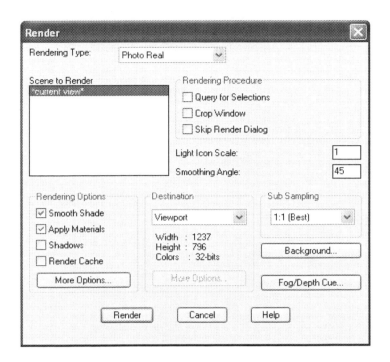

Figure 21.14

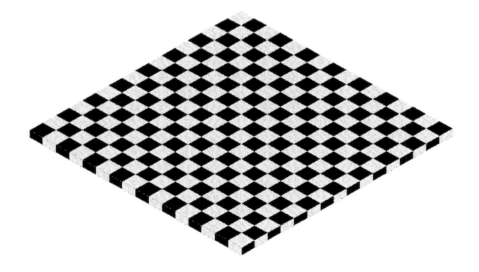

Figure 21.15

Summary:

In this Chapter you covered different topics that included:

- Using Mapping on Solid Objects
- Drawing simple 3D objects and add materials to it
- Using Projection unto Solid Objects
- Knowing of Planar, Cylindrical, Spherical and Solid Projections
- Knowing the uses of the Materials dialogue Box
- Knowing how to Insert Images
- Using the Rendering Tool
- Knowing of the New Standard Material Dialogue box
- Learning of Bitmap File Dialogue box
- Knowing the uses of the Attach option

Exercise

Draw an irregular shape, add extrusion to the sketch and attach a Landscape Material to it.

Render the Solid and save the Model

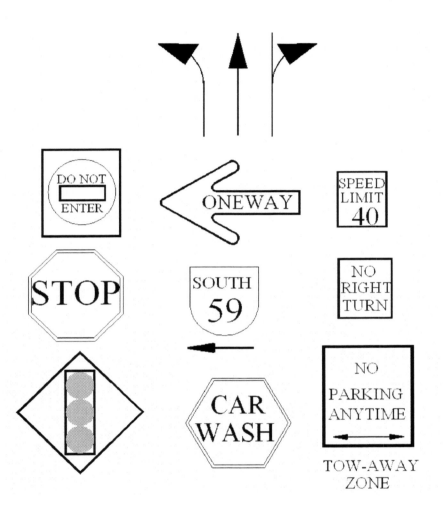

Chapter 22:

After completing this chapter, you will be able to:

- Use all the options in the Lengthen Tool, including:
- Delta
- Angle
- Percent
- Total
- Dynamic
- Convert Imperial Feet and Inches into Metric and vice versa
- Pixel
- Cover Raster Images.

Start AutoCAD if it is not already running on your computer and start a new file and click on Draw from the Main Menu and select Line. A Message pops up requesting you to:

1. **Specify first point:**
2. Type 0,0 and press the Enter key. A Message pops up requesting you to:
3. **Specify next point or [Undo]:**
4. Type 10,0 and press the Enter key twice.
5. Type **Z** and press the Enter key. A Message pops up requesting you to select from a list:
6. **[All / Center /Dynamic / Extends / Previous / Scale / Window] <real time>:**
7. Type **E** short for Extends and press the Enter key the Line should be centered on the Graphics area.

8. Click on Dimension from the Main Menu and add a Linear dimension to the Line. Refer to Figure 22.00

9. Click on Modify from the Main Menu and select **Lengthen**. A Message pops up requesting you to:

10. **Select an Object or [Delta / Percent / Total / Dynamic]:**

11. Type **DE** short for Delta and press the Enter key. You will be requested to:

12. **Enter delta length or [Angle] <0.0000>:**

13. Type **2** and press the Enter key. A Message pops up requesting you to:

14. Select an object to change or [Undo]:

15. Click on the midpoint of the Line just drawn and watch it extend 2 units to one side. Click on it again to extend 2 units to the opposite side.

16. When you press the Enter key the Dimension line should jump to the endpoints of the Line to correspond to the change.

If you would like to extend the Line in one direction, click towards the end of the Line.

Angle

The Angle under the delta option is uses the curvature of an Arc to add an extension to it. We will therefore draw an arc for this tutorial.

17. Click on **Draw** from the Main Menu and highlight **Arc** and select **Start, End, and Radius** from the list of items. A Message pops up requesting you to:

18. **Specify start point of arc or [Center]:**

19. Type **5,0** and press the Enter key. A Message pops up requesting you to:

20. **Specify end point of arc:**

21. Type **0,0** and press the Enter key. A Message pops up requesting that you:

22. **Specify center of arc or [Angle / Direction / radius]:**

23. Type **5** and press the Enter key to exit the command.

24. Click on Dimension from the Main Menu and add Linear dimension to the ends of the arc. Refer to Figure 22.01

10.0000

Figure 22.00

25. Click on **Modify** from the Main Menu and select **Lengthen** A Message pops up requesting you to:

26. **Select an Object or [Delta / Percent / Total / Dynamic]:**

27. Type **DE** short for Delta and press the Enter key. A Message pops up requesting you to:

28. Enter delta length or [Angle] <2.000>:

29. Type **A** short for Angle and press the Enter key. A Message pops up requesting you to:

30. Enter delta angle <0>:

31. Type **55** and press the Enter key. A Message pops up requesting you to:

32. Select an object to change or [Undo]:

33. Click on the arc to extend the arc line. When you press the Enter key, the Dimension should jump to the endpoint of the arc.

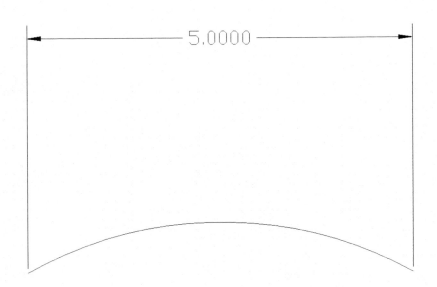

Figure 22.01

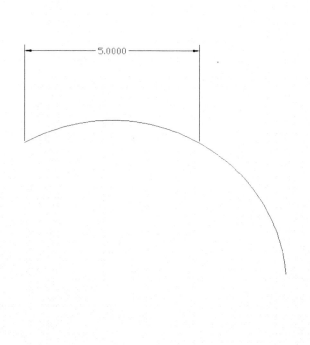

Figure 22.02

Percent

The next Tutorial will cover Percent. This option request the user to enter a percent value, which is used to convert the line to an equal length as indicated.
You will use the same Line you worked with on creating the Delta length.

34. Click on **Modify** from the Main Menu and select **Lengthen**. A Message pops up requesting you to:

35. **Select an Object or [Delta / Percent / Total / Dynamic]:**

36. Type **P** short for Percent and press the Enter key. A Message pops up requesting you to:

37. **Enter percentage length <100.0000>:**

38. Type **50** and press the Enter key. A Message pops up requesting you to:

39. **Select an object to change or [Undo]:**

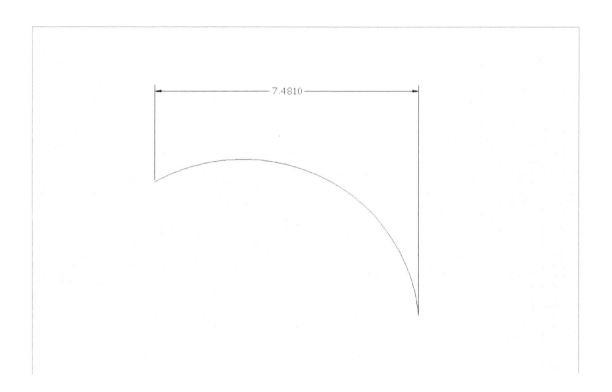

Figure 22.03

40. Click on the endpoint away from the Origin and the dimension Line will adjust to fit a reduced Line of 50 percent.

__Total__

The next Tutorial will cover Total. Total reduces the Line a Total of the entered value. You will use the same Line to go through this tutorial.

Figure 22.04

41. Click on Modify from the Main Menu and select **Lengthen**. A Message pops up requesting you to:

42. **Select an Object or [Delta / Percent / Total / Dynamic]:**

43. Type **T** short for Total and press the Enter key. You will be requested to:

44. Specify total length or [Angle] <1.0000>:

45. Type **2** and press the Enter key. A Message pops up requesting you to:

46. Select an object to change or [Undo]:

47. Click on the end of the Line away from the Origin and press the Enter key. The Line should be reduced to a total of 2 units.

48. When you press the Enter key the Dimension line should jump to the endpoints of the Line to correspond to the change.

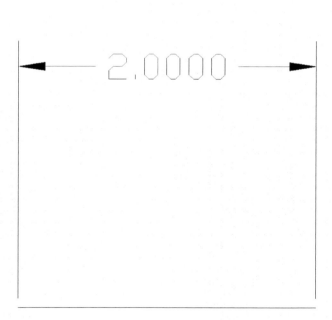

Figure 22.05

Dynamic:

You will use the same Line you drew to start the Lengthen operation in this tutorial. Click on Modify from the Main Menu and select Lengthen. A Message pops up requesting you to:

49. **Select an object or [Delta / Percent / Total / Dynamic]:**

50. Type **DY** short for Dynamic and press the Enter key. A Message pops up requesting you to:

51. **Select an object to change or [Undo]:**

52. Click on the 2-inch Line. A Message pops up requesting you to:

53. **Specify new end point:**

54. Type 8 and press the Enter key 2 times.

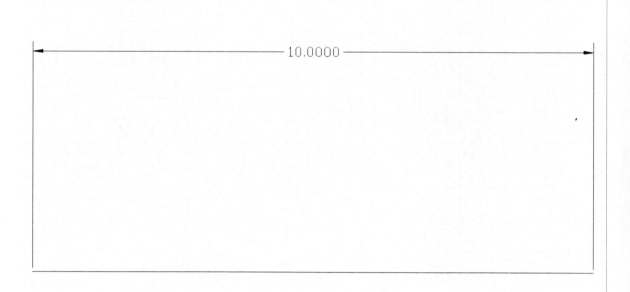

Figure 22.06

Units conversion:

Designers often start a Drawing in one Unit and realize the wrong one was chosen after completing about a third of their project.

Converting Drawings from Imperial Feet and Inches to Metric and Vice Versa is very essential in design and AutoCAD allows the designer to be able to make the conversions.

The first step is to make sure the New File will open the Startup Dialogue box. Do the following to set up the Startup Dialogue Box.

With the current drawing you would like to change from Imperial Feet and Inches on your screen, right-click in front of the **Command** at the bottom-left hand corner of the Graphics area.

55. Click on **Options** to bring up the Options Dialogue box.

56. Click on **System** under the Options Dialogue Box towards the center of the Dialogue Box.

57. Expand the arrow by **Startup** and click to select **Show Startup Dialogue box.**

58. Click on Apply and click on OK to exit.

59. Click on **Edit** from the main Menu, click on **Select All.**

60. Click on **Edit** again and click on **Copy.**

61. Click on File, New and when the Startup Dialogue box opens up, click on Start from Scratch option.

62. Click inside the radio button by Metric to select it.

63. Click on Edit and select Paste from the list of items.

64. Click anywhere on the Graphics area to insert the drawing with Metric Units.

65. Type **Z** and press the Enter key and hit **E** and press the Enter key again to expand the drawing unto your screen.

66. Reverse the operation for the other units.

PIXEL

Graphic images are made of millions of Pixels, short form for Picture Element, pictures are displayed on Graphic monitors by dividing the display area into multiple of Pixels.

These tiny square-shaped elements are arranged in columns and rows, which are packed, so closed to one another that they appear to be connected to one another. Refer to the Help files for more on Pixels.

<u>Raster Images:</u>

Pixels are used to form Raster Images like small rectangular patterns, pixels are used to project shapes that appear to the eye as one image but in effect combination of multiple square dots.

Image file formats that are supported by AutoCAD include extensions of **.BMP, TARGA, .JPEG, . FF** and many more. Refer to the Help Files for a complete list of supported formats.

You will now create a drawing to be used as a Raster image insert for a 2D drawing.

67. Using the Rectangle and Circle tools, draw the sketch in Figure 22.07 and save it as Puff.

68. Draw a Horizontal Line from the Midpoint of the rectangle, to be used as a Mirror line.

69. Go to Modify on the Main Menu select Trim from the list of items and remove excess arcs and lines from your sketch. Refer to Figure 22.08

70. Click on Draw from the Main Menu and select Boundary. Click on Pick Points from the Boundary Dialogue box, click inside the shape in

Figure 22.08 and press the Enter key.

71. Click on Draw from the Main Menu, highlight Solids and click to select **Revolve. You will be requested to:**

72. Select objects

73. Click on one of the Lines of the object in Figure 22.08 and press the Enter key.

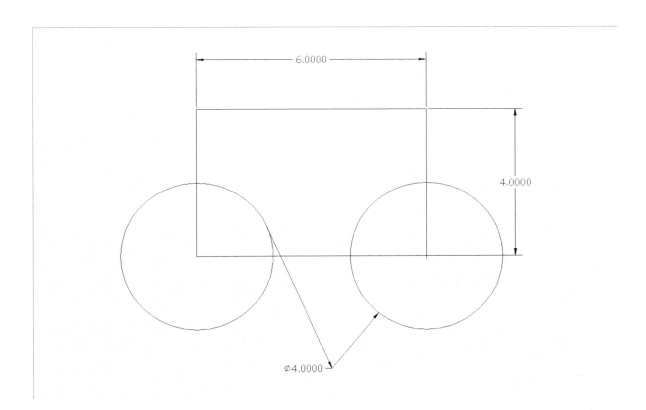

Figure 22.07

74. Define axis by [Object/X (axis)/Y (axis)]:

75. Click on the endpoints of the Top Horizontal Line and press the Enter key. A Message pops up requesting you to:

76. Specify angle of revolution <360>:

77. Press the Enter key again to complete the revolve operation.

554

78. Click on **SE Isometric** and change the color to brown or red.

79. Go to **View** on the Main Menu, highlight Shaded and select **Gouraud Shaded**

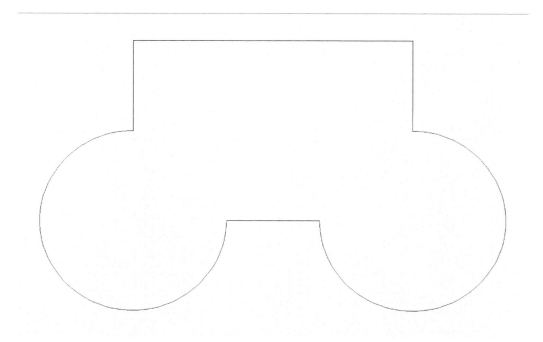

Figure 22.08

80. Save the Model as Puff2 in a known location.

81. Click on File, highlight **Export** and Save it as a **Bitmap** in a known location.

82. Open the File saved as Puff Refer to Figure 22.07.

83. Click on **Insert** from the Main Menu and select **Raster Image**

84. Open the location where the 3D image is saved and open to insert it on to your drawing.

85. When you click on Open, the Image Dialogue box opens up. Refer to Figure 22.10

86. Click on Ok. A Message pops up requesting you to:

87. Specify insertion point <0,0>:

88. Click on the Top-Right corner of the Graphics area. A Message pops up requesting you to:

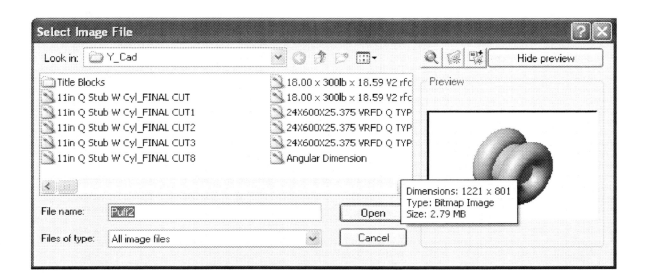

Figure 22.09

89. Specify scale factor <1>:

90. Type **10** or any preferable figure and press the Enter key.

If you prefer to retain, the **Frame** around the Model save your drawing as such.

To get rid of the Frame, click on Modify from the Main Menu, highlight object and select Image and click on Frame.

Type **OFF** and press the Enter key to remove the Frame around the Model and save your drawing. Refer to Figure 22.11

556

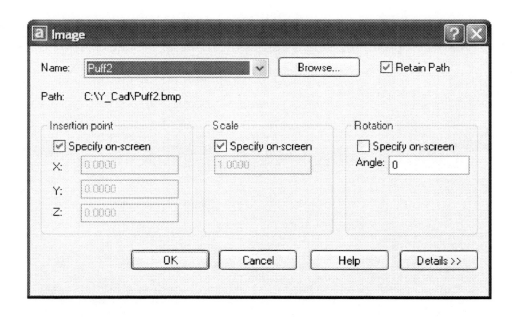

Figure 22.10

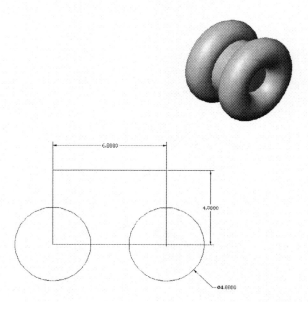

Figure 22.11

Summary:

You covered topics that included:

- Using all the options in the Lengthen Tool, including:
- Delta
- Angle
- Percent
- Total
- Dynamic
- Converted Imperial Feet and Inches into Metric and vice versa
- Learning the meaning of Pixel
- Covering Raster Images.

Exercise:

With the aid of the Tutorials, create a sketch of a Part, extrude or revolve the part and insert it as a Raster Image into the original sketch drawing.

Save your project.

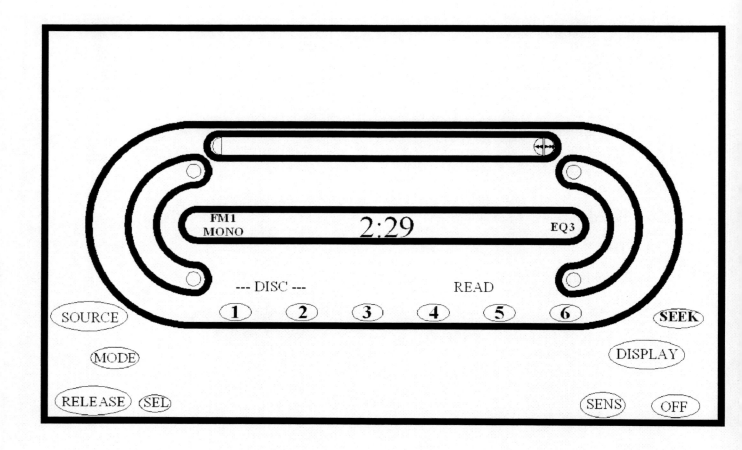

Chapter 23:

You will use the Part you designed for the Raster image found on Figure 22.11 After completing this chapter, you will be able to:

1. Take a solid Model and create a Mold Cavity with the part.

2. Properly know the many uses of Mold Cavity

3. Learn how to create a Mold Base

4. Use the Slice option for 3D objects

5. Use the Subtract option to remove parts

Mold and Cavity:

Plastic Molding, especially in the automotive industry has expanded rapidly using plastics and composite materials to replace parts forged previously from steel, thus saving cost in the manufacturing processes.

Parts that include the steering wheel, blow driers, toys, computer parts and different Gadgets are produced through molding.

To create a mold, you first design the part; create the mold base, normally, which is a little bit larger than the part it will contain, and merge the two pieces together in an assembly.

Follow these steps to create the Mold Base. Open AutoCAD if it is not already running on your computer and load the Puff Part.

6. Click on View from the Main Menu, highlight **3D Views** and select **SE Isometric View.**

7. Type **'Rec'** short form for Rectangle at the Command prompt and press the Enter key. A message pops requesting you to:

8. Specify first corner point or [Chamfer/Elevation/Fillet/Thickness/Width]:

9. Draw a Rectangle larger than the Model and extrude it to cover the Model. Refer to Figure 23.01

<u>SLICE:</u>

You are now going to use the Slice option to create the Mold Cavity

10. Type Slice at the Command prompt and press the enter key. A Message pops up requesting you to:

11. **Select objects:**

12. Click on the Box and press the Enter key. A Message pops up requesting you to:

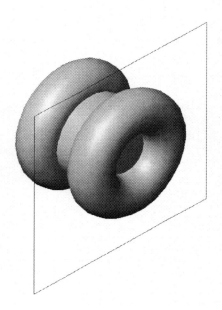

Figure 23.00

13. Specify first point on slicing plane by

[Object/Zaxis/View/XY/YZ/ZX/3points]

14. Press the Enter key to accept the '3points'. A Message pops up requesting

you to:

15. Specify first point on plane:

Figure 23.01

16. Click on the bottom edge of the box and press the Enter key. A Message

pops up requesting you to:

17. Specify second point on plane:

18. Click on the opposite edge: A Message pops up requesting you to:

19. Specify third point on plane: A Message pops up requesting you to:

562

20. **Specify a point on desired side of the plane or [keep Both sides]:**

21. Type '**B**' short for Both and press the Enter key. The Model should be sliced into two halves.

22. Type **Move** at the Command prompt and press the Enter key. A Message pops up requesting you to:

23. **Select objects:**

24. Click on the edge of the box. A Message pops up requesting you to:

25. **Specify base point or displacement:**

26. Click and hold down on the left mouse button, drag and drop one half in a different location. Refer to Figure 23.02

Subtract:

This is the point where you subtract the Puff from the box to form a Cavity Mold of the part. This action creates an imprint of the outline of the part in the box. Type Subtract at the command prompt and press the enter key.

27. Command: **Subtract** (Press the Enter key) A Message pops up requesting you:

28. **Select objects:**

29. Click on the box and press the Enter key. A Message pops up requesting you to:

30. **Select objects:**

31. Click on the inserted part, the Puff and press the Enter key again.

563

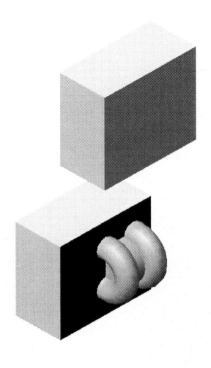

Figure 23.02

The Puff is removed from the box leaving a Cavity of the outline of the Part Imprinted in the Box. Refer to Figure 23.03

Figure 23.03

Summary:

In this Chapter, you learned among other things the uses of Mold Cavity and covered other options that included:

- Taking a solid Model and creating a Mold Cavity with the part.
- Knowing how to Properly use Mold Cavity
- Learning how to create a Mold Base
- Using the Slice for 3D objects
- Using the Subtract option to remove parts

Exercise:

Draw a Solid Model or use an already designed part to create a Mold Cavity by following the steps given in Chapter 23.

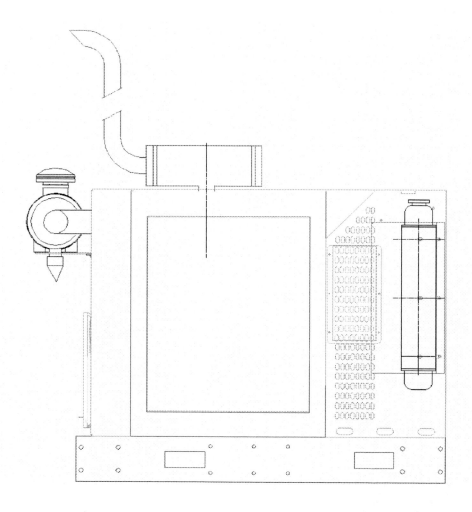

Chapter 24:

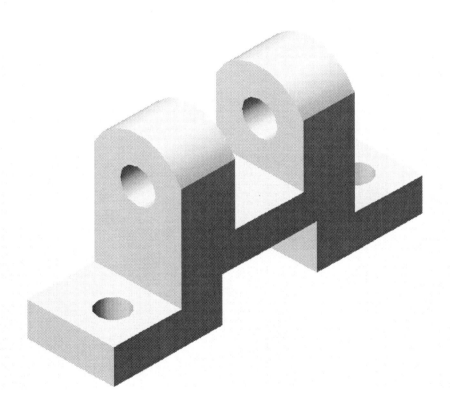

Figure 24.00

After completing this Chapter, you should be able to:

- Use Multiview Projection
- Start a new sketch and use projections to turn it into the required views
- Use Absolute and Relative coordinate to draw with the aid of the keyboard
- Set up the Top, Front and the Right-Side views
- Add Holes and extrude to form solid cylinders
- Use the Subtract command to turn the extruded cylinders into holes
- Insert Raster Images
- Create 3D drawings
- Calculate lb weight of the solid 3D part.
- Creating 3D drawings
- Using Viewports
- Learn and use Dimlfac
- Discover the Model Space
- Discover the Paper Space

Multiview Projection:

After finishing a drawing, the next step is to create different views to be able to communicate your thoughts to the end user, the drafter or the machinist. Different views of the drawing should be laid out for better understanding that include the calculated weight, properly placed dimension and tolerance and if possible a 3D view of how the finished part will look like, inserted at the upper right hand.

In 2D drawings, models saved as a **Bitmap** or **Jpeg** can be inserted into the drawing as a **Raster Image**, to represent the finished part. In a Multiview, 3D views are projected as the Top, Front, Right Side and Isometric Views.

You will be guided in all the stages from the first sketch to the finished Part.

Given a Part as in Figure 24.00 to sketch, you will first draw the Top view taken into account the position of all the holes and angular cuts.

The right side view will be represented next by also projecting construction Lines from the Front and Top views to complete the sketch.

You will start by drawing the Top View and to do that, place the part on its base on a flat surface and look on the top of the Part.

The Top will appear to have several Parallel lines, with some of the holes not in view.

You will use Hidden lines to represent the hidden holes and other openings.

Next you will draw the Front view by projecting construction Lines from the sketch of the Top view.

The Right Side view will be represented next by also projecting construction Lines from the Front and Top views to complete the sketch.

Start AutoCAD if it is not already running on your machine and load an inch Template. At the Command Prompt enter the following:

1. Command: Click on **Draw** from the Main Menu, and click to select **Rectangle.** A Message pops up requesting you to:
2. Specify first corner point or [Chamfer/Elevation/Fillet/Thickness/Width]:
3. Type 0, 0 at the Command Prompt and press the Enter key. A Message pops up requesting you to:
4. **Specify other corner point or [Dimensions]:**
5. Type **4.480, 1.260** and press the Enter key. Zoom the sketch to have control

over your drawing.

6. Click on Draw from the Main Menu and select Line. A Message pops up requesting you to:

7. **Specify first point:**

8. Type **0, 0** and press the Enter key. A Message pops up requesting you to:

9. **Specify next point or [Undo]:**

10. Type **0, 3** and press the Enter key two times, to place a Construction line at the Origin.

11. **Specify offset distance or [Through] <Through>:**

12. Type **0.984** and press the Enter key. A Message pops up requesting you to:

13. **Select object to offset or <exit>:**

14. Click on the Construction Line from the Origin and click to the right of it.

15. Press the Enter key again. A Message pops up requesting you to:

16. **Specify offset distance or [Through] <Through>: <0.984>:**

17. Type **0.748** and press the Enter key. A Message pops up requesting you to:

18. **Select object to offset or <exit>:**

19. Click on the Offset Line, click to the right of it and press the Enter key. A Message pops up requesting you to:

20. **Specify offset distance or [Through] <Through>: <0.748>:**

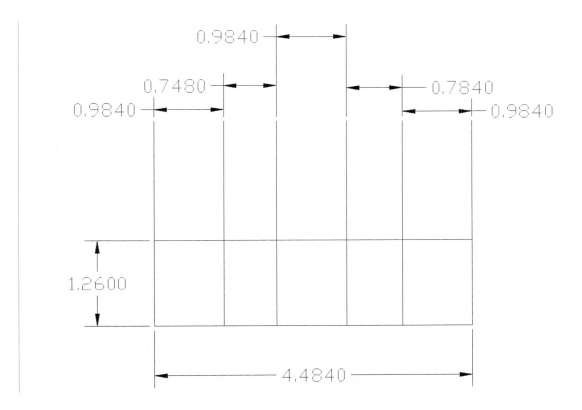

Figure 24.01

21. Type **0.984** and press the Enter key. A Message pops up requesting you to:

22. **Select object to offset or <exit>:**

23. Click on the Second Offset Line, click to the right of it and press the Enter key. A Message pops up requesting you to:

24. **Specify offset distance or [Through] <Through>: <0.984>:**

25. Type **0.748** and press the Enter key. A Message pops up requesting you to:

26. Select object to offset or <exit>:

Click on the Third Offset Line, click to the right of it and press the Enter key.

27. A Message pops up requesting you to:

28. Specify offset distance or [Through] <Through>: <0.748>:

29. Type **0.984** and press the Enter key. A Message pops up requesting you to:

30. Select object to offset or <exit>:

Click on the Third Offset Line and click to the right of it and press the Enter key, to complete the offset. Refer to Figure 24.01

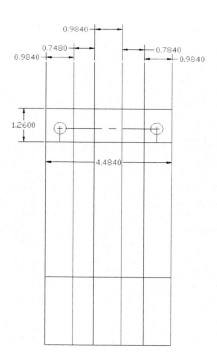

Figure 24.01

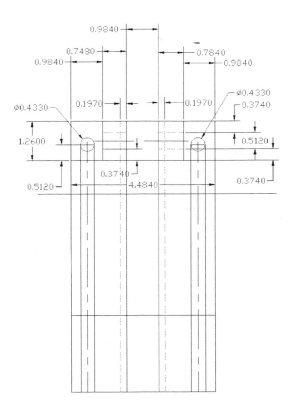

Figure 24.02

Holes:

You are now going to place circle on the part to represent holes on the part and to do that:

31. Type **'Circle'** on the Command prompt and press the Enter key. A Message pops up requesting you to:

32. **Specify center point for circle or [3P/2P/Ttr (tan tan radius)]:**

33. Type **0.502, 0.512** and press the Enter key. A Message pops up requesting

574

you to:

34. Specify radius of circle or [Diameter] <0.000>:

35. Type **'D'** and press the Enter key. A Message pops up requesting you to:

36. Specify diameter of circle <0.000>:

37. Type **0.433** and press the Enter key to place a circle on the Part.

Type **'Circle'** at the Command prompt and press the Enter key. A Message pops up requesting you to:

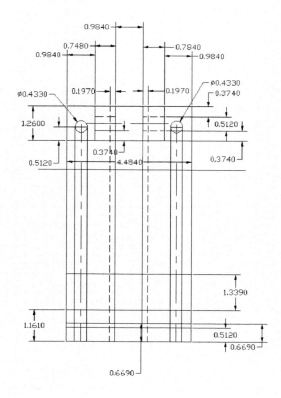

Figure 24.03

38. Specify center point for circle or [3P/2P/Ttr (tan tan radius)]:

39. Type **3.947, 0.512** and press the Enter key. A Message pops up requesting you to:

40. Specify radius of circle or [Diameter] <0.000>:

41. Type **'D'** short for Diameter and press the Enter key. A Message pops up requesting you to:

42. Specify diameter of circle <0.000>:

43. Type **0.433** and press the Enter key to place a circle on the Part.

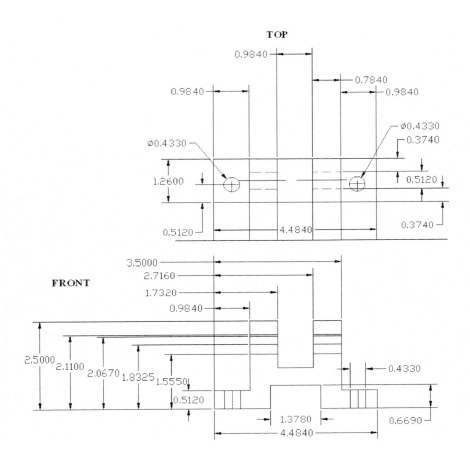

Figure 24.04

Hidden Holes and Cuts:

You will use Vertical and Horizontal Lines to represent the cuts and Hidden Holes The top Cut will be represented by a Solid Continuous line and the bottom cut represented by a Hidden line since it is not physically seen when you look on the top of the part.

Extend

You are now going to extend all the vertical lines you created as a result of the offset command to the last Horizontal Line just drawn. You will be using the Keyboard for some of the entries. Make sure you make all the entries correctly as shown below in the paragraph. Refer to Figure 24.03

44. Click on **Draw** from the Main Menu and select **Line**. A Message pops up requesting you to:

45. **Specify first point:**

46. Type **0, -5** and press the Enter key. A Message pops up requesting you to:

47. **Specify next point or [Undo]:**

48. Type **@4.484, 0** and press the Enter key two times.

49. Click on **Draw** from the Main Menu and select **Line**. A Message pops up requesting you to:

50. **Specify first point:**

51. Type **0, -7.5** and press the Enter key. A Message pops up requesting you to:

52. **Specify next point or [Undo]:**

53. Type **@4.484, 0** and press the Enter key two times.

54. Click on Modify from the Main Menu and select Extend

55. **Select objects:**

56. Click on the last Bottom-Horizontal Line (Refer to Figure 24.03) and press the Enter key.

57. Click on the **Offset Vertical** lines one at a time to extend all the lines to the Bottom Horizontal Line.

You will now extend the Top and Front Views to form the Right-Side view. Draw two vertical lines **1.260** inches apart to the side of the Front view and extend all the lines from the Top and Front view to form the Right side view. Refer to Figure 24.05

After projecting all the Lines from the edges as well as the holes, you will use the Trim tool to remove excess lines to form the Part for the right-side view. Refer to Figure 24.06

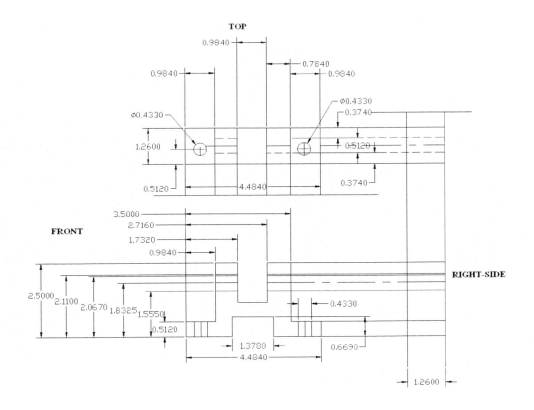

Figure 24.05

578

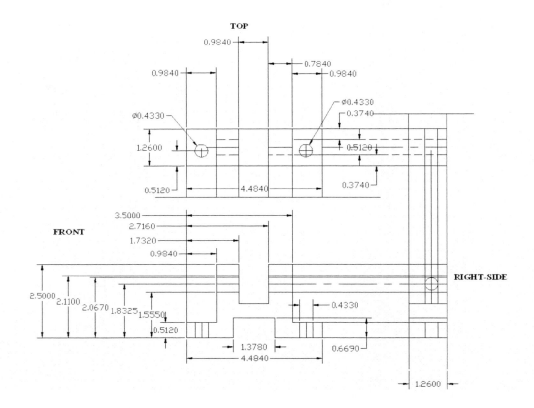

Figure 24.06

The 3D Model can be saved as a jpeg or bitmap file and inserted into the 2D drawing as a Raster Image.

<u>Creating Bitmap:</u>

To create a **Bitmap**, bring up a drawing, click on **File** from the Main Menu and select **Export**. The **Export Data** dialogue box opens up. Click on <u>S</u>ave. A Message pops up requesting you to:

Select objects or <all objects and viewports>:

Type **'All'** and press on the Enter key twice to save it as a Bitmap.

__Inserting a Bitmap:__

To add a drawing as a **Raster Image**, open the Folder containing the Bitmap drawing, drag and drop it on the 2D sketch and click to insert the Bitmap as a Raster image. Refer to Figure 24.08

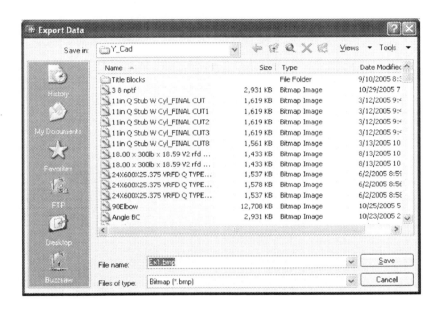

Figure 24.07

Figure 24.08 is a final view of the part with a **Raster Image** insert, of the Solid Model.

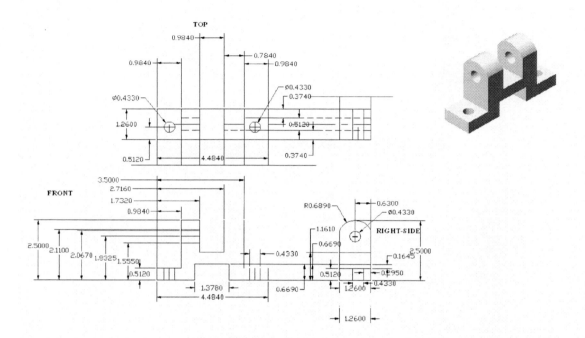

Figure 24.08

3D Drawings

Now that you have finished with the projection of the three views, let me walk you through on how to take the **Front View** and turn it into a **3D Model**.

Start AutoCAD if it is not already running on your Computer and enter the following using the Polyline tool together with **Absolute** and Relative **Coordinate System.**

One of the many uses of **PLine** is that whenever you make the wrong entry, all you have to do is type '**U**' short for undo, press the Enter key and type the correct number.

The mouse can be set-aside for now and use the keyboard to make all the entries. When finished, type '**Z**' and press the Enter key and '**E**' and press the Enter key for full view of the drawing.

58. Command: **PLine** and press the Enter key. A Message pops requesting you to:

59. Specify start point:

60. Enter **0, 0** press the Enter key. A Message pops up requesting you to:

61. **Specify next point or [Arc/Halfwidth/Length/Undo/Width]:**

62. Type **1.535, 0** and press the Enter key. A Message pops up requesting you to:

63. **Specify next point or [Arc/Halfwidth/Length/Undo/Width]:**

64. ; Type **@0, 0.669** and press the Enter key. A Message pops up requesting you to:

65. **Specify next point or [Arc/Halfwidth/Length/Undo/Width]:**

66. Type **@1.378, 0** and press the Enter key. A Message pops up requesting you to:

67. **Specify next point or [Arc/Halfwidth/Length/Undo/Width]:**

68. Type **@0, -0.669** and press the Enter key. A Message pops up requesting you to:

69. **Specify next point or [Arc/Halfwidth/Length/Undo/Width]:**

70. Type **@1.535, 0** and press the Enter key. A Message pops up requesting you to:

71.

72. **Specify next point or [Arc/Halfwidth/Length/Undo/Width]:**

73. **Type @0, 0.512** and press the Enter key. A Message pops up requesting you to:

74. **Specify next point or [Arc/Halfwidth/Length/Undo/Width]:**

75. **Type @-0.984,0** and press the Enter key. A message pops up requesting you to:

76. **Specify next point or [Arc/Halfwidth/Length/Undo/Width]:**

77. Type **@0, 2.008** and press the Enter key. A Message pops up requesting you to:

78. **Specify next point or [Arc/Halfwidth/Length/Undo/Width]:**

79. Type **@-0.748, 0** and press the Enter key. A Message pops up requesting you to:

80. **Specify next point or [Arc/Halfwidth/Length/Undo/Width]:**

81. Type **@0, -1.339** and press the Enter key. A Message pops up requesting you to:

82. **Specify next point or [Arc/Halfwidth/Length/Undo/Width]:**

83. Type **@-0.984, 0** and press the Enter key. A Message pops up requesting you to:

84. **Specify next point or [Arc/Halfwidth/Length/Undo/Width]:**

85. Type **@0, 1.339** and press the Enter key. A Message pops up requesting you to:

86. **Specify next point or [Arc/Halfwidth/Length/Undo/Width]:**

87. Type **@-0.748, 0** and press the Enter key. A Message pops up requesting

you to:

88. **Specify next point or [Arc/Halfwidth/Length/Undo/Width]:**

89. Type **@0, -2.008** and press the Enter key. A message pops up requesting you to:

90. **Specify next point or [Arc/Halfwidth/Length/Undo/Width]:**

91. Type **@-0.984, 0** and press the Enter key. A Message pops up requesting you to:

92. Type **0, 0** and press the Enter key **twice** to complete the Sketch.

Click on Draw from the Main Menu and select Boundary, the boundary dialogue box comes up. Click on Pick points, click inside the sketch and press the Enter key to turn the sketch into one object.

Extrude:

You are going to add depth to the sketch by extruding it **1.260 inches**. Follow these steps to complete the extrusion.

93. Command: Click on **Draw** from the Main Menu, highlight **Solids** and click to select **Extrude**. A Message pops up requesting you to:

94. **Select objects:**

95. Click on any of the Lines that bound the sketch just drawn and press the Enter key. A Message pops up requesting you to:

96. **Specify height of extrusion or [Path]:**

97. Type **1.260** and press the Enter key.

98. **Specify angle of taper for extrusion <0>:**

99. Press the Enter key again to accept the zero default value.

3D Model

To view the 3D Model of the Part, you will have to change the orientation of the drawing; as such you will now click on **View** from the Main Menu, Highlight **3D Views** and click to select **SE Isometric View**.

The Model should be now seen in 3D Model with the body on its side. Follow these steps to set the Model straight up on the Graphics area.

100.   Click on Modify from the Main Menu, highlight 3D Operation and click to select Rotate 3D. A Message pops up requesting you to:

101.   Select objects:

102.   Click on the body of the object and press the Enter key. A Message pops up requesting you to select:

103.   [Object/Last/View/Xaxis/Yaxis/Zaxis/2points]:

104.   Type '**X**' short for X-axis and press the Enter key. A Message pops up requesting you to:

105.   Specify a point on the X axis <0, 0, 0>:

106.   Type 0, 0 and press the Enter key. A Message pops up requesting you to:

107.   Specify rotation angle or [Reference]:

108.   Type 90 and press the Enter key to rotate the Part upright.

109.   Click on the outline of the Part on the floor and hit the delete key one at a time.

Creating 3 Model:

Next place two circles as positioned on the Top view of Figure 24.09 and extrude at a distance past the thickness of the base.

Uses Subtract option to remove the two rods formed from the main body to form a hole. Refer to Figure 24.10

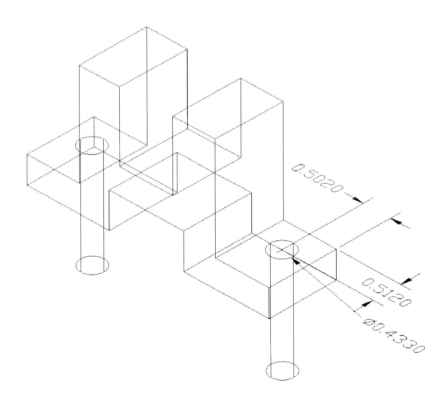

Figure 24.09

110.   Place an Arc with radius 0.689 on top part, extrude and use the Subtract option to remove excess parts from the main body.

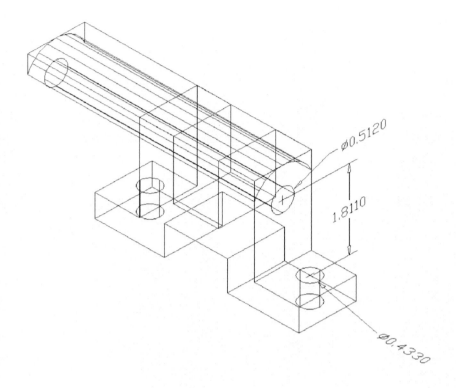

Figure 24.10

Calculating the pound Weight

You can now calculate the weight of the object with the Mass Properties option.

Mass:	5.6856
Volume:	5.6856
Bounding box:	X: 0.0000 -- 1.2600
	Y: -0.5120 -- 1.9880

Z: -3.5000 -- 0.9840

Centroid: X: 0.6269

Y: 0.4845

Z: -1.2497

Moments of inertia: X: 19.8361

Y: 18.8399

Z: 7.0232

Products of inertia: XY: 1.7400

YZ: -3.4399

ZX: -4.4535

Radii of gyration: X: 1.8678

Y: 1.8203

Z: 1.1114

Principal moments and X-Y-Z directions about centroid:

I: 9.6225 along [1.0000 -0.0069 -0.0001]

J: 7.7264 along [0.0069 1.0000 -0.0006]

K: 3.4543 along [0.0001 0.0006 1.0000]

The Volume is given as **5.6856 lb/in^3**

Multiply the value with **0.2833 in^3** to obtain **1.611lbs**

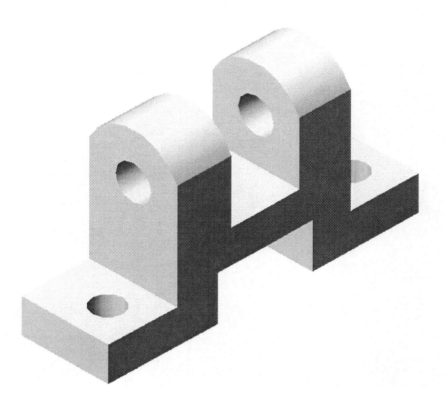

Figure 24.11

You are now going to be introduced to the uses of Viewports in printing 3D Models with different views on a Title Block. Follow these steps in achieving this objective.

After finishing a 3D drawing the next step is to turn it into a workable layout sheet, in order for the machinist to properly make the part.

Viewports also known as **VPORTS,** enables you to set up multiple Views from the Top, Front, Right-Side views and also the Isometric view, to show how the end product will look like.

You will be guided through setting up a multiple views with the aid of the VPORTS option using the Model from Figure 24.11

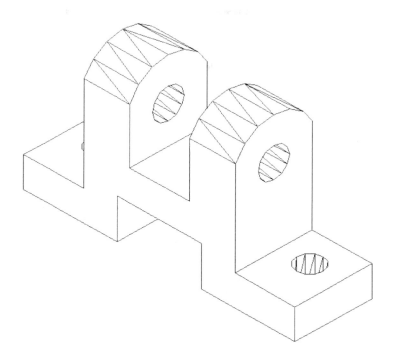

Figure 24.12

111. Using the Model in Figure 24.11, click on File, **Save as** and enter a
     Filename, Vports3D.

112. Click on **View**, from the Main Menu highlight **3D Views** and select **SE
     Isometric** to orient the Model as in Figure 24.12

113. Click on **Layout1** from the bottom of your screen, the Page Setup – Layout1
     dialogue box opens up as in Figure 24.13

114. Click on OK to insert a copy of the Model on the Graphics area.

You are now in PaperSpace mode. You can tell you are in Paper Space by the
Triangular-Shaped image at the bottom left of the screen. This normally contains a
'W' and a small cube inserted in the triangle.

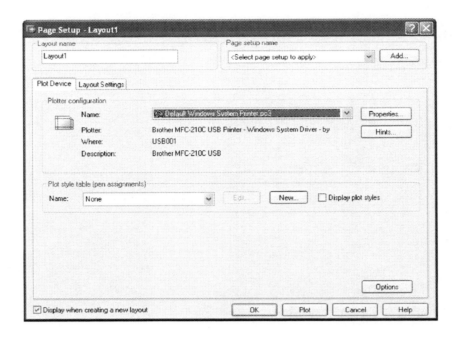

Figure 24.13

Paper Space enables you to plot your 3D drawings together with a Title Block. You will be able to add Dimensioning and Text on the Paper Space together with the 3D Model.

Similar operation in Model Space will be practically impossible.

115. Click on the outer rectangular lines that bound the 3D Model and hit the Delete button on the keyboard.

116. Click on View from the Main menu, select Viewports and click on **4 Viewports**. A Message pops up requesting you to:

117. **Specify first corner or [Fit] <Fit>:**

118. Click on the **Top-Left** corner of the dotted Rectangle, release your finger from the left mouse button, drag the pointer to the bottom right corner of the

dotted rectangle and click to place four 3D views on the Graphics area. Refer to Figure 1.05

The next step is to hide the lines in between the four models to enable properly plotted views. You will use the Layer Properties Manager to set up a layer with the lights turned off to be able to hide the lines.

Follow the steps below to set up the layer.

119. Type Layer at the Command prompt and press the Enter key twice, **Layer1** should be highlighted and blinking.

120. Click on the Light bulb adjacent to **Layer**1 to turn it **off** and click on **OK** to exit the Layer Properties Manager.

Scale:

You will have to Scale your Model to fit properly in all the views, as such you will click on **Model** at the bottom of the screen and type Scale at the command prompt to reduce your Model to half its original size.

121. Command: Scale [When you press the Enter key, you will be requested to]

122. Select objects:

123. Type 'All' and press the Enter key 2xs. A Message pops up requesting you to:

124. Specify base point:

125. Type **0, 0** and press the Enter key. A Message pops up requesting you to:

126. Specify scale factor or [Reference]:

127. Type **0.5** and press the Enter key.

When you click on **Layout1** again all the Models should be scaled down to half size.

DIMLFAC:

Dimlfac is a tool in AutoCAD used to set up the scale factor for measuring linear dimensions as well as circles, diameter and radii.

The initial value is set to **1.000** and the objective is to set up a scale factor in order for all reduced or oversized parts to correctly be dimensioned to reflect the original values.

The objective is to set up a scale for the drawing in Model space and set up the Dimlfac in Paper Space to reflect the original dimensional values.

To properly place a correct Dimension on your Drawing, you will have to Setup the **DIMLFAC** option, to enable you correctly add the original values.

For an example, a part that has been scaled down by a '¼' in the Model Space will require that you setup the Dimlfac to '**4**' in **Paper Space**, to be able to obtain the correct dimensioning on your drawing.

Paper Space:

Model Space is used in completing the drafting and design work, whereas **Paper Space** is used in creating plotting Sheet and finished layout of your drawings.

Back in the Paper Space you will type **Dimlfac** at the Command prompt and press the Enter key.

128.　Command: **Dimlfac,** when you press the Enter key, you will be requested to:

129.　Enter new value for Dimlfac <1.000>:

Remember your drawing was scaled down in half. The question therefore will be how much should be multiplied by '½' to obtain '1'?

The answer is '2'

130.　Type **2** at the Command prompt and press the Enter key

131.　Begin adding Dimension and Text to your drawing and when finished, type

Dimlfac at the Command Prompt and change the value back to the default of '**1.000**'.

The next step is to remove the Viewports Lines, using the **Layer1**, to setup the plotting sheet. The reason the light bulb was turned **OFF** is to enable us use it to turn **OFF** the Viewports.

132. Type '**PS**' short for PaperSpace at the Command Prompt and press the Enter key, to be sure the drawing is in PaperSpace mode.

133. Click on one of the Cross Lines in between the Models, to highlight it, click on the arrow by the **Layer Properties Manager** and select **Layer1**.

134. A warning pops up as in Figure 24.14

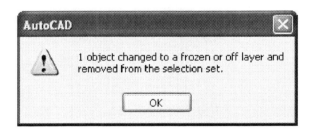

Figure 24.14

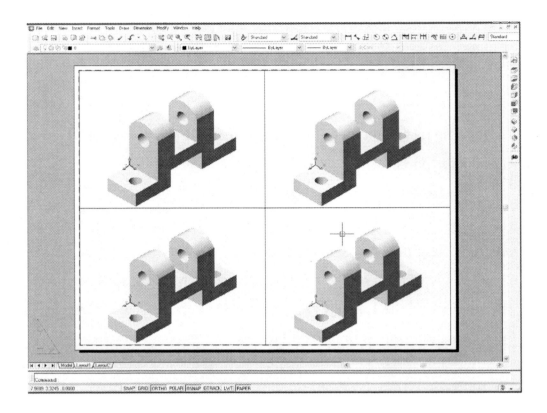

Figure 24.15

135. Click on OK to turn **OFF** the Viewports.

136. Repeat this action on #24, until all the Layers are turned OFF

It is time to insert the **Title Block**, so make sure an **Object Layer** is currently

displayed on the Layer Properties Manager and not **layer zero (0) or Defpoints.**

Type Insert at the Command Prompt, select Browse and locate a Title Block to be inserted
on your drawing.

137. Command: **Insert** [When you press the Enter key, the Insert dialogue box is

displayed on the Graphics area] Refer to Figure 24.16

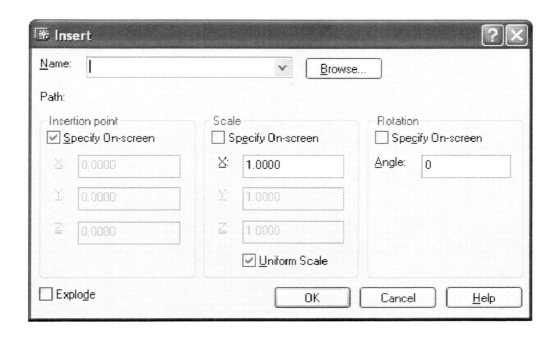

Figure 24.16

138. Click on a Corner of the Screen to Insert the Title Block. You can always use the Move command to fit it perfectly around your drawing.

139. Add all the attribute definitions and make all necessary changes on the Text.

You are now going to change the views to Top, Front. Right-Side and Isometric view.

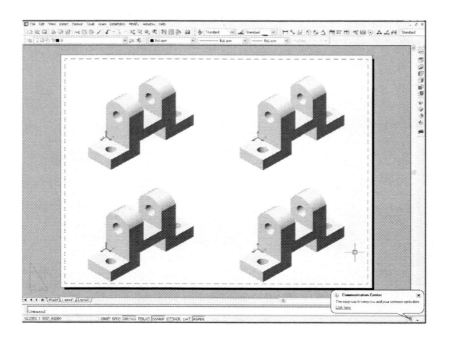

Figure 24.17

140. Double-Click on the first Model on the Top Left corner in Figure 24.17 click on View from the Main Menu, highlight 3D Views and select **Top**, the Model should change to the Top view.

141. Double-Click on the second Model on the Bottom Left corner, click on **View** from the Main Menu, highlight 3D Views and select **Front**, the Model should change to the Front view.

142. Double-Click on the Third Model on the Bottom Right corner, click on View from the Main Menu, highlight 3D Views and select Right, the Model should change to the Right view.

143. Double-Click on the Fourth Model on the Top Right corner, click on View from the Main Menu, highlight Shade and select **Gouraud Shaded** the Model should change to a Solid Model.

144. Click on the body of the Solid Model, click on ByLayer and select a lighter color.

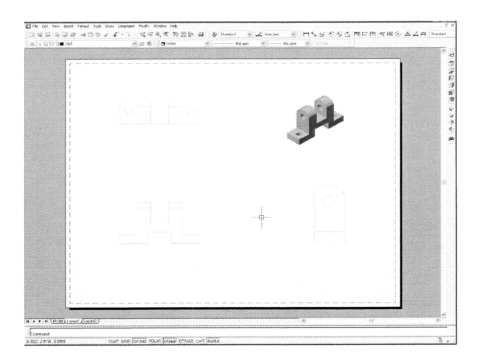

Figure 24.18

598

Dimensioning:

You can now add all the dimensioning to the three views and with the exception of the Isometric View.

Text:

You can also add Text on the sheet layout for any additional information on the Part.

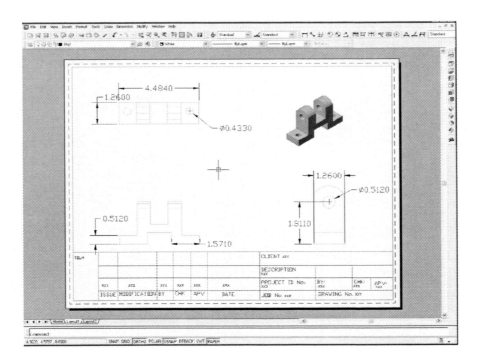

Figure 24.19

Summary:

Topics covered in this Chapter included:

- Using Multiview Projection
- Starting a new sketch and use projections to turn it into the required views
- Using Absolute and Relative coordinate to draw with the aid of the keyboard
- Setting up the Top, Front and the Right-Side views
- Adding Holes and extrude to form solid cylinders
- Using the Subtract command to turn the extruded cylinders into holes
- Inserting Raster Images
- Calculating lb weight of the solid 3D Part
- Creating 3D drawings
- Viewports
- Dimlfac
- Model Space
- Paper Space

Exercise:

- Use the sketch below to project the three views, Top; Front and the Right-Side
- Create a 3D model of the part, extrude the sketch 2inches and save as a bitmap
- Insert it into the drawing containing the three views. Refer to Figure 24.08
- Find the Volume of the Part and calculate its weight.

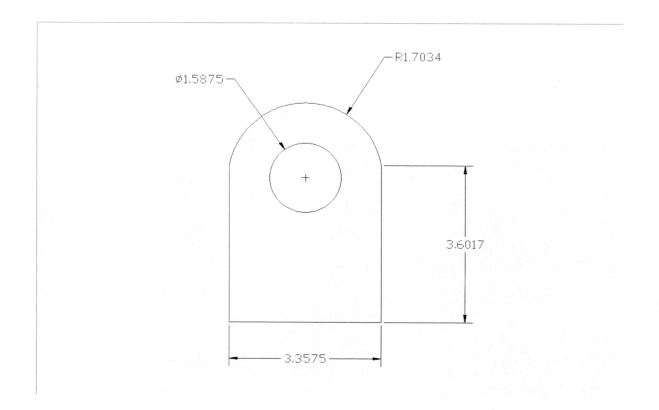

Figure 24.20

You have finally made it, and learned new terminology as well as techniques in starting a basic sketch and building it into a complex and working model.

You can now use the knowledge acquired through these pages to make your work easier as well as educate someone in your newly learned software to help create better products.

Thanks for being part of this development.

HOW DO I?

Interacting with students with different backgrounds and disciplines has made me realize that, there is more to teaching than just imparting of information to the class. I have therefore come up with a section solely to answer repetitive questions that come up in class every other day that I teach. Thus the How Do I? Section is a Q & A Session.

The difference between a Block and Xref is that the inserted Block becomes a permanent part of the drawing it was inserted into, whereas the Xref is not a permanent part of the drawing it is referenced to and both Blocks and Xref can be Moved, Scaled, and Rotated or edited.

Q. What are the uses of Attributes?

A. Attributes definition is a form of programming that allows the user to make certain entries when inserted into a Part drawing or a File.
It can be used to generate Parts Lists as well as entering DATA.

Q. How do I know which Tool is which?

A. Move the mouse pointer and rest it on any Tool for a few minutes, a brief description of that particular tool, will be displayed at the bottom. This is also known as the Tool Tip.

Q. How do I add Chamfer with a distance and angle to my sketch?

A. Click on Modify and select Chamfer from the Main Menu, a message pops up requesting you to:

a. Select first line or Polyline / Distance / Angle / Trim / Method / multiple:

b. Type '**A**' short for Angle and press the Enter key A Message pops up requesting you to:

c. Specify chamfer length on the first line<**0.000**>:

d. Type **0.125** or any preferable distance and press the Enter key again. A Message pops up requesting you to:

e. Specify chamfer angle from the first line: <0.000>

f. Type **45** or any preferable angle and press the enter key. The pointer should turn into a pick box with a message requesting you to:

g. Select first line or Polyline / Distance / Angle / Trim / Method / multiple:

h. Click on the first intersection line A Message pops up requesting you to:

i. Select the second line:

j. Click on the adjacent line to place the chamfer.

Q. How do I get rid of the Grid in the graphics area?

A. Press the '**F7**' function key.

Q. Why can't I Extrude this sketch?

A. You first have to convert the lines into one entity with PEDIT or Boundary before it could be extruded, Refer to the section on Extruding parts.

Q. How do I copy a Sketch?

A. Type copy and press the enter key. A Message pops up requesting you to:

- **Select Objects**
- Type 'ALL' and press the Enter key two times. A Message pops up requesting you to:
- **Specify base point or displacement, or [Multiple]:** The pointer turns into a cross.
- Click anywhere on the Graphics area and move the pointer to another location and click to place the copy of the sketch.

Q. How do I add Color to my model?

A. Click on Edit from the Main Menu and click on Select. Move to the arrow at the end of ByLayer, which is also the color palette and click on a color.

Q. I just finished drawing a sketch and added an Extrusion to it, but all I can see is a blank sheet on the Graphics area. Where is the Model?

A. Type Zoom at the Command Prompt and press the enter key. Type 'E' short for Extends and press the Enter key again..

Q. How do I Extrude along a Path?

A. After selecting the object to extrude, you will be requested to: **Specify height of extrusion or [Path]:** Type **'P'** short for Path and press the Enter key.
Click on the Line to complete the Path extrusion. Refer to Chapter 12 for more on Path extrusion

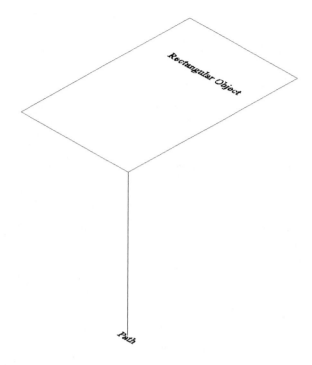

Q. How I calculate the distance of a Line I have just drawn at an angle.

A. Type DIST and press the Enter key. You will me requested to Specify the First and Second points. Click on the endpoints of the Line one after the other and press the F2 function key to view the results.

Q. What is the difference between a Block and WBlock?

A. Block is local whiles WBlock is Global, in that it could be inserted in any file, whiles the Block is only embedded in the current File that it was created in. Refer to Tutorials on Blocks.

Q. I have drawn two lines perpendicular to each other and would like to join them at the intersection. What do I do?

A. Use PEDIT to join the two Lines. Refer to the Lesson on PEdit.

Q. I accidentally deleted my entire drawing and I do not want to start all over again, what do I do to get it back?

A. Simply type UNDO at the Command Prompt and press the Enter key.

OLE

Q. What is OLE and how does it work with AutoCAD?

A. **OLE** is an abbreviation for Object Linking and Embedding. You can use OLE to configure an External database so as it could be used in AutoCAD. Bring up a Drawing you would like to add OLE to and click on Insert from the Main Menu and select OLE object.

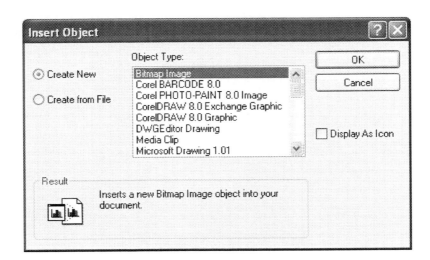

The Insert Object box opens up. Make a choice under Object type; for an example Microsoft Word Document and click on OK. An empty sheet opens up. Type in your information and when you close the File the OLE properties dialogue box pops up.

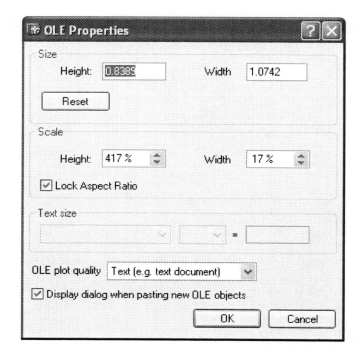

You are given the option of changing the height and width of the object to be embedded.

After making all the necessary changes in the OLE Properties dialogue box, just click on Ok and the Document gets embedded with AutoCAD.

To add an OLE to a 3D Model, you first click on Layout1 at the bottom of the screen and click on Ok.

Click on Insert from the Main Menu and select OLE object. Go through the process as aligned above to create a Worksheet or document.

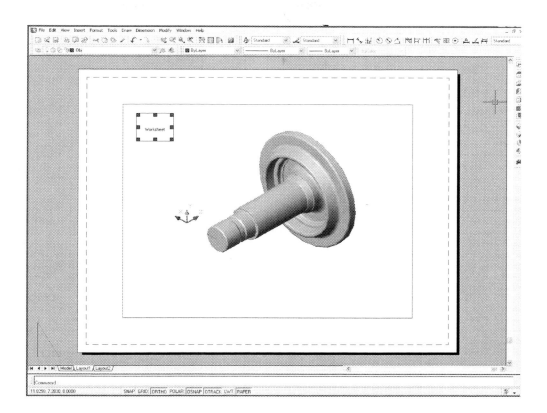

You can also add more information to it by double-clicking on the embedded document.

Q. How do I add an Angular dimension?

A. Click to highlight Dimension and select Angular Dimension. Click on the two Lines one at a time, and click in-between the adjacent lines to place the angular dimension.

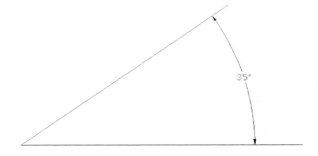

Q. The UCS icon on my computer is different from that of my co-worker, how does it get changed?

A. Type **UCSICON** at the Command Prompt and you will be requested to enter an option [On/Off/All/No origin/Origin/Properties] <ON>. Type **'P'** short for Properties and press the Enter key.

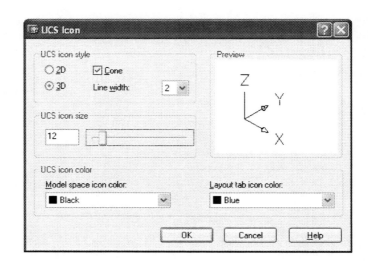

The UCS Icon dialogue box pops up, select the style and change the size by moving the dial. Click on OK to exit.

Q. Whenever I start AutoCAD the Active Assistance Window pops up, how do I get rid of it?

A. Move the Mouse pointer to the bottom right hand corner of the Graphics area and Right-click on the Assist icon and select Exit.

Q. How do I change the background color on my screen?

A. Right-Click in front of the Command Prompt and choose Options. Under current Profile under the Options dialogue box, choose Display and click on colors.
In the Color Option dialogue box that pops up, expand the arrow by Color, select a color and click on Apply & Close and OK to exit.

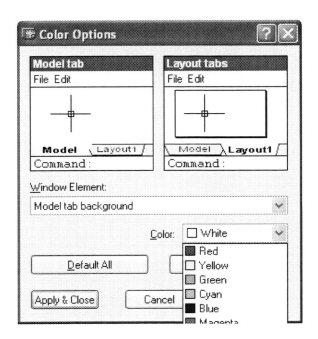

Q. How do I delete a Sketch?

A. Click on the sketch and hit the **Delete** key on the keyboard.

Q. How do I turn off a Layer?

A. Type Layer at the Command Prompt and click on the Light Bulb besides the layer to be turned off and click on OK

Q. How do I make the line thicker?

A. Click on Draw from the Main menu and select Polyline. When asked to:

- **Specify start point,** click anywhere on top of the Graphics area. A message pops up with different options
- **Specify next point or [Arc/ Halfwidth / Length / Undo / Width]:**
- Type '**W**' short for Width and press the Enter key.
- **Specify starting width <0.0000>:**
- Type 0.5 and press the Enter key
- **Specify the ending width <0.5000>:**
- Type 0.5 and press the Enter key.

You can now draw thick Lines with your sketch. You would need to reset the width back to <0.000> to exit the thick Line command.

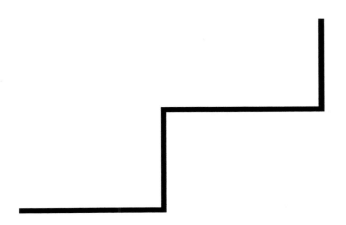

Q. I am in a middle of a drawing and the screen just went blank and my drawing is gone. What do I do?

A. Start AutoCAD again and usually you will be given the option of saving your drawing, if not click on File from the Main Menu, highlight Drawing Utilities and select Recover. It is recommended to save your drawing very often

Q. How do I send copy of my drawing?

A. Bring up a Drawing, click on **File** and select **send to**, a **New Message** from Outlook opens with a copy of the Model already attached.
Type an e-mail address and a message then click on Send

Q. How do I display inches and millimeters for my dimensions?

A. Double-Click on the Dimension you would like to apply the dual dimension. When the Properties Dialogue boxes pop up scroll to Tolerance and select Deviation and add the Upper and Lower Tolerances.

Q. The UCSICON has miraculously positioned itself in the middle of the Graphics area. How do I move it back to the bottom-left corner of the screen?

A. Type UCS at the Command prompt and a Message will pop up requesting you to select among a list of commands:
**New / Move / autoGraphic / Prev / restore / Save / Del / Apply? /World]
<World>:**
Press the Enter key to accept the default setting of World and the UCS should move back to the bottom-left corner.

Q. Will the Origin change with a change in position of the UCS?

A. No the Origin remains 0,0 wherever the UCS is positioned, therefore if you start a Line and you are requested to Specify the first point and you find the UCSICON away from the bottom-left corner, just type 0,0 and press the Enter key and the First point of the Line will be anchored at the Origin.

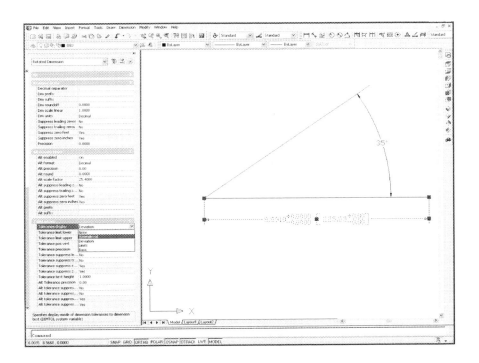

Q. How do I change the size of the 'Pickbox'?

A. Right-Click in front of the Command Prompt at the bottom left of the screen and select Options. Click on **Display** and move the slider under **Crosshairs** to increase the figure if you would like to change the size of the Crosshairs.
Next click on **Selection** and move the Slider to the right to increase the size of the Pickbox.

Q. I just finished setting up layer in the Layer Properties Manager, but all I see is the '**0**' Layer, where did my setup go?

A. Click on the arrow under **Named layer filters** and select **Show all layers** in the List of items

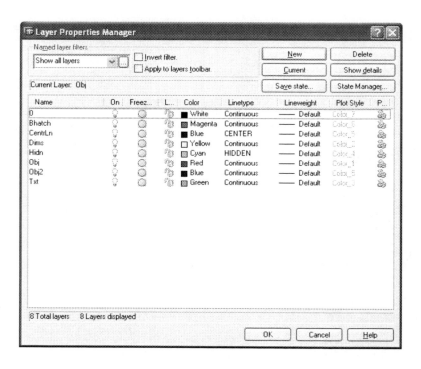

Q. I am using the Trim tool and accidentally removed a Line I would like to keep. How do I get it back?

A. Type 'Undo' at the command prompt and hit the Enter key once.

Q. I am trying to draw a Line, I can see the line on the screen but it disappears when I finish drawing the Line. What am I doing wrong?

A. You have accidentally turned off the light for the current Layer being used and all you do is to type **Layer** at the Command prompt press the Enter key to bring up the Layer Properties Manager.

Scroll to the current layer being used and click on the Light Bulb besides the layer to turn it back on.

Q. How do I draw with the Grid option?

A. Type Grid at the Command Prompt and press the Enter key. A Message pops up requesting you to:

- **Specify grid spacing (X) or [ON / OFF /Snap / Aspect] <0.500>:**
- Press the Enter key to accept the default setting of 0.5000
- Click on **SNAP** at the bottom of the Screen and click on Line from the Draw option on the Main Menu.
- When you start drawing, on the Graphics area, the pointer will jump from one point to the other 0.5 units at a time. Follow a point to generate a drawing.

Figure below demonstrates an end product of a sketch drawn with the Grid.

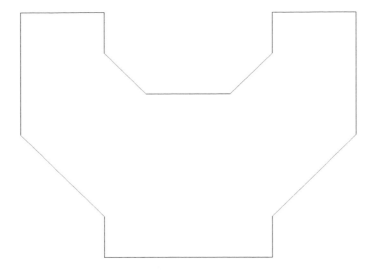

Q. How do I access shot cut for various AutoCAD Commands?

A. AutoCAD is loaded with short-cuts and is listed in the Support Files under ACAD.PGP

Find list blow a copy of the short cuts also known as known as Command Aliases.

Copyright (C) 1997-2002 by AutoDesk, Inc.

For an example when you are ready to use the Array in your design, just type **'AR'** at the Command Prompt and press the Enter key.

```
3A,      *3DARRAY
3DO,     *3DORBIT
3F,      *3DFACE
3P,      *3DPOLY
A,       *ARC
ADC,     *ADCENTER
AA,      *AREA
AL,      *ALIGN
AP,      *APPLOAD
AR,      *ARRAY
-AR,     *-ARRAY
ATT,     *ATTDEF
-ATT,    *-ATTDEF
ATE,     *ATTEDIT
-ATE,    *-ATTEDIT
ATTE,    *-ATTEDIT
B,       *BLOCK
-B,      *-BLOCK
BH,      *BHATCH
BO,      *BOUNDARY
-BO,     *-BOUNDARY
BR,      *BREAK
C,       *CIRCLE
CH,      *PROPERTIES
-CH,     *CHANGE
CHA,     *CHAMFER
CHK,     *CHECKSTANDARDS
```

```
COL,      *COLOR
COLOUR,   *COLOR
CO,       *COPY
CP,       *COPY
D,        *DIMSTYLE
DAL,      *DIMALIGNED
DAN,      *DIMANGULAR
DBA,      *DIMBASELINE
DBC,      *DBCONNECT
DC,       *ADCENTER
DCE,      *DIMCENTER
DCENTER,  *ADCENTER
DCO,      *DIMCONTINUE
DDA,      *DIMDISASSOCIATE
DDI,      *DIMDIAMETER
DED,      *DIMEDIT
DI,       *DIST
DIV,      *DIVIDE
DLI,      *DIMLINEAR
DO,       *DONUT
DOR,      *DIMORDINATE
DOV,      *DIMOVERRIDE
DR,       *DRAWORDER
DRA,      *DIMRADIUS
DRE,      *DIMREASSOCIATE
DS,       *DSETTINGS
DST,      *DIMSTYLE
DT,       *TEXT
DV,       *DVIEW
E,        *ERASE
ED,       *DDEDIT
EL,       *ELLIPSE
EX,       *EXTEND
EXIT,     *QUIT
EXP,      *EXPORT
EXT,      *EXTRUDE
F,        *FILLET
FI,       *FILTER
G,        *GROUP
-G,       *-GROUP
GR,       *DDGRIPS
H,        *BHATCH
-H,       *HATCH
```

HE,   *HATCHEDIT
HI,   *HIDE
I,   *INSERT
-I,   *-INSERT
IAD,   *IMAGEADJUST
IAT,   *IMAGEATTACH
ICL,   *IMAGECLIP
IM,   *IMAGE
-IM,   *-IMAGE
IMP,   *IMPORT
IN,   *INTERSECT
INF,   *INTERFERE
IO,   *INSERTOBJ
L,   *LINE
LA,   *LAYER
-LA,   *-LAYER
LE,   *QLEADER
LEN,   *LENGTHEN
LI,   *LIST
LINEWEIGHT, *LWEIGHT
LO,   *-LAYOUT
LS,   *LIST
LT,   *LINETYPE
-LT,   *-LINETYPE
LTYPE,   *LINETYPE
-LTYPE,   *-LINETYPE
LTS,   *LTSCALE
LW,   *LWEIGHT
M,   *MOVE
MA,   *MATCHPROP
ME,   *MEASURE
MI,   *MIRROR
ML,   *MLINE
MO,   *PROPERTIES
MS,   *MSPACE
MT,   *MTEXT
MV,   *MVIEW
O,   *OFFSET
OP,   *OPTIONS
ORBIT,   *3DORBIT
OS,   *OSNAP
-OS,   *-OSNAP
P,   *PAN

-P,   *-PAN
PA,   *PASTESPEC
PARTIALOPEN, *-PARTIALOPEN
PE,   *PEDIT
PL,   *PLINE
PO,   *POINT
POL,   *POLYGON
PR,   *PROPERTIES
PRCLOSE, *PROPERTIESCLOSE
PROPS,   *PROPERTIES
PRE,   *PREVIEW
PRINT,   *PLOT
PS,   *PSPACE
PTW,   *PUBLISHTOWEB
PU,   *PURGE
-PU,   *-PURGE
R,   *REDRAW
RA,   *REDRAWALL
RE,   *REGEN
REA,   *REGENALL
REC,   *RECTANG
REG,   *REGION
REN,   *RENAME
-REN,   *-RENAME
REV,   *REVOLVE
RO,   *ROTATE
RPR,   *RPREF
RR,   *RENDER
S,   *STRETCH
SC,   *SCALE
SCR,   *SCRIPT
SE,   *DSETTINGS
SEC,   *SECTION
SET,   *SETVAR
SHA,   *SHADEMODE
SL,   *SLICE
SN,   *SNAP
SO,   *SOLID
SP,   *SPELL
SPL,   *SPLINE
SPE,   *SPLINEDIT
ST,   *STYLE
STA,   *STANDARDS

```
SU,     *SUBTRACT
T,      *MTEXT
-T,     *-MTEXT
TA,      *TABLET
TH,      *THICKNESS
TI,     *TILEMODE
TO,      *TOOLBAR
TOL,      *TOLERANCE
TOR,      *TORUS
TP,      *TOOLPALETTES
TR,      *TRIM
UC,      *UCSMAN
UN,      *UNITS
-UN,     *-UNITS
UNI,     *UNION
V,      *VIEW
-V,     *-VIEW
VP,      *DDVPOINT
-VP,     *VPOINT
W,       *WBLOCK
-W,      *-WBLOCK
WE,      *WEDGE
X,       *EXPLODE
XA,      *XATTACH
XB,      *XBIND
-XB,     *-XBIND
XC,      *XCLIP
XL,      *XLINE
XR,      *XREF
-XR,     *-XREF
Z,      *ZOOM
```

Q. How do I use short cuts for Drafting Settings?¯

A. Right-Click on OSNAP at the bottom of the Screen and click on Settings. The Drafting Settings dialogue box opens up. If you are going to draw curves and circles, it is advisable to place check marks in Center, Quadrant or Tangent and do not overdo it.

On the other hand use Endpoint, Midpoint, Intersection for Lines and Polygons. Listed below, find short cuts to the commands in the Drafting Settings.

you would like to make it smaller than the drawing and press the enter key. You can use a preferred scale to fit your need.

6. Type Move at the command prompt and press the Enter key. A Message pops up requesting you to:

7. **Select objects:**

8. Click on the Title Block and press the Enter key, the pointer should turn into a crosshair with a Message requesting you to:

9. **Specify base point or displacement:**

10. Click on the Graphics area away from the Title Block, hold down on the left mouse button and drag to fit it on your drawing and click to exit command.

Q. After completing a sketch I realized the text of the dimensions being placed on the part, look larger than the part itself. How do I adjust the arrowhead and the Text also?

A. When you use Inches to draw on a Metric Template, the dimensioning will not come out right.

1. You can do one of two things, copy the drawing and paste it in an Inches Template or

2. Open an inches Template and draw all over again.

Q. I started a new sketch and do not remember what units I started with. How do I check whether I am in **Inches** or **Metric?**

A. Type **Limits** in front of the Command Prompt and press the Enter key. I f the Message that pops up reads:

Specify lower left corner or [ON/OFF] <0.0000,0.0000> and you press the Enter key again and it reads

Specify upper right corner <12.0000,9.0000> You are using a Template for Inches units.

On the other hand if you typed Limits and pressed the Enter key and received a Message requesting you to:

. Specify lower left corner or [ON/OFF] <0.0000,0.0000> and you pressed the Enter key again and it read

Specify upper right corner <420.0000,297.0000> You are using a Template for Metric units

Q. I just placed Dimensions on my sketch and the Text and arrows appear very small. How do I resize the Text and Arrowheads as well as add 3 decimal places to the dimensions?

A.

1. Click on Dimension from the Main Menu and select Style. The Dimension Style Manager opens up. Refer to Figure.

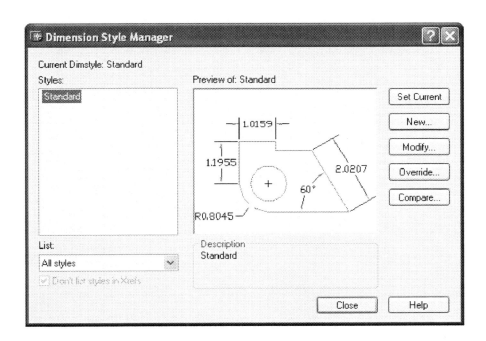

2. Click on Modify to open the Modify Dimension Style:

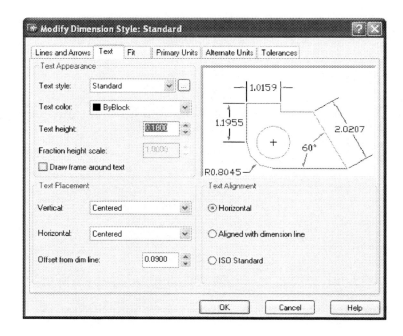

3. Click on **Lines and Arrows** and change the Arrow size to 0.500 or 0.250

4. Click on Text and change the Text height to 0.500 or 0.250

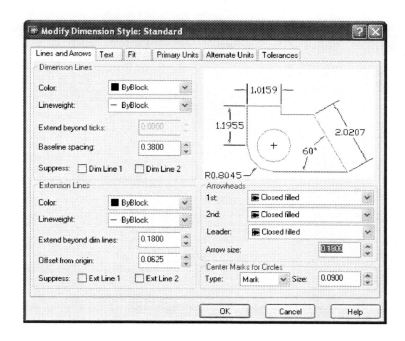

5. Click on the Primary Units and change Precision setting to 0.000

6. Click on Ok and Close to confirm the change.

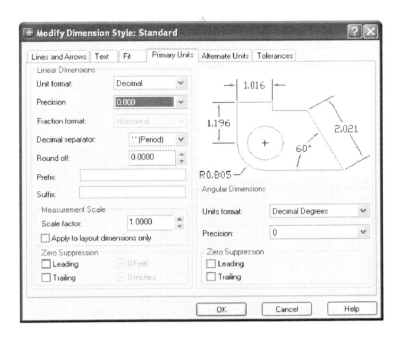

Q. How do I place Center Mark on the circle just drawn?

A. Click on Dimension and select Center mark. A Message pops up requesting you to: Select Arc or Circle.
Click on the tangent of the circle or an Arc you are trying to place the Center Mark to.

Q. The size of the **Crosshair** for the pointer is too long on my screen. How do I change it to a preferred size?

A. Right-Click in front of the Command at the bottom of the screen and select Options.

From the Options dialogue box that opens up, click on Display.

Move the pointer to the bottom of the dialogue box and slide the dial under **Crosshair size** or change the figure in the allotted box to a smaller number and click on Apply and OK to exit.

The Crosshair on the screen should change into the preferred size.

INDEX

Printed in the United States
49437LVS00001B

9 781420 896770